ANGLO-AMERICAN POLITICAL RELATIONS, 1675–1775

ANGLO-AMERICAN POLITICAL RELATIONS, 1675–1775

EDITED BY

Alison Gilbert Olson and Richard Maxwell Brown

RUTGERS UNIVERSITY PRESS

NEW BRUNSWICK · NEW JERSEY

TO MANCUR AND TO DEE

Preface

This book is an outgrowth of the Twentieth Conference on Early American History held on the Rutgers College campus of Rutgers University on October 7–8, 1966 as a part of the observance of the Rutgers Bicentennial, 1766–1966. At that time the editors of this volume were members of the Rutgers University faculty, and they acted as codirectors of the Conference. The theme of the Conference was "Anglo-American Political Relations, 1675–1775." Papers were presented by Richard S. Dunn, Stanley Nider Katz, David Alan Williams, and Michael G. Kammen. In revised form these papers appear as articles in this book. In order to round out the treatment of the subject, additional articles by David S. Lovejoy, Thomas C. Barrow, John Shy, Joseph E. Illick, and Alison Gilbert Olson were solicited for inclusion in the present volume.

We wish to acknowledge the contributions of the following persons who did so much to assure the success of the Conference: the members of the State University Bicentennial Commission; Richard Schlatter, Provost and Vice President of Rutgers University; Van Wie Ingham, the Rutgers Bicentennial Coordinator; Madison E. Weidner, Associate Dean of the University Extension Division of Rutgers; Lester J. Cappon, Director of the Institute of Early American History and Culture; and Mr. George W. Franz.

Alison Gilbert Olson
Richard Maxwell Brown

Contents

1

INTRODUCTION

Anglo-American Politics, 1675–1775: Needs and Opportunities for Further Study

ALISON GILBERT OLSON holds the B.A. and M.A. from the University of California at Berkeley and the D.Phil. from Oxford University. She has taught at Smith College and Douglass College of Rutgers University and is now Associate Professor of History at American University where she teaches English as well as American history. Her publications include *The Radical Duke: The Career and Correspondence of Charles Lennox, Third Duke of Richmond* (1961) and several articles including, "The British Government and Colonial Union, 1754" and "William Penn, Parliament, and Proprietary Government" (*William and Mary Quarterly*, 1960, 1961). She is the author of a forthcoming study of English and American political parties in the seventeenth and eighteenth centuries.

More than half a century ago Charles McLean Andrews began his lifelong efforts to convince American colonial historians that "the colonial period of our history is not American only but Anglo-American. . . . [we must] bring the mother country into the forefront of the picture as the central figure, the authoritative and guiding force, the influence of which did more than anything else to shape the course of colonial achievement." But in spite of Andrews' crusade and his own monumental studies of British colonial administration his efforts caught on slowly; it is only in the years since his death and largely (though not entirely) among a generation of historians who never knew him, that the study of Anglo-Colonial politics has come into fashion. The present volume of essays is a product of the new interest and the new generation.

This book suggests Andrews' influence not only in marking out the field of Anglo-American history but also in indicating the lines along which the field might best be developed. Before Andrews wrote, such limited interest as there was in the field concentrated, for example, on the economic effects of British mercantile restrictions, the constitutional struggles between governors and Assemblies, theories of imperial taxation put forth on the eve of the Revolution (these were largely the studies of American historians), and British struggles with the French for mastery of the colonial world (this was the interest of British historians). The papers in this book suggest few of these interests. Rather than economic repression they stress the development (and disintegration) of transatlantic economic interests; rather than legislative-executive conflict within the Colonies they stress the governors' use of transatlantic connections to maximize their support within the Colonial Assemblies; rather than comparing British ideas of imperial taxation with American ideas on the subject they discuss the alternative approaches open to British policy makers as the Revolution threatened. And rather than interpreting the military significance of Colonial history primarily in terms of the struggle between Britain and France for the balance of power in the new world, Anglo-American historians now are concerned rather with the character of the military governors sent to the colonies, with the connection between military crises and proposals for administrative reform of the Colonies (there was always a correlation), and with the British army as a force in imperial politics. In recent years the Anglo-Colonial historians have been "bringing the mother country into the forefront of the picture" in the broadest way by studying in its most varied context the effect of colonial status on local politics in the Colonies and the impact of the Colonies on domestic politics in Britain.

One of our objects in this book is to show a few of these new lines along which Anglo-Colonial research has been developing; equally important, we hope to suggest, by omission, lines along which it has not, for there are, even in this modest scaffolding we have erected, some timbers missing. The articles on Anglo-Colonial politics in Virginia, 1690–1730, and New York for the two decades following, for example, suggest an analysis of Anglo-Colonial connections which really ought to be made for all the Colonies and for the entire Colonial period. We must, in particular, study the men who made Anglo-Colonial politics work—the governors, the agents, and colonists who crossed the Atlantic on private business, especially in the first half of the eighteenth century. How did they maneuver? What were the criteria for success or failure on their various missions?

Take, for example, the Colonial governor. There is yet extensive work to be done on him. We need to know more about his friends and enemies, his early political experience, and his career after retirement. Enough has been written about the background of the Colonial governor to show that he was not inferior to the run of English patronage seekers, but a great many more questions need to be asked, particularly about the changing nature of gubernatorial appointments over the whole of the American Colonial period.

For one thing, it would be helpful to have a breakdown on these appointments by various ministers after 1689, to learn whether ministers' attitudes to and handling of governors' appointments changed. Stanley N. Katz, for example, suggests that Newcastle's appointments were abysmal, but he is writing about New York, where the Duke's appointments were at their worst. By contrast the Earl of Halifax is usually considered a superb colonial administrator. But a comparison of Newcastle's and Halifax's appointees in action suggests that, in fact, there was little difference between the appointments the two men made. If this is so, we may need to revise our assessment of Newcastle and Halifax as colonial administrators; we may also need to recognize a gap between the rapid development of British colonial policy in the 1750's and the much slower development of the means to carry it out.

It would also be helpful to know more about the early experience, particularly the military experience, of the Colonial governor. Around the turn of the century he almost certainly had experience in the English army, experience that may have been useful both in wartime operations and in bringing order to colonies torn by violent internal dissensions. As the years went on somewhat fewer of the governors seem to have come to the colonies from military careers, possibly because civil disturbances within the colonies were no longer expected to be a problem, possibly also because the attempts of well-meaning but inexperienced officer governors to assume command in campaigns against the French proved ill-fated both from the standpoint of the army itself and the standpoint of the colony they were supposed to be governing full time.

Did British governments change their minds about the role of the governors in developing and executing military strategy? Did they change their ideas about the qualifications of a good governor in general and about the importance of the governorship itself? These are questions whose answers would emerge from studies of the appointment and early experience of the Colonial governor. Once in the Colonies, the royal or proprietary governor had to develop his own support by working with, and at times creating, a combination of political factions and interest groups. From early in the eighteenth century, however, the governor was in something of the position the English monarch occupied a century later. He had almost no "King's Men"—no steady supporters—nor were his assemblies dominated by interest groups so effective they could ensure a majority of the governor who appeased them. Nor were there groups within the Assemblies who were inclined by interest always to support or oppose a royal executive.

So the governor was left, like the later English monarchs, and in many of the same ways, to manage his Assembly as best he could. How did he do it, and how well? Studies of the governors, their patronage, their handling of legislative crises, will help answer these questions. But now is also the time for some head-counting studies of the colonial Assemblies, combined with studies of their "managers" like Lewis Morris.

If the royal governor who arrived in the Colonies at the beginning of the eighteenth century brought with him the techniques of management his English patrons were developing at the same time, he also became increasingly subject to the criticism, then developing in England, of the abuses of such management. Even in the 1680's and 1690's official criticism of the corruption and rapaciousness of Colonial governors became widespread. The British government tried to improve the situation by sending roving inspectors and by dismissing governors suspected of excessive corruption. But the reforms were hardly effective—the inspectors were not above corruption themselves, they used and were used by partisan opponents of the governors in the several Colonies, they had no consistent standards for defining excessive corruption, and when they did succeed in getting a notorious governor dismissed the reasons for his dismissal were never made clear, either to the man himself or to the public.

The approach of the home government to the governorship stilled neither the Colonial nor the British critics of gubernatorial corruption; in the end the governor who was recalled for whatever reason returned to England embittered and determined to justify his behavior, demonstrate his knowledge of the Colonies by proposing changes in administration, and revenge himself on his successor and on his Colonial critics. The retired governor was an angry man—angry at the ministry, angry at his Colonial opponents, angry at Parliament for not putting teeth into his instructions and money into his treasury. If as much study were given to the governors' bitterness after they retired as has been given to their aspirations before they arrived we would be far better able to understand the tensions in Anglo-Colonial relations.

These are some of the questions most immediately raised by the papers which deal with particular Colonies; the other papers, particularly the ones dealing with the decade immediately before the Revolution, suggest an entirely different set of topics. John Shy's essay on Pownall and Knox, for example, shows how nearly impossible it was for contemporary English politicians to formulate an alternative to Lord North's Colonial policy in the decade before the Revolution. It is, in fact, in striking contrast with David Lovejoy's revelation of the fundamentally different alternative policies open to—and seriously considered by—the British government in handling Virginia during the Restoration. The articles suggest the need for study of the development of imperial policy as such, and taken together they imply that one of the themes of such a study would be the narrowing of the range of alternative Colonial policies available from the Restoration to the Revolutionary era. They also raise the question whether the English opposition was ever in a position to create a viable alternative to the policy of the existing ministry. What was the role of the English opposition in creating those alternatives and in shaping the government's approach to colonial administration? Was there ever a genuine difference of approach between the ministry and the opposition or even within the ministry itself after the beginning of the eighteenth century?

Similarly Michael Kammen's article discussing the divergence of English and American interest groups in the decades just before the Revolution points up the need for study of such groups in the earlier period. In the years just before the Revolution the development of English pressure groups hostile to the Americans undoubtedly reduced what chances there were for compromise and enhanced the feeling among English and Americans that they were in separate camps; earlier in the same century, however, interest groups had had the opposite effect—they had themselves often contributed to the compromise which held the Empire together. The landed and mercantile companies, the Anglican Church, the Dissenting Deputies: their very existence took some of the pressure off the political connections and contributed to the informal associations that made Anglo-Colonial politics workable. Only by pushing earlier in the century for a study of interest groups can we see the real nature of the change that took place in the 1760's.

Even within the rather narrow scope of this volume, therefore, there are important gaps to fill. But more important, there are the aspects of Anglo-Colonial politics which this volume cannot cover at all. Taken together the papers in this volume suggest the existence at one time of the sort of Anglo-Colonial community which had dissolved long before the Stamp Act controversy was injected into Anglo-Colonial politics. Indeed, by the 1750's, according to the essays, self-consciously English and American interest groups had begun to develop, the English *ad hoc* decisions so easily shaped by Anglo-Colonial politicians on Colonial issues had begun to crystallize into a policy or at least a less flexible approach, and the Anglo-Colonial politicians, DeLancey, Morris, Byrd, and others—who had crossed the Atlantic a generation before, were now ceasing to visit. If the line of these essays is drawn to its natural conclusions, the Anglo-Colonial community was an empty formality long before the Stamp Act controversy showed it to be so. The question is, why?

Before we can answer this, many studies need to be made. One set involves a comparative analysis of social development in England and America. Why, for example, did Americans seem to feel more at home in the England of 1700 than they did fifty years later? In the decade after the Glorious Revolution both English and colonial aristocracies were consolidating their political power. Both were in a state of flux. Although the Colonial politician like Byrd or Mather or Dummer found most of his friends among the lesser rank of politicians, colonial associations with some of the English aristocracy were by no means closed to him, nor was the occasion for his sons to meet, on terms of some intimacy, the sons of the aristocracy at an English school. By contrast even Franklin, the last Anglo-Colonial politician and as such an anachronism in his time, seems to have had few informal associations with the English nobility or lesser aristocracy, and while Robert Hunter Morris, visiting England in 1750, made the acquaintance of Bedford and Halifax he never exchanged social visits with them. The Colonial aristocrat seems to have felt far less comfortable in the Whig society of the fifties than he had in English society half a century before.

Why? Clearly a large part of the answer rests with the evolution of a self-conscious Whig aristocracy in England. But did the American aristocracy develop differently with different manners and with a different image of society and politics (and, of course, an entirely different legal position), or did it, in fact, develop along lines quite similar to the English aristocracy, and this very development enhance the Colonial aristocrat's resentment of an English snub? In part the answer varies from Colony to Colony: the DeLanceys, Livingstons, and their associates in New York, for example, seem the most English in their outlook, far more so than their contemporaries in Massachusetts—or North Carolina. And is the answer exclusively, or even primarily, in social conditions? Is not the significance of the Whig aristocracy that they were Whig, rather than that they were aristocrats, that the plethora of English placemen in the Colonies had led the Colonial aristocracy increasingly to respect the attitude of the eighteenth-century Tory gentlemen who openly decried Whig corruption and lauded their own independence from it? In any event, there is a stiffening, a formalizing of relations between Colonial and English aristocrats in the beginning of the eighteenth century which makes it increasingly impossible to work out informal arrangements and solve cases out of court.

This deterioration in personal relationships coincided in time with the increased British efforts to develop a "policy" for the Colonies; and the attempt to develop an overall policy necessarily narrowed the ability of the Colonial politician visiting London to affect day to day decisions. John Shy suggests that the major ideas shaping English Colonial policy of 1765–75 date back to the Earl of Halifax (a controversial politician long overdue for a biographical study). But Halifax's thought developed along the lines set out by Martin Bladen, and Bladen got some of his own ideas from the earliest members of the Board of Trade. A study of the evolution of British thinking about the Colonies—from the roving inspectors and Board of Trade members of the turn of the century through Bladen, Halifax, and ultimately Knox and Pownall would illustrate the obvious point—that the ideas of Grenville and his successors were not new— but it would also show that the number of issues regarded as questions of "policy" rather than of management or accommodation (although there was not a clear line between them) had grown, and with their growth inevitably came a narrowing of the areas on which the Anglo-Colonial politicians could have an influence.

Any study of the evolution of British Colonial thinking would involve not only biographical studies of the men who contributed to it; it would also involve the working of the Board of Trade and Privy Council themselves, not so much in terms of their organization, which has already been studied at length, but in terms of the way members arrived at their decisions, the information available to them (just what maps did they have, for example?), the overwhelming influence of the army and needs of defense in shaping policy, and the relations of the Board of Trade with the ministry. The fact that in the 1730's and 1740's certain important members of the Board of Trade seem actually to have developed their Colonial policy in cooperation with the English opposition rather than the ministry may explain why the later English opposition found itself at a loss to develop an alternative policy. It may also help to explain why the ministers of the 1730's, 1740's, and 1750's were reluctant to undertake stricter Colonial administration whereas Lord North was willing to do so, though the weakness of North's government suggests another correlation which seems to be general for the period of Colonial history: the stronger the leading minister was, the milder his colonial administration. North's failure to modify the plans of his undersecretaries was doubtless the result of the lack of a feasible alternative; but it was also true to the principle of Colonial history going back as far as Clarendon and Cromwell—namely, that a strong minister was inclined to disregard the recommendations of lower echelons for a hardening of imperial administration; a weak minister or the absence of a leading minister altogether (as in the last years of Charles and James) left no one to tone down, absorb, or ignore the recommendations of eager policy makers at lower levels; hence, there was often an inclination to stricter Colonial government. Thus at a critical stage in Anglo-Colonial history the British had the worst possible head of government to handle Colonial problems.

Policy and social structure are two topics touched upon by these essays. One that is not—in fact one that is quite strikingly absent in view of its importance in much outstanding recent scholarship—is the transit of radical ideas within the Anglo-Colonial community. This is largely by chance; the authors are simply more interested in politics and politicians. But is chance the only explanation? Is it not far more difficult than first appears actually to connect the transit of ideas with the development of a transatlantic political community? For one thing the transit of English ideas seems to have been fastest just at the time the Anglo-Colonial community was breaking up, an inverse correlation which is hardly surprising since it was the ideas of English radicals that most obviously affected Colonial thinking. How, if at all, was the Anglo-Colonial politician an agent for transmitting ideas? There is no direct evidence. How did the ideas get transmitted? We know, for example, that articles from *The Craftsman* were widely read in the Colonies. We do not know how they got here. Bolingbroke's works were not published in the Colonies until twenty years after they were widely known; there is no evidence of extensive importation of his works. How did he get read? Copies of the "commonwealthmen's" writings were in major libraries. How did they get there? There are many questions about the process by which ideas actually crossed the Atlantic that must be answered before we can fit the spread of ideas into a discussion of Anglo-Colonial politics.

And what elements in Colonial politics were most responsive to the English ideas—the colonists with the most experience in the English community, or the least? Before one can assess the effect of

English radicalism on Colonial politics one must study more the provincial factors leading to a native radicalism, the nature of radical politics in the Colonies as it developed in the 1730's, and the ideas put forth by Colonial radicals inside and outside of the Assemblies. A good part of Colonial radicalism had very little to do with Anglo-Colonial politics; it was often a reaction against the men who made their livings through that politics.

Moreover, to study British Colonial decisions, the men who lobbied for them, carried them out, and supported them in the Colonial Assemblies is usually, though by no means necessarily, to study the politics of interest and interest groups, hence, perhaps unconciously, to conceive of Empire as held together by common interests, not common theory. Theory, in the form of radicalism in the Colonies and policy in England, was the enemy of those informal connections and decisions which made the Empire work. As such, the intellectual origins of American radicalism are a vital part of the story of Anglo-Colonial politics, but it is perhaps not surprising that political historians have not found the direct connections which might seem so obvious.

Pushed to their natural conclusion, the studies in this book suggest a new dating in Colonial history. If Anglo-Colonial politics was the cement that held the Empire together, it began to crack in the 1730's. Through studying it we may revise backward the origins of the American Revolution; we may find ourselves blocking out anew all the periods of American Colonial history.

Beyond this the studies in this book suggest some new directions stemming from the earlier work of Charles McLean Andrews. They may, however, suggest more—taken along with other new strands of Colonial scholarship they may indicate that we are ready to go beyond Andrews' conceptualizations, ready to take Anglo-Colonial politics into a new stage of comparative studies, over both time and place. We are far overdue for a comparative study of European Colonial methods in the seventeenth and eighteenth centuries. A comparison of the Anglo-American and the Franco-American communities in the early eighteenth century would reveal more similarities in the patterns of Colonial decision-making than are usually acknowledged; it would also show why British Colonial reformers were particularly impressed by the French administration of their colonies and eager to emulate the details of French management. And certainly it is time to bring material from the American Colonies into general studies of the relative development of representative institutions, the army, the creation of political factions, the forms, definitions, and uses of corruption, and the effectiveness of the mother country in controlling its own colonial officials in underdeveloped countries. Not until we can better fit the Colonies into eighteenth-century European politics on the one hand and into the contemporary pattern of developing countries on the other, can we begin to assess the American Revolution in its relation to other types of revolutions.

Meanwhile we are reaching the time in Anglo-Colonial politics when, in Andrews' words, the "duality of interest will be regarded as a necessary part of the stock-in-trade of every serious writer on the subject who deals with [Colonial history] in a fair minded and comprehensive way . . . not until that time has come will this long and eventful period of our country's past receive its merited treatment as history."

The Anglo-American Political System, 1675–1775:
A Behavioral Analysis

RICHARD MAXWELL BROWN is a graduate of Reed College with his A.M. and Ph.D. from Harvard University. He has taught at Rutgers University and is now Professor of History at The College of William and Mary and a member of the Council of the Institute of Early American History and Culture. He is the author of *The South Carolina Regulators* (1963), the editor of *American Violence* (1970), and has contributed studies on "Historical Patterns of Violence in America" and "The American Vigilante Tradition" to *Violence in America: Historical and Comparative Perspectives: A Report to the National Commission on the Causes and Prevention of Violence*, ed. Hugh D. Graham and Ted R. Gurr (1969). He is currently at work on a history of colonial South Carolina and on a history of American vigilantism.

. . . behavioral research in politics . . . seeks to describe and explain the political behavior of a group, an organization, a community, an elite, a mass movement, or a nation, but also assumes that such collectivities do not exist apart from the conduct of their individual members. The interactions and transactions of these members make for systemic relationships that are structurally discrete and functionally specific and can be meaningfully studied.*

* Heinz Eulau, "Political Behavior," p. 203, in David L. Sills, ed., *International Encyclopedia of the Social Sciences* (17 vols.; New York, 1968), Vol. XII.

1. The Rise of Anglo-American Politics, circa 1675–1700.

The period from about 1675 to 1700 was the era in which the Colonies were forcibly made aware of their existence in a tightening imperial setting. Elements of the system that would mature after 1700 made their appearance, but the main significance of the era was the revolution in consciousness thrust on the colonists by the aggressive new imperial trend. The trend was signaled in many ways: by the abortive but significant Dominion of New England, by the forging of the mercantilist economic system in the Acts of Trade and Navigation, and by the establishment of a series of colonial supervisory bodies climaxed by the creation of the Board of Trade in 1696. All developments focused on one point: that the Colonies must accept a more circumscribed role in a taut new transatlantic imperial system.

The implications of their new role were impressed on the colonists at every turn: in Massachusetts Bay by the royalizing of the previously autonomous Bay Colony,[1] in Jamaica where the Crown took control of the executive and cracked down on the Assembly,[2] and in Virginia by royal rejection of the colonists' self-drawn charter of self-government.[3] Acting through the ambitious new Colonial agency, the Lords of Trade,[4] the Crown struck body blows at the hitherto nearly perfect autonomy of the three Colonies. In Massachusetts, for example, there had been no official communication of any sort with the home government for almost a decade from 1666 to 1674.[5]

The strategy of Crown administrators was to break the power of the factions, which had manipulated the autonomy of their respective Colonies to serve their own interests. Thus the old Puritan faction of Massachusetts was pushed aside by the revocation of the Charter of 1629, the basis of its authority.[6] In Jamaica the dominant pirate faction that had been led for years by Sir Thomas Modyford was warned "in plain terms" by Secretary of State Coventry that "the King intendeth to make a Plantation" of the Colony "and not a Christian Algiers."[7] About the same time Charles II and his ministers turned against the Virginia regime of Governor William Berkeley whose rapacious self-interest had provoked rebellion and sent the royal revenues on tobacco spinning downward.[8]

Many in the Colonies sensed the new trend and were anxious for closer union with the home government. They "perceived that the traditional autonomy was out of date, and that liaison with the crown opened new avenues to wealth and power." [9] It was to these impatient, opportunistic new interest groups that the King's government turned. In Massachusetts the "moderate" faction of "non-Puritan merchants and land speculators" supported the efforts of royal agent Edward Randolph to cancel Massachusetts' "precious chartered liberties." [10] In Jamaica "a compact group of large-scale sugar planters" had long chafed under buccaneer domination, and hence were willing to exchange a reduction in autonomy for the end of pirate power. With the pirates ousted the sugar planters moved in, and, as sugar profits and customs revenues soared, Sir William Beeston, a big planter, governed the remodeled Jamaica "to the satisfaction of the Jamaicans and the plantation office" alike.[11]

The situation was more amorphous in Virginia where the short-lived opposition faction of Nathanael Bacon had been shorn of its leadership by the death of its chieftain and the hanging of his lieutenants. But in 1677 the royal commissioners found a bedrock of local hostility which could be appeased only by the ouster of Berkeley.[12] In the general satisfaction over the shattering of the oppressive Berkeley machine, the colonists paid little heed to Charles II's rejection of the draft charter of 1674 which had enshrined "the principle of self-government" and had confirmed the old autonomy of Berkeleyan days.[13]

In Massachusetts the sudden appearance in 1686 of Royal Governor Sir Edmund Andros in his scarlet laced coat at the head of two companies of soldiers was a traumatic experience for Samuel Sewall and the other Bostonians who stood gaping at the sight.[14] The shock wore off, but Bay colonists—like other Americans—were now conscious of certain changes that would never be reversed. Although "the Glorious Revolution ended Stuart despotism in the colonies," the "Stuart idea of the English Empire as a self-contained unit" survived. The next stage involved a "natural interaction between English and American politics" which produced something greater than either: Anglo-American politics.[15]

2. The Anglo-American Political System, circa 1700–1765.

The interpretation of the Anglo-American political system which follows is a gloss on the historical essays in this book. The essays drive home the point that a political system was involved. Reference to the literature on political systems reveals that Anglo-American politics, ca. 1700–1765, does indeed conform to the political-system model as developed by David Easton and other political scientists.[16] Figure 1 in this essay is based upon Easton's model of a political system, and its general characteristics are those diagrammed by Easton.[17] Its specific terms are those delineated by the contributors to this book and by other authorities on Anglo-American politics in our Colonial period. In this instance the contribution of political theory is to validate the insight already gleaned from the work of historians: namely, that Anglo-American politics embodied a complete, fully developed system—a system that did more than merely encompass the politics of the mother country and the Colonies but transcended it in a configuration that was the Anglo-American political system.

The procedure has involved a dual test of the concept of the Anglo-American political system through the measures of historical evidence and political theory. The concept is verified by both criteria. A part of the testing process was the case of the Virginia Tobacco Act of 1730 and the defeat of Robert Walpole's Excise Bill in 1733—events that are analyzed in this book by David Alan Williams.[18] This case was applied to the paradigm of the Anglo-American political system as sketched in Figure 1, and the result was Figure 2. Williams' account of the case described the way in which pressures stemming from the Virginia tobacco interest, the English tobacco merchants, and the English landed gentry in conjunction with the initiatives of Virginia Governor William Gooch and English first minister Robert Walpole (in interaction with other officials and agencies) led to three crucial political actions: the Tobacco Act of 1730, the English Colonial Debt Law of 1732, and the defeat of Walpole's excise. The details of Williams' narrative fit perfectly into the theoretical terms of the political-system model encompassing environment, inputs,[19] outputs,[20] demands,[21] decisions and actions, and

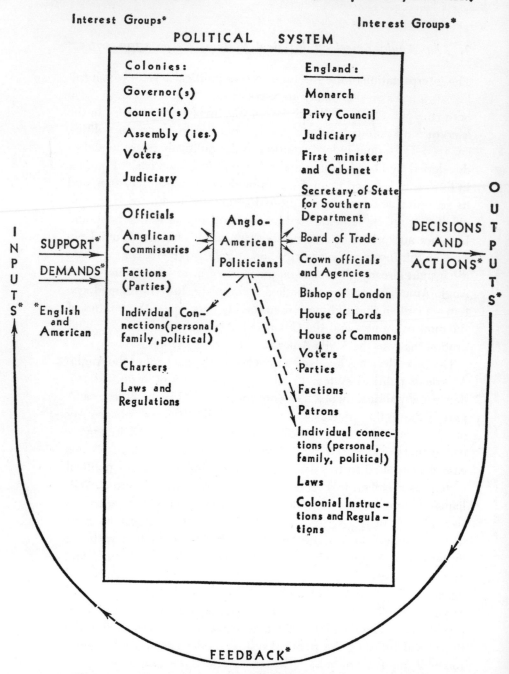

ENVIRONMENT
(Social, Economic, Intellectual)*

ENVIRONMENT
(Social, Economic, Intellectual)*

Interest Groups*

Interest Groups*

POLITICAL SYSTEM

Colonies:

Governor(s)
Council(s)
Assembly (ies.)
Voters
Judiciary

Officials
Anglican
Commissaries

Factions
(Parties)

Individual Con-
nections(personal,
family, political)

Charters

Laws and
Regulations

England:

Monarch
Privy Council
Judiciary
First minister
and Cabinet
Secretary of State
for Southern
Department
Board of Trade
Crown officials
and Agencies
Bishop of London
House of Lords
House of Commons
Voters
Parties
Factions
Patrons
Individual connec-
tions (personal,
family, political)
Laws
Colonial Instruc-
tions and Regula-
tions

Anglo-
American
Politicians

INPUTS*

SUPPORT*

DEMANDS*

*English
and
American

DECISIONS
AND
ACTIONS*

OUTPUTS*

FEEDBACK*

FIGURE 1. The Anglo-American Political System, *ca.* 1700–1765.

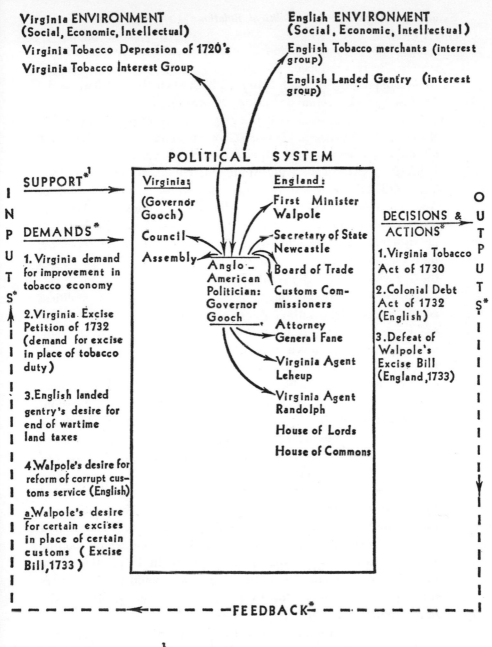

POLITICAL SYSTEM

Virginia ENVIRONMENT
(Social, Economic, Intellectual)

Virginia Tobacco Depression of 1720's

Virginia Tobacco Interest Group

English ENVIRONMENT
(Social, Economic, Intellectual)

English Tobacco merchants (interest group)

English Landed Gentry (interest group)

INPUTS*

SUPPORT*[1]

DEMANDS*

1. Virginia demand for improvement in tobacco economy

2. Virginia Excise Petition of 1732 (demand for excise in place of tobacco duty)

3. English landed gentry's desire for end of wartime land taxes

4. Walpole's desire for reform of corrupt customs service (English)

a. Walpole's desire for certain excises in place of certain customs (Excise Bill, 1733)

Virginia:
(Governor Gooch)
Council
Assembly

Anglo-American Politician: Governor Gooch

England:
First Minister Walpole
Secretary of State Newcastle
Board of Trade
Customs Commissioners
Attorney General Fane
Virginia Agent Leheup
Virginia Agent Randolph
House of Lords
House of Commons

DECISIONS & ACTIONS*

1. Virginia Tobacco Act of 1730

2. Colonial Debt Act of 1732 (English)

3. Defeat of Walpole's Excise Bill (England, 1733)

OUTPUTS*

FEEDBACK*

*English and American   [1]Inputs of Support are actions and orientations

FIGURE 2. The Anglo-American Political System in Operation, 1730–1733. A case: The passage of the Virginia Tobacco Act of 1730 and the defeat of Walpole's Excise Bill, 1733. Based on Figure 1 and Williams, "Anglo-Virginia Politics," pp. 89–91.

feedback.[22] The combination of historical evidence with political-system theory produced, therefore, Figure 2. Hence, the Anglo-American political system is observed both in an abstract flow model (Figure 1) and in actual operation (Figure 2).

Figures 1 and 2 reveal that the Anglo-American politician was at the center of the system. He was the one who made it function. Like all politicians driven above all else to succeed, the necessities of his political survival defined the limits and boundaries of the system. The poles of the system were in London and the Colonial capitals of America. For the politician the difficulty—and thus the challenge and complexity of Anglo-American politics—was that he had two constituencies. To cultivate one at the neglect of the other was fatal, for each was an unrelenting master. The "complete politician" [23] was the one who mastered the system by satisfying each.

One constituency was the politician's own colony. The political colony by mid-eighteenth century had come to a focus in the Colonial lower house, the Assembly. The vibrant factionalism of the typical American colony was a study in itself for the politician and has in turn been the subject of numerous studies by historians.[24] The other constituency—the one with which the essays in this book are mainly concerned—was that of Whitehall and Westminster in London: Parliament, the Cabinet, and the Colonial administrators. Here the "connections" of the Anglo-American politician were crucial. Without them he would have soon been swallowed up in the grinding maw of the British sector of Anglo-American politics.

A decline of standing with one constituency was instantly detected by the other, for the constituents were as aware as the politician of the seamless nature of the transatlantic political web. A loss of connections (family, personal, or patronage) in England would soon be known in America, and a consequent reduction in the prestige of the politician would follow.[25] On the other hand, should the politician's rapport with his always "touchy people" [26] in America dissolve the news would reach England and his reputation there would be subject to discount, for in this period British authorities strongly desired stability in the colonies.[27] Among both constituencies the factions, parties, connections, officials, and interest groups were the operational units in the Anglo-American political system in which the politician nursed his career (see Figure 1).

Interest group proliferation on both sides of the Atlantic was a basic fact of the system.[28] A host of British interest groups had a continuing concern with the colonies. American interest groups kept a weather eye on their political and economic flanks in Whitehall and the City. Many interests were truly transatlantic. Thus the Jamaican sugar interest stretched from the slave plantations of the island colony to the sumptuous English residences of their absentee owners. Another important, though by no means unitary, transatlantic interest was the Anglican Church whose key figure in the Colonies —the Commissary of the Bishop of London—is treated in this book by Alison Gilbert Olson.[29]

Perhaps more common were the interest groups of one locale which of necessity were cognizant of and interested in developments in the other. On the English side, the iron manufacturers were interested in protecting their markets from nascent Colonial competition. The British financial, mercantile, fishing, and textile interests, among others, maintained a like viewpoint on Colonial affairs. By the same token, American interest groups—large merchants in Massachusetts, tobacco planters in Virginia,[30] land speculators, and the like—were ever aware that the edicts of Whitehall might affect them crucially, nor were they bashful about carrying demands unsatisfied in America to the higher authority of Cabinet and Commons. The complexity of now competing, now complementing interest groups might seem to be a source of ineradicable chaos, but, on the contrary, Michael G. Kammen has shown that between the interest groups and government "an equilibrium" prevailed.[31] The result was that interest groups when "viewed in broad perspective" [32] lent stability and cohesiveness to the Anglo-American political system.

As the system evolved in the eighteenth century the politics of the mainland Colonies became more and more linked with the politics of Whitehall and Westminster. Colonial politicians began valuing their English connections more highly than ever and increasingly sought English decisions for the settlement of their own factional disputes. The politics of the mainland Colonies became closely integrated with the politics of England. Politicians on both sides of the Atlantic found themselves as never before working for the same objectives, for provincial politics had changed and adapted to changes in English politics.

With the original issues which had divided the early colonists dying down and a local aristocracy developing in the various provinces, Colonial politics ceased to be a life-and-death struggle between religious or economic groups fighting for survival. Now the well-to-do provincial leaders played the game of politics for patronage and prestige, or for the land grants, commercial contracts, and other spoils involved. Sources of such rewards were the English governors or even English politicians in London. Initially the governors owed their appointments to the support of English patrons.[33] Once in the Colonies they found it essential to win the support of influential politicians and the Assembly factions with which the latter were associated. This they did by a judicious distribution of land grants, commercial contracts, judgeships, council positions, and other provincial offices.

Offices such as that of Chief Justice or councillor had to be approved at Whitehall, and important court cases were appealed to London. For a while colonists were even willing to appeal their local disputes to Parliament. Not only did Colonial politicians thus become involved in English politics, but English officials sent to the Colonies found themselves drawn into local politics. That governors became involved with provincial factions is not surprising, but customs officials, military commanders, and even ministers of the Church of England also took active roles in the factional struggles within the colonies and often, surprisingly, found themselves among the leaders of the opposition to Colonial governors.[34]

Colonial political factions or parties[35] represented the merged efforts of interest groups and politicians stemming from the linkage of socioeconomic forces with the forces of personal ambition. The Colonial faction had many arrows in its quiver. Aside from the constant need to dominate the Colony through ceaseless activity in Assembly and Council chamber, the faction brought many pressures to bear in England. The lobbying of cooperating or constituent interest groups in Whitehall or Westminster was effective. Agents—nominally representing the Colony as a whole but usually the exclusive servant of the dominant faction in the Assembly—were sent to London (or employed there) for the purpose of cultivating the politically influential wherever they might be found. But the most effective instrument of the Colonial faction or party was the Anglo-American politician.

The Anglo-American politician brought his skill to bear in the British arena where all depended on his connections and the talent with which he maintained and manipulated them. The Anglo-American politician was not a frequent visitor to England. He usually held an official position in the Colony that required his constant presence. Moreover, the security of his position in the Colony depended heavily upon his ability as a political leader and organizer. To function effectively in these roles he had to be present personally in America. His British connections depended not upon his personal presence, then, but upon the importance of his patrons, the standing of his family relations, and the potency of his political friends. If on all counts his connections were good, he could maintain their strength and tenacity with an attentive correspondence and, when necessary, the dispatch of an emissary. If his connections were not of the first rank, personal attendance would have done little to improve matters.

An Anglo-American politician without a patron was a contradiction in terms. In Massachusetts Jonathan Belcher and William Shirley competed for the favor of the Duke of Newcastle, a patron made preeminent by his crucial position as Secretary of State for the Southern Department.[36] The leading Anglo-American politicians in New York were strongly identified with their British patrons: George Clinton with Newcastle, George Clarke with William Blathwayt and the great Robert Walpole, and Cadwallader Colden with the Marquis of Lothian.[37]

The Anglo-American politician at his best possessed British connections with all the permutations of a deck of cards. As the occasion demanded he played tricks and trumps with the cunning of a cardsharp. Stanley N. Katz has recorded the virtuoso performance of James DeLancey, who built a career and served his faction well in New York.[38] DeLancey had the connections to cover all bets. By marriage he was related to Sir John Heathcote (brother-in-law of a Newcastle crony and friend of Walpole) and to enormously wealthy Admiral Peter Warren who was ever willing to enlist his efficacious political connections in the interest of DeLancey's career. By long standing ties of personal friendship the fortunate DeLancey was linked to the primate, Thomas Herring, Archbishop of Canterbury, and to the Baker brothers, powerful London merchants who cut a swath in both politics and economics. Such were the variety of De-Lancey's connections and the guile with which he manipulated them that he was able to bring off the near miracle of undercutting George Clinton with Clinton's own patron, Newcastle.[39]

No ideology emerged to support the unified whole that was the Anglo-American political system. The system was purely operational in character. Interest groups, factions, parties, politicians, and imperial administrators blended together in a functioning unity. There were tensions and strains, to be sure, but compensating forces checked and balanced each other. The result was an equilibrium, an interaction of forces and men, a *system*.[40] The Anglo-American politicians were the brokers who made the delicately geared system function so well for more than half a century.

3. *The Collapse of the Anglo-American Political System, circa 1765–1775.*

The dissolution of Anglo-American unity in the 1760's and 1770's is a familiar tale. Stringencies of the French war's debt, economic change, and imperial reorganization brought on a mounting crisis in which the multiform interests of the old Anglo-American political system polarized into American and English blocs.[41] Thus Anglo-American politics "died of strangulation." [42] Many sensed that something was in the wind. Thomas Pownall was witness in 1764 to the postwar mood in England wherein "some new state of things" was arising in regard to relations between mother country and colonies.[43]

Straws in the winds of change revealed the maturation of "hard line" thinking on the part of imperial officials. The attitude was new, but some of the premises were old. As far back as 1716 the idea of a Colonial civil list based upon an augmented colonial revenue had been developed.[44] Traced back to the Earl of Halifax's presidency of the Board of Trade, 1748–1761, is an increasingly prevalent belief that the somewhat ramshackle and disorderly Empire should be rationalized and made more efficient.[45] Tendencies along this line are seen in a Board of Trade collection of reports which spelled out in detail in Colony after Colony the unseemly disorder in imperial relations and in the Treasury letter of 1763 to the Privy Council which argued that English authority was simply too weak in America.[46]

Left in the lurch was the Anglo-American politician who had acted as broker and fixer in the old transatlantic political system. A few—like Benjamin Franklin—made the transition to the new era, but most of the old Anglo-American politicians fell by the wayside, their positions made untenable by the decline of the system that had produced them. The DeLancey family went into political eclipse, eventually and typically—marching down the dead end street of American loyalism. The future in America belonged to those politicians "who were more completely identified with American interests." [47]

While the Anglo-American politician was becoming more and more isolated during the 1760's, one of the paragons of the breed, Thomas Pownall,[48] was attempting to remedy a grave deficiency of the Anglo-American political system: its lack of an explicit and commonly accepted ideology or doctrine upon which basis the crumbling structure might be firmly cemented together. The lack of an ideology was the fatal flaw in the system which had functioned so well in an operative sense. In the absence of a widely held doctrine of Anglo-American unity, the stage was set for the naked clash of irreconcilable American and English interests. To bridge the doctrinal gap was the task which, as John Shy shows in this book, Thomas Pownall set for himself in several editions of *The Administration of the Colonies*. Although an Englishman himself and long schooled in imperial government and administration, from an American point of view no one could have been better for the difficult job than Pownall, for he was a true friend of the Colonies and, for his time, a political radical. During the quarrels of the 1760's and early 1770's Pownall was ever pro-American and on the "liberal" side. He could never agree with the likes of Henry Ellis, the "hard line" former governor of Georgia. But as Shy has shown there was no essential difference in basic premises between the liberal Pownall and the irreconcilable Ellis. Thomas Pownall could never go beyond the dogma of a rationalized and more efficient Empire based, crucially, upon the recognition of Parliamentary sovereignty.[49] For all his good will, understanding, and sympathy for the colonists, the rationale of Pownall by its insistence upon Parliamentary supremacy simply did not reflect the bivalent reality of the Anglo-American political system.

With the failure of Pownall—or any other—to develop a theory that would jibe with the practice of Anglo-American politics, Englishmen and Americans could only fall back on stale and hidebound constitutional shibboleths: "the one prevalent in America emphasized the equal rights of all Englishmen, while the other, held widely in Britain, stressed the necessary subordination of colonies." [50] The impasse in doctrine prepared the way for the final clash.

In his theoretical work on the political system David Easton has emphasized the concept of *inputs of support,* by which he asserts that actions or orientations which promote goals, ideas, institutions, actions, or persons constantly enter the political system and thereby support it.[51] In theoretical terms the Anglo-American system ultimately broke apart because its inputs of support gradually withered in the period 1765–1775. The withdrawal of the inputs of support is described in part by Michael G. Kammen in his narration of the fragmentation of interest groups in the 1760's and 1770's and by John Shy in his sketch of Thomas Pownall's doomed attempt to provide a theoretical basis for the Anglo-American political system. Had Pownall succeeded, his contribution would have been to provide a crucial input of support for the system by which (following Easton) an *orientation* (Pownall's) would have promoted a *goal* (the prevention of Anglo-American rupture) and an *institution* (the system itself).

While interest groups were spinning apart and Pownall was floundering a series of *outputs* (decisions and actions such as the Stamp Act, Townshend Acts, Tea Act, Coercive Acts, Non-Importation, Boston Tea Party, and the Continental Association) from the political system were having a disastrous *feedback* that fostered not only new, negative inputs of demand but cumulative erosion of the inputs of support. The result was the collapse of the Anglo-American political system.

A NOTE ON METHOD

For the behavioral analysis of politics the work of David Easton has been most important, beginning with his pioneering book, *The Political System . . .* (New York, 1953), which was an incisive critique of the older, nonbehavioral political science and theory and an influential call for more study of two types of behavioral data: the situational and the psychological. In a classic article, "An Approach to the Analysis of Political Systems," *World Politics*, IX (1956–57), 383–400, Easton published his diagrammatic model of a political system (*ibid.*, p. 384) in which the main terms were environment, inputs, outputs, demands, support, and feedback. Easton has used his paradigm (upon which Figures 1 and 2 in this essay are based) in two important recent books, *A Framework for Political Analysis* (Englewood Cliffs, N. J., 1965), p. 112, and *A Systems Analysis of Political Life* (New York, London, and Sydney, 1965), p. 32, in which he has elaborated his behavioral conception of politics. The Easton paradigm has had a wide impact. See, for example, Bertram M. Gross's adaptation of it for his "general system model" on p. 182 of his monograph, "The State of the Nation: Social Systems Accounting," in Raymond A. Bauer, ed., *Social Indicators* (Cambridge, Mass., and London, [1966]).

Significant contributions to the behavioral theory of political systems have also been made by Gabriel A. Almond in three widely cited works: "Comparative Political Systems," *Journal of Politics*, XVIII (1956), 391–409; "A Functional Approach to Comparative Politics," pp. 3–64, in Almond and James S. Coleman, eds., *The Politics of Developing Areas* (Princeton, 1960); and Almond and G. Bingham Powell, Jr., *Comparative Politics: A Developmental Approach* (Boston and Toronto, 1966). S. N. Eisenstadt, *The Political Systems of Empires* (New York, [1963]) deals largely with non-European "historical bureaucratic empires" and gives only passing attention to the old British Empire.

The new *International Encyclopedia of the Social Sciences*, ed. David L. Sills (17 vols.; New York, 1968) includes four articles that present fine summaries of the state of scholarship in regard to their respective subjects. The articles are: David Easton, "Political Science," Vol. XII, pp. 282–298; Heinz Eulau, "Political Behavior," Vol. XII, pp. 203–214; Bertram M. Gross, "Political Process," Vol. XII, pp. 265–273; and William C. Mitchell, "Political Systems," Vol. XV, pp. 473–479. The excellent bibliographies of these articles comprise the most convenient guide to the literature of the behavioral approach to political systems.

A penetrating and comprehensive book, *A Behavioral Approach to Historical Analysis* (New York and London, 1969), has just been published by Robert F. Berkhofer, Jr. Berkhofer's footnotes constitute the most up-to-date and inclusive bibliography of the behavioral approach to historical interpretation.

II

ESSAYS ON ANGLO-AMERICAN
POLITICAL RELATIONS, 1675–1775

Virginia's Charter and Bacon's Rebellion, 1675–1676

DAVID S. LOVEJOY is a graduate of Bowdoin College and he received his A.M. and Ph.D. from Brown University. He has taught at Marlboro College, Brown University, and Northwestern and is now Professor of History at the University of Wisconsin. His publications include *Rhode Island Politics and the American Revolution, 1760–1776* (1958), "Rights Imply Equality: The Case Against Admiralty Jurisdiction in America, 1764–1776" (*William and Mary Quarterly*, 1959), and a reader called *Religious Enthusiasm and the Great Awakening* (1969). He is now preparing a book on the Glorious Revolution in America.

The history of Colonial America is more explicit about the emerging British policy than it is about colonists' response to it and their experience as settlers. Policy was a matter of laws, proclamations, and instructions; what went on in the minds of colonists is not always easy to determine. The period between the Restoration and the Glorious Revolution was a time of new regulations and centralization of control. Sometimes rules handed down by the planners clashed with the colonists' self-interest and assumptions—even presumptions—about what they were doing in the New World and how they ought to be treated. Certainly, most Englishmen could agree that Colonial policy was based generally on concepts of what we now call mercantilism, but these were not precise and could be worked out in a variety of ways. Doubtless, too, Colonies existed for the benefit of the Mother Country, but colonists believed they were Englishmen who happened to live outside the realm and therefore ought not to be discriminated against.

Rapid development after 1660, both economic and political, often created uncertainty in the minds of colonists about the bases of their settlement. The effect of intensification of policy was to force them to seek guarantees and assurances against what they believed were "mutacons." In searching for guarantees they came to a number of conclusions about the Empire and their place in it, and what rights and privileges colonists in America ought to enjoy.

Each Colony responded in its own way to new policies of the Restoration, depending, of course, on its local circumstances. New York lacked a representative Assembly, and its history from the conquest in 1664 was colored by an intense struggle to secure one. But the struggle itself and the charter which resulted have meaning only in terms of New York's needs and assumptions.[1]

Virginia affords an even better example of a Colony which attempted in the latter half of the seventeenth century to define the limits of its relation to the Crown and the Mother Country. It did so in a drive to secure a charter in 1675. Like New York, Virginia's response was in constitutional terms, and the content was dictated by its peculiar conditions. What makes Virginia's experience more striking is that in these same conditions, which produced the struggle for the charter, lay also the causes of Bacon's Rebellion.

I

Virginians confronted a number of problems after Charles II was restored to the throne in 1660. Chief among these was their tobacco economy, which suffered under surpluses that had drastically forced down the price the planter received for his crop. Parliament in 1660 aggravated the problem by forcing all Colonial tobacco to England where it became an even greater drug on the market. Governor William Berkeley, who found the Navigation Acts "Mighty and destructive" to Virginia's economy, preached diversification in the hope that

it would afford the colonists a better life and through broader economic efforts still serve the King.[2] But diversification was not easy,
particularly since Virginia's climate and geography presented excellent conditions for tobacco. Moreover, once Virginians commenced
production when the price was high, it was next to impossible, or at
least seemed so, to give up and start over with other crops since
money, land, time, and labor were already heavily invested. On top
of this, revenue to the Exchequer depended not on the price but on
the amount of tobacco shipped to England, and as the Colonial policy intensified in the middle 1670's under the Lords of Trade's
guidance, the Crown became more and more dependent upon the
annual tobacco customs. Berkeley was well aware of this and found
it a difficult obstacle to overcome in directing diversification. Earlier
the Crown had encouraged his efforts, but as customs mounted,
royal support became increasingly disingenuous. By 1676 tobacco
customs amounted to probably £100,000 a year, although several
other figures, some higher, were mentioned. Revenue from the tobacco colonies alone was estimated at a third of all English customs
in 1670.[3]

In arguing against restrictions, Governor Berkeley tried hard to
impress the King with the Colony's real value to the realm. In doing
so he doubtless impressed yeoman farmers even more, for he reported about 1675 that Virginia and the King's revenue from it had
increased to the point that "there is not one laborer here that does
not pay the king five pounds sterling yearly." [4] Eight years earlier a
member of Berkeley's Council had estimated that 1200 pounds of
tobacco was average for one man to produce in a year. If the planter
received a half-penny a pound for it (as he did in 1667), his total
income for the year was fifty shillings, or two and a half pounds, out
of which came taxes and other necessities. This was precious little for
a poor man who had a family to keep, and it probably seemed even
less when he learned that what he produced in Virginia paid the
King five pounds each year in England. Profits were so small in the
1660's that Secretary Ludwell could "attribute it to nothing but the
great mercy of God . . . that keeps [the poor people] from mutiny
and confusion." [5] It is revealing to learn what the cost of Empire was
to those in Virginia who did the work.

Politically, Berkeley found ways to get along with Virginians, at least with the Assembly, the people who made up the government, if not the people as a whole. Virginia boasted not a government of the people anyway, nor did it mean to. It was the "better sort" whom the Burgesses increasingly represented and the very best who found a voice in the Council. This was particularly true after 1670 when the Assembly restricted suffrage to the freeholders, that is, property owners, eliminating the propertyless freemen who had elected Burgesses for some time.[6]

Berkeley and the Assembly worked well together and saw eye-to-eye on a number of things. But placid relations between the governor and his Assembly did not hide the growing uneasiness of Virginians as a whole during the 1670's, and doubtless the growing elite quality of the government was one cause. There were other causes, too, and some were vital to the well-being of large numbers of colonists. First, of course, was the price of tobacco, which had tumbled some time before and had remained generally depressed despite attempts at diversification and even cessation of planting. The effect of low prices was universal throughout the Colony and bore upon all levels of society, for all of Virginia was tied to a single crop.

The normal trade in tobacco at best was unrewarding, but war with the Dutch interrupted even this. In 1673 a squadron of bold Dutchmen sailed up the James River and without opposition burned six vessels laden with Virginia tobacco and made prizes of five more. All told, the loss in this one-sided engagement was 5,600 hogsheads, a sizeable portion of the total production.[7]

Acts of God always had plagued Virginia, but they seemed to accumulate in the middle 1670's. The winter of 1674–1675 was particularly severe, destroying a good many cattle. As a result, food was dear until new crops provided more. There was "much distress for victuals," since the bad winter was followed by an extreme drought which played havoc with the Indian corn and spoiled provisions for hogs. In one plantation area a multitude of squirrels swept down out of the woods and devoured what corn was left and most of the potatoes. Reports circulated in England that Virginia's "condition is much worse than it has been for many years." [8]

Already suffering from a lack of food, Virginians were convinced that the Plantation Act of 1673, which placed a duty on intercolonial trade in tobacco, worsened conditions, limiting their outlets through

New England. Yankee shipmasters were wary of the penny impost, and when they did not come to load tobacco, they did not bring corn and "other necessaries" more cheaply supplied than from other places.[9]

Taxes were burdensome, and this was universal, too, but the poorer sort believed they were the sufferers, for Virginia taxes were levied *per poll* at the colony, county, and parish levels. A Virginian paid taxes in proportion to the number of tithables he supported, family, servants, and slaves. Granted the large planter who kept more servants and slaves paid more than his humbler neighbor, the difference was not in proportion to relative wealth and ability to pay, since the size of one's holdings had no effect on the levy. The smaller farmers and poorer sort were sure that the tax system discriminated against them, and they were probably right, although maybe not as absolutely as they imagined.[10]

With Dutchmen marauding their coasts and Indians disturbing the frontier—a reverberation from King Philip's War in New England—[11] Virginians' taxes were raised abruptly in the 1670's to build castles and forts against invasion from the sea and attacks from the hinterland. The threat of war was unsettling enough, but an increase in taxes, unevenly distributed, physical hardships, characteristic of early Colonies anywhere, and then acts of a distant Parliament which confined their trade and seemed to force them for survival to grow more of the very crop which tended to suffocate them—all these and more created an uneasiness and uncertainty which Virginians found hard to live with in the 1670's.

While these problems were accumulating, Charles II contributed another which further undermined Virginians' confidence in what they were doing and sharply aggravated the uncertainty of the times. In the early 1670's they grew increasingly aware that Virginia belonged not altogether to them and the King as a royal Colony but to two different groups of proprietors to whom Charles in feudal manner had granted rights to land over several years' time. The first gift, the Northern Neck, a long stretch of land between the Rappahannock and Potomac Rivers, a desperate and newly exiled Charles had granted in 1649 to several royalists, including John Lord Culpeper, Sir John Berkeley, and several others. Virginia had gained these proprietors nothing during the Commonwealth and Protectorate periods, but upon the Restoration, with their King back on the throne, they had trotted out their patent for all to see and made preparations to exercise authority and collect quitrents. Despite some modification in 1669, the proprietors still enjoyed rights to divide the land into manors, to hold courts baron, to have markets and fairs, collect tolls, customs, fines, and other perquisites including quitrents.[12]

In the midst of their wondering and complaining about the King's generosity to his courtiers, Virginians were thunderstruck when Charles in 1673 granted to Lords Arlington and Culpeper the remaining part of Virginia to the south "with all rights appurtenances . . . jurisdictions . . . and royalties whatsoever." Again, this was not the right to govern, but who knew what it might become. It did include escheats and quitrents—these last in specie rather than tobacco—and a lot more.[13]

There is no doubt that granting away to proprietors land already settled and planted bred "infinite discontents" and "sad effects." Thomas Ludwell, one of Governor Berkeley's right-hand men, put it succinctly when he wrote home that he had "never observed anything so much move the people's grief or passion, or which doth more put a stop to their industry, than their uncertainty whether they should make a country for the King or other Proprietors." If the King had wanted to discourage his subjects in Virginia, he could not have hit upon a surer way.[14] What *was* Virginia, and what right did people there have to their lands if the King could grant them away and allow proprietors to gobble them up? Were not colonists the King's subjects like any other Englishmen? Or were they in a class by themselves whose rights no one seemed to respect?

Jamestown was a busy place in September 1674 when the Virginia Assembly met to discover some scheme which would protect Virginians from their enemies, the proprietors, or maybe even from their best friend, the King. The scheme hit upon was the appointment of an agency of three men to treat with the King and the powers-that-be for the purpose of buying out the proprietors and coming to terms with the English government about the rights of Virginians. In the fall of 1674, three agents, Francis Moryson, Thomas Ludwell, and Robert Smith, left Jamestown armed with petitions, letters, and instructions to commence their campaign in London against the proprietors and in behalf of Virginians' rights.[15]

Before and after the agents arrived in London, Governor Berkeley sent a barrage of arguments against the proprietors' claims, ranging from high principle to common horse sense. Virginians, wrote Berkeley, ought to "have something out of their sweat and labour to supply their necessities," and this they could not if the proprietors exercised to its utmost the authority included in their patents. As it looked to the governor, the proprietors' agents had begun already to "grind" the people and leave only "disorder" behind them. Besides Berkeley, most Virginians were apprehensive lest the proprietors seriously disturb the headright system, which worked in Virginians' favor, and insist upon the collection of quitrents heretofore spotty and paid in tobacco not specie.[16]

Once in London, the Virginia agents had their hands full. First they negotiated with Lords Arlington and Culpeper and exacted their promise to reduce claims in the larger, southern grant to just quitrents and escheats. Then they petitioned the King, requesting Letters Patent which would allow the Colony to incorporate—in order to buy out the proprietors of the Northern Neck—and at the same time to guarantee Virginians the "future security" of their "rights, properties, and privileges." Either the Assembly or the agents organized the latter request under ten "Heads" which accompanied the petition and which, the agents hoped, would form the bases of a charter.[17]

The original charter, granted to the Virginia Company of London, had been revoked by James I in 1624 when he took the settlement under his wing, making it the first royal Colony in America. Since that time, except for the Puritan interlude, Virginia had functioned through commissions and instructions to its governors, a system which guaranteed the settlers very little and left them to the whim of the King, as the proprietary grants sadly demonstrated. Virginia, through her agents, now asked the King to approve a royal charter which would tie down the Colony's relation to the Crown and the realm and explicitly define the rights of Virginians and their place in the Empire.

What did the Virginia charter draft contain? It granted to the Assembly a very marked degree of local power and authority. It permitted the Colony to incorporate for the purpose of buying out the proprietors of the Northern Neck. It assured the colonists immediate dependence upon the Crown, eliminating any middle authority such as present or future proprietors. The King promised not to grant away their lands in the future, and he confirmed to Virginians and their heirs forever all land possessed by them at the time. Headrights of fifty acres would continue; escheated land could be repossessed and enjoyed forever after compounding at a moderate rate in tobacco. The charter gave power to the governor and Council to try all treasons, murders, felonies, and other crimes, with full pardoning power to the governor except in cases of treason and murder. What is more, it confirmed and ratified the power and authority of the Virginia Assembly, reserving to the Crown only a review of its laws. Lastly, and probably most important, the charter guaranteed that no taxes or impositions would be laid upon Virginians but by the "Comon Consent of the Governour Concil and Burgesses," excepting only customs on Virginia's goods sent to England.

Confirmation of the authority of the Assembly, an assurance of the rights of Englishmen, and a guarantee against taxation without consent were the heart of the new charter. The agents in negotiating in London argued that these would not alter the Colony's government, for it had functioned for some time in this manner, but only with an apparent authority. All they asked now was confirmation of a working system, the making of their own laws, as close to those of England as conditions allowed, subject only to the governor's veto and review by the King. Taxation by consent was the custom in Virginia, practiced for over fifty years. It was also one of the liberties of Englishmen, guaranteed by Parliament in England, a right which planters and their heirs ought "to enjoy by law." After all, the agents claimed, Colonies were "but in nature of an extension or dilatation of the realm of England," and colonists should possess "the same liberties and privileges as Englishmen in England." In the Virginia Company charter James I had declared that settlers and their descendants should be regarded as "natural born subjects of England" as, in truth, the agents added, "without any declaration or grant, they ought by law to be." The first charter was revoked, to be sure, but James had promised to issue a second that would renew the "former privileges of the planters." Although he had failed to do so, since that time no King in England had ever imposed taxes upon Virginia without consent of the people there. By the new charter Virginians sought a guarantee of this right in black and white. Heretofore, the power to tax themselves was given only through instructions to their governors, which, the agents conceived, "ought to be confirmed under the great seal." And, too, they argued, other colonies, so much less deserving than Virginia, "New-England, Maryland, Barbadoes, &c. are not taxed but of their own consent."

The Virginia charter draft very clearly stated what one Assembly in America believed were the rights of Colonies and settlers—the rights of Englishmen overseas. Dependence upon the Crown had a specific meaning to Virginians. To be "unseparably affixt to the crown" guaranteed to them, they believed,

those just rights and privileges as were their due whilst they lived in England, and which they humbly hope that they have not lost by re- moving themselves into a country where they hazarded their lives and fortunes, so much more to the advantage of the crown and kingdom, than to their own. . . .

This was a declaration of equality, of equality within the Empire, for Virginians felt themselves equal to the people who stayed at home as well as to other colonists in America as far as treatment from govern- ment was concerned. In addition, they believed they were entitled to quiet possession of their property, with the prospect of adding to it, without threat from alien proprietors with power to manage the land and collect quitrents. They believed their Assembly was autonomous except for the King's right to review their laws, and there was no doubt in their minds that as Englishmen their rights included taxa- tion by consent.

Life in the Colonies was hard enough without encroachment upon it from home, intensifying the uncertainty, instability, and the haz- ards of living in a wilderness three thousand miles from a govern- ment which attempted control but not responsibility. Indians, the Dutch, geography and climate, high taxes, the vicissitudes of a single crop, all were difficult to contend with, sometimes impossible, when the price of tobacco sank far below existence levels. At very least, the home government ought to treat Virginians as Englishmen and by so doing lessen the uncertainty of a frontier existence, not add to it. Legalize our relationship so that we may have a foundation upon which to build. Don't keep us guessing about our identity as colonists. Guarantee us our property and Englishmen's rights, make permanent and legal the system of government we have worked out over two generations of Colonial life, and we will benefit the Crown as well as ourselves and increasingly so—this is what the Assembly seems to be saying in the draft of the charter which attorneys, Lords, Councils, and King scrutinized and then approved during the winter of 1675–1676.[18]

His Majesty's royal Colony of Virginia had made a very definite statement in defining the role of its government and people in the Empire. As Maryland, New York, and Massachusetts would do later, Virginia in 1675 demonstrated in no uncertain terms that in the first century of colonization a number of American colonists had decided who they were and what their relation was to the government and people at home.

Disappointingly, despite the several approvals, the charter got only as far as the Great Seal but not through, for there it was stopped for reasons that have never been adequately explained. In March 1676 both Secretaries of State, Coventry and Southwell, made inquiries, and the next month the Lord Treasurer and Lord Chancellor brought the matter before the Privy Council, but they were unable to pry the charter loose. It was stopped in the Hanaper Office, probably by the King himself.[19]

II

Was Bacon's Rebellion the cause of the Virginia charter's failure? Probably not. It is almost certain that Charles II and his advisers had turned thumbs down on it before they learned of the rebellion in Virginia, news of which arrived in England some time in June of 1676. By this time the King had already changed his mind, and the Privy Council's order annulling the charter was dated May 31.[20]

The charter failed for other reasons. Although the Lords of Trade had agreed to it in the fall of 1675, they were very new to their jobs, having just been appointed, and may well have withdrawn their approval by the spring of the next year. They doubtless found the power and authority about to be given to Virginia at odds with their schemes to centralize and intensify Colonial policy for England's advantage. More specific evidence supports this contention. When scrutiny turned into delay and delay into a complete halt in negotiations in the early spring of 1676, the agents sought reasons for the stoppage, hoping to beat them down with their arguments. But Moryson, Ludwell, and Smith found it very difficult to learn what the objections were and who their authors. In some manner, not explained in their letters, they discovered that one reason for the charter's failure was its supposed threat to the Navigation Acts, something the Lords of Trade would be very likely to notice. In response Ludwell and Moryson drafted a lengthy Remonstrance, reviewing the "Heads" of the charter draft in light of the Acts of Trade. They pointed out an obvious proviso which preserved "the power of the laws of navigation, and all future acts of parliament, of that nature. . . ." In other words, the charter itself excepted the Acts of Trade, and therefore, said the agents, there should be no argument about it on that score. True or not, it made little difference; by this time no one was listening.[21]

A more significant cause for the halt in charter proceedings was doubtless Thomas Lord Culpeper who may have had a hand in persuading the King and Privy Council to reverse their earlier approval of Virginia's bid for power. There is some indication that Culpeper and his friends made several objections to the charter, particularly to the right of Virginians to tax themselves.[22] But there were more personal reasons why Culpeper might oppose it. First, he was a proprietor of both grants, north and south, which the King had given away at two different times, and although he had compromised with the agents and agreed to incorporation for purchase of the Northern Neck, there remained the right to quitrents for the huge southern grant. (In 1677 the agents were surprised to learn that Lord Culpeper still was pushing plans for reviving the business of the patents and sometime later worked out a very favorable compromise with the King.)[23]

Second, and more surprising, Lord Culpeper already possessed a commission from King Charles to be *governor* of Virginia upon the death or removal of Berkeley. The commission was dated July 8,

1675. Throughout much of the time the agents were negotiating in London, Culpeper knew full well that he would be governor of their Colony when Berkeley gave it up.[24] A strong charter propping up the authority of the Assembly would have stripped a new governor of much of the power of his office. Culpeper, an outsider, was no Berkeley and could not possibly identify himself with Virginia and a strong faction in the Council and Burgesses as had Berkeley. What is more, an aggressive Assembly with a good deal of room to move around in would be difficult for a proprietor to manage when it came to the issue of quitrents. Culpeper's best interests would be served in Virginia with the power of the prerogative behind him, not the chartered authority of an Assembly confronting him. There were several reasons, then, for the charter's failure before the bloody news of rebellion reached the King's ear. If not cause of the charter's defeat, Bacon's Rebellion did prevent renewal of negotiations by the agents, for they found the King deaf to continued talks after the serious nature of the rebellion became common knowledge in London.

III

To attribute the drive for the charter wholly to political and constitutional principle would be sadly to misunderstand the Assembly's motives and at the same time some of the causes of Bacon's Rebellion. Encroachment by proprietors with power to control the land could only damage the economic and political interests of those who had already won themselves places of power and profit. The Virginia charter, while guaranteeing the rights of Englishmen in Virginia, would have guaranteed also considerable power and control in the Assembly, power and control which Berkeley and his people had acquired over years of experience and wielded for their own sakes. Moreover, in the hands of Berkeley and his party, this power, through politicking, persuasion, and patronage, proved to be enormous, great enough to endanger local rights, strong enough to provoke rebellion in 1676.

Sir William and the agents, although they had kept pretty much to the high ground of principle in their arguments against the patents, were not blind to the proprietors' threat to the headright system. Legally practiced, headrights were an encouragement to immigrants, guaranteeing them land to commence life as colonists. At the same time, the custom rewarded with land older settlers who sponsored newcomers, helping in this way to increase population and extend settlement. When abused, the headright system presented several splendid opportunities for those already settled to acquire more property than the law allowed and greatly augment their estates. Who knew but what the proprietors would stick their noses into the system as it was practiced and alter Virginia's customs? A guarantee of headrights held a prominent place in the "Heads" presented by the agents in London and remained a significant item in the final form of the charter draft.[25]

An equally serious threat to Virginia's way of doing things was the proprietors' authority under the patents to collect quitrents on the land already settled. All land in Virginia was subject to quitrents paid to the King, for he was ultimate owner of the soil. Fortunately for the colonists, collection had been spotty. Actually, the Crown never saw the quitrents which Virginians paid since as early as 1650 the King had given over the profit of them to Colonel Henry Norwood, an exiled royalist, who had come to Virginia the year before.[26] Collection, however, according to an old practice, was in the hands of members of the Council who had been "Farmers" of the quitrents in their home counties for some time, and although "not a certain Place, yet it is a certain yearly Profit and Favour." Proprietary quitrents, strictly collected, would strike a telling blow at the colonists' pocketbooks, to say nothing of the councilors' income.[27]

Along with quitrents the proprietors were allowed escheats, too, taking the business out of the hands of Berkeley's favorites, council members Francis Moryson and Thomas Ludwell, two of the three agents, who had been mixed up in the matter of escheats for sometime. The charter draft directed that the Colony revert to its earlier practices, allowing Virginians composition of escheats at favorable rates.[28]

Suddenly, headrights, quitrents, and escheats were all subject to proprietary control, "in prejudice of many royall concessions and grants . . ." which the Virginia government and certain individuals had acquired by several means over the years. Not only did proprietary interference in these matters divest the local government of its "just powers and authorities by which this colony has hitherto beene kept in peace and tranquility . . ." but it cut deeply into the perquisites of office which successful Virginia officials had been pocketing for years. No wonder, then, that the Assembly demanded in the charter draft a "dependence upon the crown," for such dependence in the past, despite quitrents, had been fairly easy to live with and profitable to a few in power. A liberal concept of Empire, if written into a royal charter, guaranteed a very favorable share of self-government. It also assured concrete advantages to those who directed that government.

The very origins of the charter seem to have stemmed from an elite group already strongly entrenched in Virginia's government. Agents Moryson and Ludwell had come to Virginia as royalist veterans and exiles in the 1640's, Moryson with the King's commission in his pocket to command the fort at Point Comfort along with its profits. Governor Berkeley warmly received them, and it was not long before they, with the governor's help, had firm positions in government and considerable land around them. Moryson was at different times Speaker of the House of Burgesses, deputy governor during Berkeley's mission to England, and for several years a powerful member of the Virginia Council. Ludwell, a distant relative of Berkeley, received his first grant of five hundred acres in 1648 and by 1660 was the colony's Secretary and a leading councilor. Their companion, General Robert Smith, also an army officer under Charles I, was an active Virginia landowner and became a Council member in 1663. He served several times on commissions to treat with Maryland over cessation of tobacco planting and soon owned a good deal of land. All royalists, the agents to London were closely tied to Berkeley and owed him personally for their advancement and estates.[29]

During the winter 1675–1676, with negotiations going in their favor, the agents showed a boldness which must have surprised a number of Englishmen. Despite the liberal grant of power already in the charter draft, the agents had asked for more. Once the "Heads" were approved, probably some time in the fall of 1675, the agents sent them back to Virginia in a report of their progress which at that point was encouraging. The agents explained to the Assembly that they had "come very little short" of what they desired. What they had not been able to swing was a permanent incorporation. The obstacle here was the government's experience with Massachusetts, a corporate Colony whose virtual independence had antagonized for some time the King, Council, and ministry to the point that they were desperately looking for a way to revoke the Bay Colony's charter. Therefore, the bold request for permanent incorporation smacked of Massachusetts and colored Virginia's demand with the same kind of independence, a stand it was politic to recede from. Convincing critics of their good intentions was difficult, for it was well known in London that the "New England disease is very catching." The result was that the charter limited incorporation exclusively to purchasing lands from the proprietors of the Northern Neck.[30]

At the same time, the agents had tried to incorporate Virginia in the name of the Governor, Council, and Burgesses, but the Privy Council quickly substituted "commonalty" for "burgesses," remarking, that this was in "favor of the country, as being more called in law." The shift in wording may have been simply a legal point, but it offers some grounds to suspect that the agents represented the Assembly rather than the people and were very willing that *it* become the incorporated body, not Virginians as a whole. In inserting the change the Privy Councilors argued that such a grant ought not be given to an order of men which could be dissolved or discontinued, a statement in itself not very encouraging to the permanency of the Burgesses.[31] Did the Privy Council suspect some kind of "grab" on the Assembly's part and believe it necessary to preserve the rights of the "country", the "commonalty", an attitude it later took respecting Bacon's Rebellion?

The next year the Collector of Customs in Virginia, Giles Bland, indicated that the agents' support in the Colony was confined to a smaller body even than the Assembly. In a report to the Secretary of State, Bland referred once to the agents as "those Gentlemen who are Employed as Com'rs from ye Governor and Councell to his Ma'tie" and later to those persons "who were employed hence by ye Governor." This may have been simply oversight on the Collector's part, but it is curious that in two references he should omit even a nod to the Assembly as a whole, let alone the Burgesses or the people.[32]

In their report to the Assembly, the agents found it necessary to make two other explanations. One was of the King's power to review laws which, the agents remarked, they could not reasonably object to since "it is a power due him" and insisted upon in England in order not to exclude the Crown altogether from authority in Virginia. That question of the King's veto needed comment hints that the agents arrived in London ready to suggest that the Colony get along without it.[33] Lost somewhere in the shuffle was another clause limiting the King to a period of two years only to exercise his veto over an act of the Assembly, the law being valid in the meantime. Doubtless the agents agreed to suppress this once they had sampled opinions of those in power.[34]

That Berkeley's hold on Virginia's government was great hardly needs proof. A governor of his stamp, after years of experience, knew what string to touch and how to use those about him to concentrate power into a solid faction. Berkeley was the " 'sole author of the most substantial part' of the government, 'either for Lawes or other inferior institutions,' " wrote Secretary Thomas Ludwell in 1666, and Ludwell certainly must have known, for he had been at Berkeley's side for a generation or more.[35] Although Hartwell, Blair, and Chilton wrote their *Present State of Virginia* several years later, they based their conclusions about government on a retrospective view of the Colony's history. All the great offices in Virginia, they wrote, "were at first heaped upon one Man, and, which is stranger, continues so to this Day." The normal checks on these "very large Powers" had disintegrated, leaving the Council in particular "at the Devotion of the Governor" and the ready instruments to advance what he desired.[36] Through various means he and the Council had secured the support of a majority of the House of Burgesses particularly through the efforts of Robert Beverley, clerk of the lower house, who exercised great influence over the members. The government's restriction of the suffrage to freeholders in 1670 tended to reduce opposition, and by the time of Bacon's Rebellion Governor Berkeley and several members of the Council, through a majority of the House of Burgesses, pretty much called the turn in Virginia. It was common knowledge then and now that the governor had not called an election of Burgesses for some dozen years.[37]

The causes of Bacon's Rebellion were multiple and make most

sense when examined on several planes of Virginia society. No one would doubt today that Indian war precipitated the rebellion which in turn laid bare other serious grievances apparent at parish, county, and provincial levels.[38] But most of these grievances the colonists laid at the door of Berkeley's Assembly, the same Assembly that fought hard to secure the charter in 1675.

Besides fear of the Indians, most grievances stemmed from the high cost of provincial government which seemed to benefit the colonists not at all. Increased taxes for protection against the Indians failed to produce a successful Indian policy. Taxes levied to build forts and castles along the coast were inefficiently—maybe corruptly —spent and exposure to a seaborne enemy continued. The very cost of government seemed exorbitant to colonists whose tobacco was collected each year to support it. Particularly galling was the 250 pounds of tobacco it took each day to keep a delegate in the House of Burgesses which, it was generally agreed, met more often than necessary anyway. Some of these grievances were long standing, but they were aggravated when the bloody Indian war commenced and taxes rose again. And then, in the midst of this bad feeling, the Virginia Assembly levied an additional tax of fifty pounds of tobacco *per* tithable for two years running to support the agents in their negotiations against the proprietors and for the charter. To colonists, already complaining that they derived no benefits from increased taxation, that their tobacco was taken for public causes, but neither improvement nor strict accounting followed, the additional tax to support the charter agency, despite its alleged rewards, was another overwhelming burden and pointedly so when news of the mission's failure reached Virginia.[39] But by this time Bacon's Rebellion was on in earnest.

When news of the rebellion sifted into England in the spring of 1676, the agents refused to admit that the outburst in Virginia had killed any hope of securing the charter. In fact, they desperately tried to use the Indian war and the rebellion to persuade the King that now, more than ever, Virginians needed the charter to allay their fears and settle their condition. How seasonable it would be if the King would apply the charter to the "present distractions," they declared! How hazardous in the present circumstances to refuse Virginians any part of it! Actually, the Virginia agents were in a very tough spot, for they could not admit in London that the upheaval in Virginia was a rebellion against the governor and Assembly who had sent them to England in the first place and who had instructed them to extract a charter which would guarantee tremendous local power to that government. What possible chance would there be to reopen negotiations with the King if he thought that a great many people in Virginia were violently opposed to the very government the charter would confirm? And so the agents supported Berkeley and played down the scope of the rebellion. Not only had Virginians always been loyal to the Crown, they pled, but even now the trouble in Virginia had nothing to do with disaffection to the King's government in England *or* Virginia. What is more, they claimed that the "better or more industrious sort of people" were not the abettors of the mutiny; rather, the cause was the "poverty and uneasyness of some of the meanest whose discontents render them easier to be misledd." Truly, this was "the sole cause and foundation of these troubles. . . ." The most effective way to bring Virginia to a "lasting obedience" was first to revoke "those graunts wch have and still doe soe much disturb theire mindes . . ." and then settle the people's "just priveledges and properties . . . on a sollid foundacon . . ." in other words, grant the charter they had come over to secure.[40]

The tensions of the rebellion brought out more evidence of its causes. Although the county grievances, requested by the Royal Commissioners in 1677, were somewhat after the fact, their reiteration of complaints against the government pointed directly to the Assembly and claimed it to be the primary source of the trouble. Again and again the counties asked questions about where the tax money went and why there was no accounting of it. Nansemond County put it succinctly: Its people complained "against the great Taxes imposed these 3 or 4 years last past, and they know not for what." [41]

The most direct statement of this kind can be found in the grievances of Charles City County whose complaints flatly blamed Sir William Berkeley for subverting the government. He had forced his will on the Council and then assumed to himself the appointment of all civil and military officers and other places of profit, giving them to people who would carry out his designs. And then to bind them even more closely to himself and to attract others to his party, he permitted them locally "to lay and impose what levies and imposicons upon us they should or did please," which they "converted to their owne private lucre and gaine." By these means the governor got the upper hand over a majority of the "men of parts and estates," and these were the very people whom the voters found necessary to send to Jamestown as their Burgesses. Berkeley strengthened his authority over the people and deprived them of great quantities of tobacco which were "embezelled and consumed betwixt him and his officers." Ordinarily Charles City people sent their grievances to Jamestown with their Burgesses, but lately they feared their representatives had "been overswayed by the power and prevalency of the sᵈ Sʳ Wm. Berkeley and his councell," neglecting their grievances and using them to "putt under their Pyes." [42] Some counties refused even to submit grievances while Berkeley remained in power, "so overawed & biassed" were they by him. The "general cry" of the country was that Virginia "would not be quiet so long as he continued Governor and Ludwell, Secretary." [43]

Berkeley did remain governor for several more months and, once the rebellion was over, vindictively sustained his power by hanging a number of his enemies and confiscating their estates. A Maryland observer wrote home to Lord Baltimore in January 1677 that the coming warm weather could very well produce another swarm of Virginians who "may have as venomous stings, as the late traytr had." It could happen again, he commented, if the King did not settle Virginia's affairs, for certainly those in power could not do it. His next comment went to the heart of the problem:

There must be an alteration though not of the Government yet in the Government, new men must be put in power, the old ones will never agree with the common people, and if that be not done, his Majtie in my opinion will never find a well setled Government in that Colony. . . .[44]

At the time the King ordered a Commission to suppress the rebellion and investigate its causes, he ordered Berkeley home to answer for all the trouble.

After the governor's departure Colonel Herbert Jeffreys took his place temporarily, supported by the Commission and their troops. The same Maryland writer reported to Baltimore that if Jeffreys built on the "old foundations" neither he nor his soldiers could "satisfy or rule these people." If there was anyone in Virginia brave enough to stick out his neck, he wrote, the "Commons would immure" themselves in rebellion as deep as in Bacon's time.[45] About a month before Berkeley left for England, his Green Springs faction, again in control of the Assembly, implored the Secretary of State in London to revive the business of their charter with the King. But the King's mind about the causes of trouble in Virginia was clearly expressed by the Privy Council when it flatly asserted "that the Rebellion of Virginia was occasioned by the Excessive power of the Assembly. . . ."[46]

Ironically, Charles II did grant Virginia a royal charter in 1676, but it fell far short of what was expected, and this was owing primarily to Bacon's Rebellion, which was a slap in the face to the prerogative. More telling, the Rebellion reduced drastically the King's customs on tobacco, besides costing him dearly to send commissioners and troops. The new charter met several of the original demands respecting headrights, escheats, the governor and Council's power to try cases of treason and murder, and significantly, confirmation of the colonists' land. At the same time it stressed the Colony's dependence upon the Crown, a dependence the Assembly had hoped to achieve but which now had a wholly different meaning. Without the other guarantees, so important in the earlier charter draft, there was little protection afforded the assembly of Virginia against the power of the Crown.

The most glaring omissions in the new charter were a confirmation of the authority of the Colonial Assembly, a guarantee to Virginians of the rights of Englishmen, and specifically the right to consent to taxes. The King had confirmed their property but not their rights.[47] The charter Charles granted to Virginia in the summer of 1676 very clearly defined a royal concept of empire, a concept which simply viewed colonists as a subordinate people not equal in rights to Englishmen in England and not entitled to the same treatment from government. An empire was made up of superiors and inferiors, and the inferiors enjoyed only the rights the superiors were willing to give them. It was this kind of thinking which laid the basis for the Crown's attempt, shortly after Bacon's Rebellion, to exact a permanent revenue from Virginia and to dictate laws to the Assembly in the manner of Ireland after Poynings' Law.[48]

Had King Charles granted to Virginians the charter the Assembly sought, they would have won, in the agents' words, "those just rights and privileges as were their due whilst they lived in England," a position in the Empire equal to that of Englishmen at home. Such a grant would have been contrary to the whole tenor of colonial policy as it emerged in the 1670's. But the new charter would have protected only the government of Virginia from an arbitrary King and Parliament. It would not have protected the people of Virginia from their own government whose arbitrariness was altogether apparent at the time of Bacon's Rebellion. The charter of 1675 would not have eliminated the grievances which caused the Rebellion. On the contrary, it would have aggravated them, for it placed additional power and authority in the hands of the very people against whom Bacon and his followers rebelled. By vetoing the charter and substituting a weaker document in its place, the King guaranteed Virginians their land, but he kept their government in leading strings. Given the conditions which obtained at the time, given the fact that in over thirty years of rule Sir William Berkeley had fused a governing body which seemed to work first for its own ends and only secondly for those of other Virginians, one might argue that Charles II did a majority of Virginians a favor. What was good for those in government was good for all Virginians, or so the Assembly seemed to reason in 1675. That it was not became painfully clear the next year. Berkeley and the Assembly also reasoned that what was good for Virginia's government was good for the King in England, too. But they misjudged the King as they had Virginians. After vetoing the Assembly's charter, Charles then blamed its members for provoking rebellion and destroying his revenue. While the violence and complexity of Bacon's Rebellion have obscured the significance of the Virginia charter, the principle of self-government, which the charter contained, has obscured the self-interest which lurked behind it.

Imperial Pressures on Massachusetts and Jamaica, 1675–1700

RICHARD S. DUNN received his A.B. from Harvard and his M.A. and Ph.D. from Princeton. Professor of History at the University of Pennsylvania and a former member of the Council of the Institute of Early American History and Culture, he is the author of *Puritans and Yankees: The Winthrop Dynasty of New England, 1630–1717* (1962) and *The Age of Religious Wars 1559–1689* (1970). Dr. Dunn's articles include "The Downfall of the Bermuda Company: A Restoration Farce" and "The Barbados Census of 1680: Profile of the Richest Colony in English America" (*William and Mary Quarterly*, 1963, 1969). He is currently writing a book on the rise of the planter class in the English sugar islands, 1640–1713.

The American colonists during the late seventeenth century, as we all know, experienced a prolonged time of troubles, punctuated by wars, insurrections, and witch-hunting, reflecting a deep-seated sense of social malaise and political instability. It is not easy to generalize about this crisis period. To find out why Bacon's Rebellion erupted so suddenly and briefly in Virginia, or why Leisler's Rebellion cast such a long shadow over New York politics, or why the witchcraft mania reached its climax at Salem, one has to burrow into the local peculiarities of Virginia, New York, or Massachusetts social behavior. As a result, we have an atomistic series of monographs and articles on various episodes leading up to and away from the Glorious Revolution in America. There is, I think, an overall pattern to events in English America between 1675 and 1700.[1] But the pattern does not emerge clearly unless we take into account the development of the English West Indian Colonies during these years, together with the rising imperial ambitions of the home government. By examining two strikingly different Colonies, Massachusetts and Jamaica, and comparing their respective relations with the Crown, we can see how social patterns in the islands as well as on the mainland were disrupted and reconstituted by centripetal imperial pressures from England during the last three decades of the seventeenth century. At first blush it seems impossible to compare the Puritan preachers of Boston with the daredevil buccaneers of Jamaica. What links the Puritans and buccaneers in the 1670's is their independence of home control and their isolation from home-based values and standards. Starting around 1675, the royal government, aided and abetted by important interest groups within Massachusetts and Jamaica, launched a campaign to break the Puritans and buccaneers. The campaign was by no means confined to these two Colonies. But the struggle in Massachusetts and Jamaica illustrates the general crisis which engulfed late seventeenth-century English America.

Down into the 1670's, let us remember, English colonization everywhere in America had been pervaded by a spirit of *laissez faire*. At least 100,000 Englishmen had fanned out into some twenty separate New World plantations, from Newfoundland to Guiana, with immense variety of motivation and no overall plan. There was much coming and going between the islands and the mainland. Virginia and Bermuda were founded by the same sponsors, who incidentally thought Bermuda the more promising of the two. The first planters of Massachusetts and Barbados formed part of a single migration. The early settlers of Carolina came from the Caribbean, and some of the first planters in Jamaica came from New England. All the Colonies, mainland and island, grew slowly and from the viewpoint of Englishmen back home they looked insignificant, not to say downright disappointing. Hence every little English society in America was permitted to develop its own identity in an atmosphere of virtually complete autonomy. The colonists did not yet have a rooted fear of the French, nor any compelling need for dependence on England. Then suddenly, during the last three decades of the seventeenth century, all this changed. Charles II's government started to enforce the navigation acts, to collect more American revenue, and to regulate the heretofore autonomous American plantations. Some colonists welcomed closer ties with England. Others fiercely objected. The years 1675–1700 saw intoxicating economic growth, feverish political experimentation, and fundamental social change throughout English America. These years also saw the opening of the Anglo-French contest for control of North America and the West Indies. Imperial politics became crucial for the first time, as the colonists gradually adjusted themselves to a new dependent status within the English mercantilist system. Doubtless the change-over brought greater gain than pain. Certainly the Caribbean planters reacted to the new conditions quite differently from their North American cousins. By 1700 the island and mainland plantations had coalesced into two distinct communities. Each community worked out its own role within the Empire, to be maintained thenceforth until the 1750's.

It is thus evident that the closing decades of the seventeenth century constitute a pivotal period in the history of Anglo-American imperial politics. This period also invites comparison between North American and Caribbean Colonial social development. To illustrate these two points as succinctly as possible, I will discuss parallel developments in Massachusetts and Jamaica, because these two Colonies offer the most pointed comparison. The Crown had a stormier struggle with the Puritans of Massachusetts than with any other North American colony during the late seventeenth century, and likewise a stormier struggle with the buccaneers of Jamaica than with any other West Indian colony. But I believe that the same general conclusions would emerge from a comparison between any other pair of mainland and island English colonies during this period.

By way of background, we need a capsule description of late seventeenth-century Massachusetts and Jamaica.² In physical appearance, the two places were (and are) totally dissimilar. Jamaica is about half the size of modern Massachusetts, but much harder to traverse, since it is one of the most mountainous and thickly jungled islands in the Caribbean. Along Jamaica's south coast, where the first

English colonists settled, the broad savannas are ideal for cattle ranges and sugar plantations. Lushly verdant hills and rushing streams line the north coast, and misty blue peaks taller than the White Mountains in New England range the 150-mile length of the island. The incredibly green tropical foliage, rich soil, constant heat, heavy rainfall and frequent hurricanes are all a far cry from Massachusetts' hard-etched, rock-ribbed, northern terrain. In 1670 the settlement of Jamaica was barely started, and Massachusetts was not much further advanced. Both Colonies had small populations; Massachusetts had approximately 30,000 inhabitants and Jamaica 15,000. Practically all the settlers in both places lived within a few miles of the seacoast, in primitive habitations which have long since disappeared. Three-quarters of the present state of Massachusetts was Indian country. Jamaica's north coast was almost empty, and her interior mountains were inhabited by runaway Negroes.[3] In the 1670's, most colonists in both places were subsistence farmers, though Massachusetts had already established the outlines of her distinctive eighteenth-century economy: fishing, shipbuilding, and overseas trade. The merchant community in Boston, Salem, and Charlestown was already prosperous. In 1675 these three seaports paid half as much in taxes as all the other forty-six farming villages put together. By contrast, the Jamaica colonists were only just starting to concentrate on their eighteenth-century staple, sugar production. In the 1670's, Jamaica exported far less sugar to England than the much smaller islands of Barbados, Nevis, and St. Kitts.[4]

In moral tone, the contrast between Puritan Massachusetts and tropical Jamaica was truly extraordinary. Jamaica had been seized from the Spaniards in 1655. Since the island is strategically situated in the heart of the West Indies, the English found it a perfect base for plundering expeditions against the Spanish islands and mainland. Jamaica's population was dotted with ex-soldiers and surplus talent from the London streets and jails. Several thousand of these drifters turned into buccaneers, still in a state of private war against Spain. Buccaneers were a law unto themselves. Led by the redoubtable Henry Morgan, they preyed on Spanish commerce or robbed the coastal settlements of Cuba, Hispaniola, and Central America, then came roaring home to roister away their booty in the taverns of Port Royal. There were plenty of taverns to choose from. Forty persons in this small seaport were licensed to sell strong drink, and the large number of onion-shaped seventeenth-century liquor bottles that have been dredged up from the harbor floor by skin divers lends credence to Port Royal's boast that it was once the wickedest city in the West.[5] In austere Massachusetts, there was no such outlet for daredevil adventure. Two generations of Puritanism had inculcated habits of community introspection and discipline. Few people have suffered so much guilt over so little sin. No doubt the preachers' endless warnings of divine wrath and punishment had become a comforting routine or ritual to many Massachusetts churchgoers. The Colony employed upwards of one hundred clergymen as against four in Jamaica. An Irish schoolmaster who found his way to Jamaica wrote Increase Mather that he must look for a new occupation, since no one in the island was willing to study humane literature.[6] Probably not even Perry Miller could write a book about the Jamaican mind in the seventeenth century.

Between 1670 and 1700 both Massachusetts and Jamaica expanded very rapidly in size and wealth. In these thirty years Massachusetts doubled her population—without the aid of much new immigration. The Colony was still a community of small farmers, but Boston now displayed considerable surplus wealth and social snobbery. Massachusetts merchants were beginning to match Massachusetts clergymen in their energy and ingenuity. It was no easy matter to import the European goods which the colonists wanted, for the Massachusetts merchants could not sell New England commodities on the English market in exchange. Furthermore, Massachusetts businessmen were harrassed by a chronic shortage of specie. Yet by building ships for English customers, by selling provisions to the Caribbean sugar planters, and marketing fish and timber in southern Europe, not to mention the middle-man profits from carrying these commodities, they acquired the necessary purchasing power in England.[7] The Massachusetts merchant, however, could by no means match the dazzling prosperity of the Jamaica sugar planter. By 1700 Jamaica sugar production was catching up to Barbados, and would soon surpass it. Sugar was far and away the most lucrative commodity produced in English America. Already by 1700 sugar accounted for 70 percent of the total value of American imports to England, and this amazing percentage held firm until the American Revo-

lution. Jamaican exports to England in 1700 were approximately
ten times the value of Massachusetts exports to England. Sugar
profits permitted the chief Jamaica planters to retire grandly to
England as absentee landlords—a luxury beyond the aspirations
of the Boston merchant community. Those unfortunate planters who
stayed in the tropics, deprived of the English climate, compensated
for their loss by spending conspicuously more money than their
northern neighbors, as is shown by the fact that Jamaica imported
more goods than Massachusetts from England, despite her far
smaller white population.[8]

Jamaica's total population was rising as rapidly as Massachusetts',
but the figure is deceptive, for it disguises the fact that fewer white
men lived on the island in 1700 than in 1670. Big planters who cultivated their fields with armies of Negro slaves were squeezing out the
buccaneers, the small planters, and the indentured servants. Thus
Jamaica's population rise was owing entirely to a massive importation of African slaves, one thousand per year in the 1670's and four
thousand per year in 1700. By this later date, perhaps 80 percent of
Jamaica's population was black.[9] These Negro slaves were fed so
skimpily and worked so hard that their death rate far exceeded their
birth rate. The planters reckoned that it was cheaper and more efficient to restock regularly with fresh slaves from Africa than to raise
living standards to the point where the existing slave population
would live longer and breed better. Horses and cattle, of course, they
managed on a different principle, giving them enough care to keep
the strain healthy and fertile. It is true that a slave was better off on
Jamaica than on the smaller islands, because he had a plot of land
for growing food, and he had a chance of escape into the mountains.
Still, there were big slave revolts in 1676, 1685, and 1690, and the
Jamaican slave codes of 1664, 1683, and 1696 were progressively
more elaborate and brutal—a sure index to rising insecurity within
the master class.[10]

Against this general background, let us compare Jamaica's and
Massachusetts' respective relations with the home government during the period 1675–1700. Into the 1670's, both Colonies enjoyed virtually complete autonomy. In Jamaica as in Massachusetts, the
planters practiced full self-government, evolving their own local institutional pattern and social structure, undisturbed by effectual

supervision from Whitehall. Massachusetts' belligerently independent attitude toward Charles I in the 1630's, Parliament in the 1640's,
Cromwell in the 1650's, and Charles II in the 1660's, is well known.
For the eight years between 1666 and 1674, the Colony records list
no communications of any sort between the Massachusetts Bay
Company and the royal government.[11] The best proof of Massachusetts' proud isolation is that the colonists asked for no help from
home in fighting the bloodiest Indian war of the century, King Philip's War, in 1675–1676. The normal Massachusetts public revenue
was scarcely adequate for the Garden of Eden, yet in this war crisis
the colonists assessed themselves the staggering sum of £50,000 to
fight the Indians and repair property damage.[12] The New Englanders
wanted their Dissenter friends at home to know all about their
agony. Between 1675 and 1677 at least a dozen books and pamphlets
describing the war were published in London. But Governor
Leverett barely bothered to mention the subject to the King's ministers.[13]

Jamaica's behavior was equally independent. To be sure, the islanders did not have chartered privileges of self-government, as in
Massachusetts. Jamaica had been conquered from Spain at government expense, and was a Crown possession. The governor was appointed by the King. Yet like the popularly elected governor of Massachusetts, he was an entrenched local magnate who served himself
first, his community next, and the King last. From 1664 to 1671 Sir
Thomas Modyford governed Jamaica. The Modyfords were the biggest planters on the island, with ten thousand acres and four hundred slaves and servants. Sir Thomas openly invited the buccaneers
to make Jamaica their headquarters and collected handsome fees
and kickbacks from them. Since he acknowledged receiving £1,000
a year from the buccaneers, he probably received a good deal more.
In 1666 and again in 1670 Modyford declared war between Jamaica
and Spain so as to justify open attacks on Spanish commerce. In 1670
he dispatched Sir Henry Morgan with a fleet of thirty-six ships to
plunder the enemy. Morgan, in his most daring stratagem, led 1400
men across the Isthmus and sacked the city of Panama. He returned
to Jamaica in 1671 reputedly with £70,000 in loot.[14]

This extravaganza persuaded Charles II's government to suppress
the buccaneers and reverse the traditional English policy of war

against Spanish America. Morgan's buccaneering was by no means as attractive to the Crown as Sir Francis Drake's privateering had been a century earlier. Morgan's profits stayed in America, whereas Drake's had been channeled to England. Furthermore, Morgan collected less booty than Drake had found, because Spanish wealth in America had greatly declined since the late sixteenth century. To Charles II a war with Spain over the buccaneering issue was not worth risking. Instead, in 1670 England pledged peace with Spain in America, and the two powers opened the possibility of limited legal trade. Even the Jamaicans could see that France, rather than Spain, was now England's prime antagonist in the Caribbean. English merchants argued that there was more profit in selling slaves to the Spanish colonists than in vandalizing them. For these reasons, Jamaica's aggression under Modyford and Morgan was highly vexing to the home government, more vexing indeed than Massachusetts' isolationism.

Charles II's ministers soon discovered that it was not so easy to correct the situation in Jamaica. In 1671 and again in 1675 the King sent out a new governor instructed to suppress the buccaneers. But royal policy was hamstrung by the Jamaica Assembly. This body was by no means as powerful as the Massachusetts General Court, but it aspired to all the legislative and taxing rights enjoyed by the Puritans. During the early 1670's the Jamaica Assembly challenged the governor's authority, it revised the whole body of colony laws every session, it sent home copies of these laws only after they had expired, and it ignored all commands from the King. In 1674 it voted to enforce some English statutes, while rejecting others. No English law, the Assembly declared, could be put into execution in Jamaica without its consent.[15] This was essentially the position adopted concurrently by the Massachusetts colonists. The Puritans supposed that they might ignore any English law they disliked, since English laws "do not reach America," and the Massachusetts Bay Company had sole legislative jurisdiction within the Colony.[16]

In the late 1670's the home government proceeded to crack down hard on Jamaica and Massachusetts. This was part of a new general policy toward English America, designed to shatter Colonial autonomy by binding each plantation more directly to the Crown. Recognizing that Colonial production was rising in importance, English mercantilists were determined to gear it to the needs of the home market. Furthermore, Charles II and his successor James II were both eager to free themselves from dependency on parliamentary taxation, and they hoped to collect a sizeable American revenue. Thus between 1675 and 1688 the Stuarts freely revamped their American territories, trampling local habit and defying local opinion. Since Jamaica was a royal Colony and Massachusetts a private corporation, the home government handled the two cases somewhat differently. But both colonies experienced the same inexorable pressure from the King's newly created colonial board, the Lords of Trade.

The royal remedy for Jamaica's problems was engagingly simple—to castrate the Assembly. As the Lords of Trade viewed the situation, representative self-government not only bolstered Jamaica's political autonomy, but encouraged the islanders to operate a pirate den rather than a sugar colony. "In plain terms," Secretary of State Coventry said, "the King intendeth to make a Plantation of Jamaica and not a Christian Algiers." [17] The Lords decided in 1677 to send out an imposing new governor, the Earl of Carlisle, and arm him with a new body of forty permanent laws prepared by the plantation office, including a perpetual revenue act. Once Carlisle got the Jamaica Assembly to ratify these laws, he must ask the King's permission before summoning any further Assemblies. Further legislation, if needed, would be drafted by the governor and his council, not the Assembly.[18] This drastic surgery was by no means wholly successful. When Carlisle presented his body of laws to the Jamaica Assembly in 1678, the Assembly voted down every single one, reserving their sharpest denunciations for the perpetual revenue act. The colonists perceived that Carlisle had an empty purse as well as a lordly title. So, they bribed him to lobby the home government for the restoration of Jamaica's ancient legislative privileges.[19] Having been double-crossed by their hand-picked governor, the Lords of Trade were compelled to settle for more modest changes in Jamaica. Carlisle's successor, Sir Thomas Lynch, conceded full legislative power to the Assembly, while continuing to press for a settled revenue. In 1683 he wheedled the Assembly into passing a twenty-one-year revenue act which guaranteed fiscal independence to the royal governor.[20] From 1683 to 1688 the Jamaica Assembly met infrequently and did little. Though the old institutional pattern survived, the planters had lost control of their executive, and local self-determination seemed a thing of the past. The Lords of Trade had not emasculated the Assembly as they had hoped to, but—if we may pursue the analogy—Jamaicans now spoke with a new falsetto tremolo.

It is easy to sentimentalize the rise of Stuart autocracy in Jamaica (and elsewhere in America) by telling horror stories about grasping governors, emasculated Assemblies, and the destruction of beloved constitutional liberties. The fact is that many colonists were anxious for closer union with the home government. The English imperial system could hardly have developed, let alone survived, without the voluntary cooperation of leading planters in every Colony. In Jamaica, a relatively compact group of large-scale sugar planters played a leading role in the 1670's and 1680's, because they welcomed the royal campaign against the buccaneers. Many of these planters owed their start in Jamaica to Governor Modyford; during his freewheeling administration they had received very large land grants.[21] But they were not as grateful to Modyford as might be expected, because his encouragement of buccaneering drained off their labor force of indentured servants and reduced the inflow of African slave ships. Sugar production required stable conditions in Jamaica, and sugar profits depended on a home market guaranteed by Whitehall and a harmonious partnership with slavers and merchants in London. Therefore the big Jamaica sugar planters were anxious to cooperate with Charles II. They protested against Governor Carlisle and his body of laws, to be sure, but this was at least partly because Carlisle, like Modyford before him, solicited support from Sir Henry Morgan and his buccaneering faction. Sir Thomas Lynch's administration (1681–1684) was very much more to the sugar planters' taste. Governor Lynch was a big planter himself, whole-heartedly committed to the sugar staple, and determined to end the buccaneers' long dominance. Lynch's twenty-one-year revenue act of 1683 was opposed by Morgan's buccaneering faction, and when Lynch crushed this faction, he secured political control of the island for the sugar interest.

Yet the big Jamaica planters soon began to regret their dependence on Whitehall courtiers and London merchants. Their supply of Negro slaves was manipulated by a London corporation, the Royal

African Company. Charles II granted this company a monopoly on the African slave trade, and James II was the chief stockholder and company president. Both royal brothers gave the company full government support. It was useless for the sugar planters to complain that the Royal African Company shipped them too few Negroes, of inferior quality, at too high a price. Jamaicans felt particularly aggrieved, because the company sold its cargoes as much as possible in Barbados and the Leeward Islands, to avoid the longer trip to Jamaica. From 1684 to 1687 the Royal African Company agent in Jamaica, Hender Molesworth, was also governor of the Colony. The Jamaica planters did not appreciate Governor Molesworth's efforts to stop interlopers from importing Negroes in violation of his company's monopoly. In 1685 Parliament imposed a heavy new duty on sugar. This produced a strangled cry from the Jamaica Assembly; even Governor Molesworth protested, though in vain. The new duty was designed to fall on the English consumer, but it seems to have reduced the planters' profit margin, while returning a handsome revenue to the Royal Treasury.[22] In 1687 and 1688, James II contemplated the incorporation of a new West India Company, a scheme which promised additional profits to the Treasury and further economic subjugation for the sugar planters. Details are shadowy, but it seems that the projected West India Company was intended to operate rather like the Royal African Company. It would be financed by a group of London stockholders. It would be granted exclusive right to buy sugar from the island planters and sell it in England. The King would be guaranteed an annual dividend equivalent to his present customs revenue from sugar. Thus the company could manipulate sugar prices and achieve a strangle hold on all commerce between the West Indies and England. Plans for this West India Company fell through. But the Jamaica Assembly's grateful address to James II, thanking him for rescuing the island from total destruction, shows how helpless the colonists felt.[23]

Even this brief account of Jamaica's losing struggle against imperial centralization, 1675–1688, should suggest the strong parallel with events in Massachusetts during these years. The Massachusetts crisis looks more dramatic, to be sure, because of the flamboyant manner in which the zealous royal agent, Edward Randolph, challenged the hidebound Puritans and broke their precious chartered liberties. The big issue in Massachusetts, however, was not Puritanism but the colonists' open violation of the navigation acts. In 1676 the Lords of Trade first sent Randolph to inspect New England. By 1678—the year after they had decided to remodel Jamaica—the Lords had decided to remodel Massachusetts also. They wanted to repeal the Colony's charter of 1629 so as to install a royal governor.[24] But it is worth emphasizing that the plantation office hounded Massachusetts less tenaciously than Jamaica, because Massachusetts was considered to be a less valuable Colony. Several times between 1678 and 1683 the Lords of Trade offered to revise rather than repeal the Massachusetts Bay Company charter. Some of the Puritans, including Governor Simon Bradstreet, told the home authorities they would rather compromise than lose their chartered privileges altogether. But the majority—like the Jamaica buccaneers—preferred to sink with all flags flying. The Massachusetts colonists knew all about Charles II's persecution of Dissenters in England. They feared that any admission of royal control in New England would expose them to equivalent persecution. And since they had repeatedly outbluffed the home government in the past, they risked doing so again.

In the end, Charles II handled the Massachusetts corporation as he handled scores of English corporations in the early 1680's. Crown lawyers used the ancient writ of *quo warranto* to detect irregularities in any and all chartered groups whose privileges interfered with the centralization of royal power. Most English corporations "voluntarily" surrendered to the Crown, but the Massachusetts Bay Company hid behind three thousand miles of ocean and never answered the King's charges. Some of the Colony leaders derisively called the King's writ "a poore, toothlesse creature." [25] They were wrong. In 1684, shortly after Jamaica had been reorganized, Charles II liquidated the Massachusetts Bay Company and the Lords of Trade set about drafting a royal government for the Colony.

Edward Randolph supposed that Massachusetts would welcome royal government. Numerous non-Puritan merchants and land speculators had assured him how eager they were to dismantle the Bible Commonwealth and establish better relations with Whitehall and London. These friends of Randolph—sometimes labeled the "moderate" party in Massachusetts—had much in common with the sugar planters in Jamaica who wanted to get rid of the buccaneers and attain closer economic and political ties with the mother country. In both Colonies, an important interest group perceived that the traditional autonomy was out of date, and that liaison with the Crown opened new avenues to wealth and power. It is important, therefore, to note differences between the situation in Jamaica and Massachusetts in the 1680's, suggestive of larger differences between West Indian and North American society. The Jamaica sugar planters were anything but self-sufficient. They depended on the outside world for much of their food, all of their Negro manpower, and all of their manufactured consumer goods. They depended on the home government for military support against the French and Spanish in the Caribbean and protection against foreign sugar competition. Under Charles II and James II, they were paying an extortionate price for these services, but they had no choice. Their grievances, which were real enough, could not be corrected by rebellion against the imperial system. In Massachusetts, on the other hand, the business community was considerably more self-sufficient and correspondingly less dependent on the mother country. It is of course true that Massachusetts' commercial prosperity required good connections with English officials and merchants. But those Massachusetts businessmen who agitated against Puritan rule were unwilling to pay a very high price for union with England. Edward Randolph's "moderate" party turned out to be far less cohesive and cooperative than he had supposed. Once James II established his authoritarian Dominion of New England, most of the "moderates" disliked it very much more than the old Puritan charter government. In fact, they were soon ganging together with the dispossessed Puritans in rebellion against Stuart despotism.

The atmosphere in both Massachusetts and Jamaica during James II's reign had an eerie quality of living death which is hard to convey in a few sentences. James's American empire was a sort of Potemkin village, an imposing façade with nothing behind it. The King and his ministers treated Massachusetts and Jamaica with a curious blend of autocracy and ennui. The Lords of Trade showed slight interest in either Colony, once their independence was broken.[26] There is no evidence that anyone in the plantation office paid close attention to the design for the Dominion of New England, by which Massachusetts was casually amalgamated with her Puritan neighbors into a single political unit. The defunct Massachusetts charter government continued to operate for nearly two years because the Lords did not send over a royal governor. As a stopgap measure, they put Edward Randolph's "moderate" friends in charge of a provisional government. Though this provisional government functioned for only a few months in 1686, it lasted long enough for poor Randolph to discover that his colonial partners were scarcely more obedient to the King than the Puritans had been. The arrival of Sir Edmund Andros, with his scarlet laced coat and his two companies of soldiers, made the Dominion of New England for the first time a reality. Unencumbered by a representative Assembly, Governor Andros steam-rollered opposition within his council—where legislative and executive decisions were made—and jailed and fined those colonists who dared to protest his tax levies. Yet Andros was perilously isolated. The Puritans hated his religious policy, which favored the Church of England. The merchants hated his enforcement of the navigation acts, which crippled trade. The landowners hated his policy of challenging all patents issued under the charter government. And all the colonists hated the loss of self-government. Perhaps because Andros minimized these difficulties in his reports home, the Lords of Trade never bothered to write him letters of inquiry, advice, or instruction. Instead, they gave him additional territories to govern, which naturally increased his problems. By 1688 the Dominion of New England had ballooned into a sort of Spanish viceroyalty, covering the whole of English America from Maine to the Delaware. The northern frontier needed a single energetic military commander, in the face of rising French and Indian threats. But like a balloon, Andros' Dominion was hollow inside.[27]

James II did not combine his sugar islands into a single viceroyalty like the Dominion of New England. Probably he would have done so had his regime lasted another few years. In 1686, when Andros was sent to New England, a much more august personage, the Duke of Albemarle, was commissioned Governor General of Jamaica. Albemarle received a bigger salary than Andros and all sorts of honorific privileges, such as the power to confer knighthood. The Duke wanted still greater power, amounting to sovereign authority over Jamaica. But though James II was a notoriously poor judge of character, he could see that Albemarle was a profligate man, who wanted to go to the West Indies only because he hoped to dig up buried treasure there and replenish his squandered fortune. The Duke had, in fact, already gained £90,000 by investing in the recovery of a sunken Spanish silver galleon, and he was looking for another bonanza. It would be most accurate to say that James II sent Albemarle to Jamaica to get rid of him.[28] The Duke proved to be as autocratic as Andros and considerably more reckless. He turned out of office the big sugar planters who had dominated Jamaica under Governors Lynch and Molesworth, and replaced them with the remnants of the old Port Royal buccaneering faction which had lost power during Charles II's reorganization of the island a decade before. Finding that the big planters also controlled the Assembly, Albemarle used an armed gang to secure the election of his own supporters to a new Assembly.[29] In addition to the buccaneers, Albemarle patronized the Irish Catholic small planters and indentured servants on the island. The King had instructed him to protect and encourage a Catholic priest named Dr. Thomas Churchill. Albemarle made Father Churchill his chief advisor and sent him back to England as the Colony agent.[30] The grievances and fears rising from Jamaica's political, religious and social factionalism were papered over in the toadying letters and groveling addresses which the colonists sent to Whitehall. Each notable English event, the King's accession, Monmouth's defeat, the Queen's pregnancy, was received with mounting spasms of rapture. When the fateful news arrived in September 1688 that the Queen had given birth to a son, the Massachusetts Puritans sullenly ignored Andros' order to observe a day of public thanksgiving. In Jamaica, Albemarle toasted the Prince of Wales so immoderately that he plunged into a fit of jaundice and shortly died.[31]

Soon after Albermarle's demise, during the winter of 1688–1689, rumors filtered into America that William of Orange had invaded England. The reaction to this news in Massachusetts was utterly different from the reaction in Jamaica. In Massachusetts, the colonists grabbed the chance to participate in the Glorious Revolution. On April 18, 1689 they rose up against Governor Andros and toppled the Dominion of New England in a *coup d'état* as bloodless and expeditious as the revolution at home. The Boston revolt inspired parallel risings in most of the other mainland colonies, notably in New York and Maryland. But the planters in Jamaica and the

other sugar islands took no part in this rebellion. For them, the upheaval at home was more alarming than stimulating. They felt rud-
derless and abandoned. In 1689, for the first time, an explicit dividing line was drawn between Englishmen in North America and the
West Indies.

The Massachusetts rebellion of 1689 was a virtually unanimous
act. Puritans and non-Puritans worked together to carry out the
coup. Andros, Randolph, and a handful of colonists loyal to the Dominion were helplessly isolated and easily imprisoned. A combination of charter magistrates, turncoat Dominion councilors, and
heretofore private citizens—the new Massachusetts ruling class—
formed an interim administration, the Council of Safety. In May
1689 this Council of Safety summoned a convention of forty-four
Massachusetts towns which voted overwhelmingly to resume the old
charter government. But the convention elected several prominent
non-Puritans to the panel of charter magistrates, and hence preserved bipartisan support for the rebellion.[32] In Jamaica, by contrast,
there was political paralysis. Governor Albemarle's death left the
Colony torn between two factions, the pro-Albemarle buccaneers
and small planters, and the anti-Albemarle big planters, both factions totally bereft of leadership. The Duke's supporters kept control
of the Jamaica government, and as tension mounted in the spring of
1689 they ruled by martial law. Everyone waited nervously for
orders from England. In May 1689 it was learned that the home
government had cancelled all of Albemarle's proceedings. Both
James II (in November 1688) and William III (in February 1689)
had agreed that the Duke's governorship was a total disaster. This
cancellation produced a general turnover in Jamaica, for Albemarle's
enemies reoccupied their former posts, while Albemarle's friends
tamely surrendered control. A revolution, perhaps, but not a very
spontaneous one.[33]

How is this contrast between Massachusetts and Jamaica in 1689
to be explained? The easiest answer is that Massachusetts had
greater grievances, but as I have tried to demonstrate, this was not
really the case. The two Colonies had experienced very much the
same political and economic pressure from England. In Massachusetts the pressure fused the colonists against Governor Andros,
whereas in Jamaica it more nearly caused civil war. The Massachu-

setts rebellion cannot be ascribed simply to Puritan militance. The Puritans, I believe, only dared to act so boldly because they had the active cooperation of non-Puritans, particularly merchants, who had changed their minds about the benefits of closer union with England. By the same token, Jamaica's paralysis in 1689 cannot be ascribed simply to tropical torpor. Some of the most energetic and successful sugar planters no longer lived in Jamaica, but in England, leaving their plantations under the care of overseers. The planters who still lived on the island were not eager to give their slaves a lesson in insurrection. There had been a very big Negro revolt in Jamaica in 1685, and smaller ones during the next three years. The sugar planters could ill afford the luxury of tumults within the master class.

They had reason, also, to be nervous about the international situation in 1689, with William III leading England into war against Louis XIV. This Anglo-French war posed a much graver threat to Englishmen in the West Indies than to those on the North American mainland. Many of the buccaneers recently expelled from Jamaica had transferred to French St. Domingue, from where they could easily strike at their old base, knowing that the Jamaican fortifications were in poor shape. Jamaica's indentured servants, who constituted the bulk of the island fighting force, were few in number and entirely untrustworthy, being mainly Irish Catholics and likely to support the French in any invasion. Recent Caribbean wars had shown how easily the islands changed hands, with thousands of settlers captured or dispersed, their slaves stolen and their plantations wiped out. It is scarcely surprising that the sugar planters wanted military and naval protection from the home government even more than they wanted political and economic concessions. New England, by contrast, was so much stronger than Canada that the colonists could attempt independent military ventures against the French reminiscent of the good old days before 1676. The Massachusetts rebels saw the Anglo-French war as a golden opportunity to prove their loyalty and value to William III, and thus justify their rising against Andros. They captured the Acadian Port Royal in 1690 and tried to storm Quebec in 1691. The commander of these expeditions was Sir William Phips, a crude sailor cast in the mold of a Jamaica buccaneer, with no previous affiliation with Puritanism nor with the old

Massachusetts charter. Indeed, Phips made his reputation as the Duke of Albemarle's employee, by extracting sunken treasure from a wrecked Spanish galleon. His campaigns against the French were ineptly executed, yet he had the right strategy for the conquest of Canada, a stroke beyond the dreams of Sir Edmund Andros.

The irony is that the active Massachusetts rebels benefited less from the Glorious Revolution than the passive Jamaica sugar planters. Three years passed before William III's government settled on a definite line of policy toward either Colony, but in the end the new pattern of Anglo-American imperial relations suited the island more than the mainland planters. In Massachusetts, the rebel unity of April 1689 quickly evaporated. As the colonists waited from 1689 to 1692 without getting William III's endorsement of their revolt, or his validation of their charter, their anxiety and frustration rekindled. The charter government which they had hastily resumed was clearly suspect. Their governor, Simon Bradstreet, was nearly ninety years old and senile. Sir William Phips' ambitious naval expeditions against Canada did nothing to protect the inland frontier against French and Indian raids. The French War was interrupting trade, and it was forcing the Colony to levy much heavier taxes than Andros had ever imposed. Some people refused to pay taxes. Long before the arrival of the new royal charter in 1692, a number of the merchants who had earlier befriended Randolph were calling for the restoration of Andros and the Dominion of New England. On the other hand, most of the Puritans were still hoping against hope for a definition of relations with the Crown that would permit total self-determination. To these covenant-minded people, the new charter came as the climax to a series of bewildering shocks. Massachusetts was now just another royal province, with much less independence than Connecticut or Rhode Island. Why was God so specially angry with Massachusetts? Small wonder that an introverted religious community, so repeatedly buffeted by divine wrath and punishment, fell victim in 1692 to the mass hysteria of the Salem witch craze.[34]

Massachusetts' agents in England did not fail for lack of effort. Before, during and after the English revolution, spokesmen for the Bay Colony lobbied furiously at Whitehall, trying to extract concessions from James II and William III. In 1688 the principal Boston preacher, Increase Mather, teamed up in London with the principal

New England land speculator, Richard Wharton. This curious pair of agents beseeched James II to deliver Massachusetts from Governor Andros. Mather assiduously cultivated such courtiers as the Catholic Sir Nicholas Butler and the Quaker William Penn, men he must have loathed. He managed to obtain several interviews with the King. But though James II promised to make his New England subjects comfortable, he did not recall Andros. By the fall of 1688 the King was surrendering desperately to every English interest group in a last minute effort to rally support against the invading Prince of Orange. But Mather and Wharton did not represent an English interest group. Accordingly, the Massachusetts Bay Company was one of the few corporations James did not restore. Mather was not much downcast by this, for the Glorious Revolution brought to power a new King and a new Parliament who would surely be more kindly disposed to the Massachusetts Puritans. In 1689 Mather lobbied harder than ever, and he had excellent contacts with William III, such as his friend Sir Henry Ashurst who had personally lent the new King a large sum of money. But William had more important things than Massachusetts to worry about, and he fobbed Mather off with some more empty promises.[35] His ministers, likewise, had no leisure to shape new policy toward the plantations in 1689. When the Lords of Trade learned about the Massachusetts revolt in July 1689, they merely directed that Andros be sent home. In 1689 and 1690, Mather's friends in Parliament tried to include the Massachusetts Bay Company in a bill designed to restore all corporate charters liquidated by Charles II and James II. But the House of Lords dropped colonial corporations from the bill, and William III refused to accept the corporation bill in any form.[36] Thus, when Andros and Randolph arrived on the scene in April 1690, the Massachusetts agents suddenly found themselves on the defensive, forced to justify the insurrection in Boston. Half a dozen Massachusetts men joined Mather in London to besiege the Lords of Trade with bundles of depositions against the Dominion of New England, and to write pamphlets vindicating their treatment of Andros. All this effort, however, merely stiffened the plantation office's resistance to radical change. The Lords of Trade summarily dismissed all charges against Andros. William III might relax his predecessor's arbitrary style of rule in America, but he was not going to let the colonists revert to their original political autonomy. Neither Crown nor Parliament would validate the charter government which the Massachusetts rebels had resumed.

Meanwhile, the Jamaica lobby in London was also barraging the government in 1688–1689, with far greater success. As many as sixty Jamaica merchants and planters, resident in England, could be mustered to sign petitions charging that the Duke of Albemarle had subverted the Jamaica constitution. Their essential complaint was that the substantial planters had been driven from office in the island and replaced by "needy and mechanick men such as tapsters, barbers and the like." Both James II and William III respected the political leverage of the Jamaica lobby, and both also needed the Jamaica customs revenue. Accordingly, one of James's last orders in November 1688 was that Jamaica be restored to the condition she was in at the Duke of Albemarle's arrival. The Massachusetts agents found out about this. "Letters were writt," they pointed out in January 1689, "that the Government of Jemaica should be managed as it was before the sending of the Duke of Albemarle thither. . . . The very like is now desired as to New England, namely that they may be restored to their Government by their ancient Charters." [37] But William III confirmed James's orders concerning Jamaica, and did not restore the old Massachusetts charter. The Lords of Trade in 1689 and 1690 took the Jamaica petitions against Albemarle much more seriously than the Massachusetts depositions against Andros. Indeed, the only Massachusetts petitions recorded in the plantation office entry books are complaints by Andros and his supporters against the rebel government.

Throughout the 1690's, William III took pains to appease the Jamaica lobby. When his first appointee as governor of Jamaica, Lord Inchiquin, failed to please them, the King gave the post to one of the chief lobbyists, Sir William Beeston, a very big absentee planter, who had often served as the Colony's agent at Whitehall. Back in the 1670's, when Charles II had tried to remodel the Jamaica Assembly, Beeston had been an Assembly leader and a vigorous spokesman for local self-determination. Now, backed up by his absentee colleagues in London, Beeston symbolized the return of big planter home rule in the English West Indies. Beeston steered Jamaica through a difficult period. In 1692, shortly before his arrival, an earthquake destroyed Port Royal, symbol of so much in Jamaica's early history. French marauders continually raided the coastline. In 1694, a large French expedition invaded the island, and except for Beeston's energetic defense might have captured it. Sixteen hundred slaves were lost, and scores of sugar works wrecked. Yet, so elastic was Jamaica's growth at this time that during the decade of Beeston's governorship, 1692–1702, all wartime losses were rapidly made up and sugar production soared. Despite his wartime problems, Beeston governed to the satisfaction of the Jamaicans and the plantation office, happily combining the diverse roles of planter, merchant, lobbyist, and King's servant.[38]

It was much harder to devise a formula for Massachusetts that would suit both colonists and Crown. The charter of 1691 provided a new secular constitution for the Colony. When this document had finally been hammered out, clause by clause, after many months of strenuous negotiation between the Massachusetts agents and the Lords of Trade, neither side was at all happy with the result. The Lords of Trade regretted giving somewhat fuller self-government to Massachusetts than to other royal Colonies such as Jamaica, and the Massachusetts agents hated the royal governor's extensive independent authority.[39] Increase Mather recorded in his Diary his bitter disappointment at losing "all the old dearest priviledges" of the bygone Bible Commonwealth. But Mather did accept the necessity of compromise, which he had scorned back in 1683, when he would rather have Charles II annul the charter than revise it. Now Mather realized the permanence of the English imperial system. If the people of Massachusetts should refuse to accept this new charter, he argued, "that which is worse will be imposed," and another Andros and his creatures would take control of the colony government, courts and laws.[40] Mather was permitted to nominate Sir William Phips as the first charter governor. But the King was quickly disenchanted with Phips and recalled him in 1694. The next royal governor of Massachusetts, the Earl of Bellomont, was an outsider imposed on the colonists by the home government. Bellomont administered New York and New Hampshire as well as Massachusetts, hence his appointment was a partial reincarnation of the Dominion of New England. He was followed in 1702 by Joseph Dudley, an insider with a difference. For Dudley was the one prominent colonial who had been jailed along with Andros and Randolph by the Boston rebels. He had the distinction of being—until Thomas Hutchinson—the most ardent royalist born and bred in Massachusetts. Dudley was an able man and an effective governor, but his appointment was a calculated insult to the memory of 1689.[41]

The contrast between Massachusetts and Jamaica in the 1690's should not be overdrawn. In certain important respects they looked more alike than they had a generation earlier. With the breakup of their old autonomy, both colonies lost some of their original distinctiveness. Massachusetts, with her new admixture of worldly Anglicans and rationalists, was now a less cloistered community. Jamaica, sans buccaneers, was more respectable. By 1700, so the plantation office believed, it was easier to find pirates in any Massachusetts port than buccaneers in Jamaica. Thanks to a generation of imperial pressure, the two Colonies were also more uniform institutionally than they had been in the 1670's. The planters in both places stood in about the same constitutional relation to the Crown. On paper at least, the distribution of power between royal governor, Council, and Assembly was roughly equivalent, though the Jamaica governor had more executive and fiscal independence. Legislation, subject to review by the Crown, was also more standardized in style and content. Anything beyond the inspection range of the home authorities, such as town or parish structure, or land distribution, continued to vary enormously from Colony to Colony. There was, however, considerable similarity between the role of the big planters in Jamaica and the big merchants in Massachusetts. The leading entrepreneurs in both colonies enjoyed political power commensurate with their social pretensions. In Jamaica under Governor Beeston, the victory of the planter class was plainly evident. In Massachusetts, under the new charter, the big merchants and land speculators had to share power with the small farmers and share prestige with the clergy. But the Massachusetts merchants enjoyed a much stronger political and social position than they could claim in the 1670's. Of all Massachusetts interest groups, they were the best pleased with the Colony's new secular constitution and her new dependent status within the Empire.[42]

Yet when one compares the Massachusetts merchants with the Jamaica planters, it is evident that the West India sugar lobby had made a better bargain with the home government. William III continued the mercantilist assumptions of Charles II and James II. His Colonial advisers continued to believe that by consciously and artificially shaping the Empire into a self-sufficient economic unit they were fostering community wealth and power.[43] In the 1690's, King and Parliament invested most heavily in those plantations that offered the biggest commercial and strategic returns to the mother country. By this measure, the sugar islands were more profitable than the tobacco colonies, and far more so than New England. Jamaica, as the biggest English sugar island, promised the richest yield of all. Accordingly, during King William's War the Crown supplied Jamaica with a great deal more military assistance than Massachusetts. In 1694, for instance, the home government sent one thousand soldiers to Jamaica at a cost of £50,000.[44] Even more helpful to the Jamaica planters was the home government's opening of the African slave traffic to private traders. After 1688 the hated Royal African Company, patronized by Charles II and James II, no longer enjoyed its monopoly. The volume of Negro traffic to the English islands, particularly to Jamaica, greatly increased as a result. In 1693 the government even dropped James II's sugar tax of 1685, while retaining James' companion tax on Chesapeake tobacco. At the same time that the Jamaica planters were benefiting from these government measures, the Massachusetts merchants were being harassed by the punitive provisions of the Navigation Act of 1696. In this same year the King constituted his aggressive new Board of Trade, which completed the evolution of the imperial administrative system. The Board maintained generally cordial relations with the West Indian sugar lobby, and especially cordial relations with Beeston's Jamaica government, while it campaigned incessantly against merchants from Boston and the other mainland ports who evaded or defied their mercantilist rules. Judging by the complaints against Massachusetts merchants received by the Board in 1700, nothing seemed to have changed since Edward Randolph first reported to the King how Boston was ignoring the navigation acts in 1676.

Of course a great deal had changed. Twenty-five years of Anglo-American tension had produced two varieties of Colonial dependency, a West Indian kind and a North American kind. The sugar planters wanted and needed a close union with the mother country.

In the 1680's they had felt helplessly victimized by Charles II and James II, as they saw all the Caribbean profits and power going to the king and his court friends. The Glorious Revolution gave them the chance to press for a more balanced arrangement. Like all colonists, they wanted lower taxes and more local self-government. But equally important, they wanted better military support and better protection against foreign sugar competition. The revolutionary settlement gave them these things. In the 1690's the West Indian planter class entered its golden age. During the course of the eighteenth century, the sugar interest assumed a dominating voice within the American Empire out of all proportion to its real strength. As for the North American colonists, they wanted a different sort of liaison with the mother country. Their notion of an imperial partnership was much more vague. They wanted to be left alone as much as possible, to get more breathing space. Here was a source of permanent friction with the Crown. The revolutionary settlement in the 1690's relaxed imperial pressure on the mainland Colonies, but not very much. In short, the Glorious Revolution ended Stuart despotism in the Colonies, which was what all Englishmen in America wanted. And it continued the Stuart idea of the English Empire as a self-contained unit, which suited the islanders far more than the mainland colonists. This division of interest between North America and the West Indies, significant enough in 1700, would break up the Old Empire in 1775.

Anglo-Virginia Politics, 1690–1735

DAVID ALAN WILLIAMS holds his B.A. from Westminster College (Pennsylvania) and his M.A. and Ph.D. from Northwestern University. He is Dean of Student Affairs and Associate Professor of History at the University of Virginia. The subject of Dr. Williams' doctoral dissertation was "Political Alignments in Colonial Virginia, 1698–1750," and his current research interest is the emergence of the planter gentry in colonial Virginia. His publications include "The Virginia Gentry and the Democratic Myth" in *Main Problems in American History* (1968).

Historians have long recognized the impact of the Civil War, the Glorious Revolution, the great wars for Empire, and the instability of English politics in the 1760's on Virginia. And they have dealt at length with the major mercantile and imperial policy decisions and the Colonial reactions to them. But general opinion is that the English and Virginians lived politically in "two separate worlds" set apart by great distances, tenuous communications, ignorance bred from lack of contacts, and the coming-of-age of a colony in a wilderness environment. Occasionally the two worlds met at the Virginia Coffee House, at the Board of Trade, perhaps in the Privy Council should some rash action by the Assembly tread on the vested interests of English merchants. These spheres were joined in the gentry tradition of the Virginia planter and the English country squire.

A fairly standard picture developed for Virginia politics from the

Glorious Revolution to the Golden Age of the 1740's: nearly overrun by the despotism of Francis Lord Howard of Effingham, archspokesman for Stuart policy, Virginians rejoiced in the Revolution and its triumph of Whig principles; as Parliament gained ascendancy over the Crown, so the General Assembly successfully neutralized the royal governors. Acknowledging that political considerations were involved, historians have assumed that most governors gained the office as a reward for executive capabilities demonstrated in military service or in some lesser Colonial office. Little attention has been paid to the real significance of the governors' political patrons. Political preferences are frequently designated as "A Whig" or "A Tory." The governor's future was largely determined by political conditions in Virginia. If he were amenable to Virginia planters, not overly zealous in enforcing his instructions, conscious of the perquisites of the councilors, and deferential to the rising planters in the Burgesses, he would get along well as did Colonel Francis Nicholson in his first administration (1690–92) or Major Hugh Drysdale (1722–1726) and Major William Gooch (1727–1749). If he were not, or if he pushed his instructions fully, challenged the councilors' preeminence, defended Crown prerogatives against the encroachments of the Burgesses, thwarted the schemes for reform of Church and college proposed by Commissary James Blair, or wounded the enormous vanity of the gentry then he was harassed out of the Colony, as was Howard in 1688, Colonel Edmund Andros in 1698, Nicholson in 1704, and Colonel Alexander Spotswood in 1722. In each case the pressure for removal came from Virginia and was applied by Virginia representatives operating through political allies in England. In this picture gleaned from the standard works on the period by Thomas Jefferson Wertenbaker, Richard Morton, Philip Bruce, Leonidas Dodson, Louis B. Wright, and George M. Brydon day-to-day politics in England had little to do with the Old Dominion.[1]

This political portrait of eighteenth-century Virginia is being redrawn. Recent probing into the roots of power in Virginia has shown that they go to ground in England. At the same time English historians, their own neat view of parties forever shattered, have shown the degree to which personalities, patronage, and patrons constantly pushed parties and principles aside. New questions must be asked about the Virginia political structure to coincide with the new structure apparent in early eighteenth-century English political life. Thus, Michael Hall demonstrates the intimate relation between the Chesapeake tobacco trade and the Navigation Act of 1696, Peter Laslett discovers John Locke breathing life into the Board of Trade, and Michael Kammen connects Locke to Commissary James Blair and the famous *History and Present State of Virginia.* John Hemphill finds the origins of Walpole's Excise Bill in letters of Governor William Gooch defending a Virginian tobacco law.[2]

And most recently Stephen Webb has joined Virginia governors to the English army, army attitudes, and military policy. In this new scheme of things Locke, the Bishop of Norwich, the Battle of Blenheim, the Scottish Squadrons, John Lord Somers, the Earls of Rochester or Nottingham, and the Dukes of Bolton and Newcastle, are every bit as important for Virginia history as Blair, the Byrds, Ludwells, Harrisons and Randolphs. Where credit has been given Blair and his fellow councilors for ousting their governors, British politics were far more influential than Virginia pressure. Political patronage and rewards to politically significant officers were the sole criteria for the appointment and dismissal of Virginia governors. Each shift in English politics brought a similar shift in the administration of Virginia. Behind this observation lurks a much larger thesis, which contends that from 1660 on English Colonial policy was directed toward instituting military control over the Colonies. Only fortuitous events kept the officer-governors from achieving this goal by 1715.[3]

The real point that now needs to be made is that the politics of both Virginia and England were interconnected; that unless you had political disturbances or changes on both sides of the Atlantic at about the same time, you were not apt to have change in the Virginia governorship. It is obvious that not every political upheaval in England after 1688 brought a new governor to Virginia and not every Virginia protest turned out a governor.

The Virginian view of Empire was one of an intimate, organic union. Wrote the elder William Byrd following the hectic events of 1688: "When the body is disturbed, the members needs must be effected, therefore, we here can expect no settled times till England is in peace. . . ." English politics influenced very much the course of events in Jamestown and Williamsburg, and occasionally difficulties in the "members" distressed the "body politick" in London.[4]

Virginia was spared the spectacular outbursts which swept over Massachusetts, New York, and Maryland during the Glorious Revolution. But it had been a near miss. Many Virginians had been thoroughly alarmed by the behavior of Governor Howard in administering Stuart policy. By 1688 the Burgesses, after being at complete loggerheads with the Governor, decided that they must have a charter defining their rights and privileges. Over the opposition of the Governor's loyal councilors they sent to London their personal agent, deposed councilor Philip Ludwell, Sr.

Arriving after the Revolution had taken place, Ludwell quickly noted what recent historians have been rediscovering—the Glorious Revolution was not very revolutionary, at least not in 1689. William, after his sallies with the Dutch States-General, was no more willing to yield to Whig republicanism than James had been. The coalition which surrounded the new monarchs was reluctant to oust anyone. Howard, although out of sympathy with the new regime, was not so disenchanted as to throw away a lucrative sinecure and he agreed to send out Colonel Francis Nicholson as his lieutenant governor. Ludwell, after seeing his charter revisions set aside and Nicholson's instructions left virtually unchanged from Howard's, decided to live by the First Commandment of the statesman, Protect Thyself. He took appointments as the proprietary governor of North Carolina and the resident agent for the proprietors of the Northern Neck.[5]

The thirty-five-year-old Nicholson had blended a military career with political preferment. The orphaned son of lesser Yorkshire gentry, a page in the household of Charles Paulet (later Lord Bolton), he had first attracted attention as a diplomatic courier in Morocco. As with most career officers and colonial governors he had learned to live by his wits and his contacts, shifting political liaisons as the times demanded. Despite a monumental temper and a vulgar tongue, the Governor was a devoted Church member, a keen student of Colonial affairs, a gregarious man with many friends, and above all a scrupulously honest and loyal servant of the Crown. His indecisive behavior during Leisler's Rebellion had not injured his reputation in England. Fortunately his prime patrons and friends had successfully bridged the Revolution and ended up in places of influence around William and Mary.[6]

In these same years there came to Virginia the Reverend Mr.

James Blair, the famous *bête noire* of Virginia governors. A tough-minded Scotsman, a fervent Anglican in a Presbyterian homeland, he had drifted south to London after refusing to adhere to the Test Oath in 1681. Securing a clerkship at the Rolls Office, he soon made friends with Gilbert Burnet and through Burnet came into contact with a group of divines standing in opposition to the King. One of them, Henry Compton, Bishop of London, took a liking to Blair and in 1685 sent him out to a Virginia parish. Within two years he had married into one of the most powerful families, the Harrisons. The Revolution brought Compton, Burnet, and their associates into favored positions in the Church and at Court. Blair was made Compton's commissary in Virginia.[7]

Historians have made Nicholson and Blair carry too large a burden in the story of the following years. They were not the only Virginians who were known in England. Most of the larger planters were English born or educated. Many traded with merchant relatives whose credit had subsidized their early years. Travel to England was surprisingly frequent. Seldom did a year go by without one or more councilors being in London on personal business, and there he could always find several members of the Burgesses. A generation later such intimate contacts with "home" were disappearing.

If Nicholson's instructions were virtually unchanged from Howard's his style was certainly different. He toured the countryside, surveying the colony's needs, winning the plaudits of the people and the Assembly, which voted him large gifts in pounds sterling. Although he could not get them to support his major militia reorganization, he enthusiastically backed the colonists' plans for the College of William and Mary at Middle Plantation. Nicholson soon learned what it meant to be lieutenant-governor, for Howard out of sorts in health and politics gave up the governorship in early 1692. The new governor was Sir Edmund Andros. The unhappy Nicholson moved over to Maryland as the lieutenant-governor. Blair, in England at the time, understood that Nicholson was believed not to be ready for a full governorship; Nicholson, who had grown to hate Andros since the debacle of the Dominion of New England, blamed his transfer on the Earl of Nottingham, the Tory-oriented Secretary of State and Andros patron.[8]

Bad luck and poor timing dogged Andros throughout his administration. By 1692 King William's War had thoroughly disrupted the tobacco trade and closed European markets. Admiralty press gangs swept the English docks and reduced the merchant fleet to a shadow of itself. In some years no tobacco ships at all appeared in the upper reaches of the Potomac, tobacco rotted on the wharfs and in ware-houses, and colonists were reduced to growing cotton and weaving their own linsey-woolsey. The tobacco crisis forced desperate Virginia planters to break with their London merchants and open new trade lines with the West Country ports or enter into the clan-destine Scots trade. In 1695, a very poor crop year, London ship captains found themselves beaten out by the interlopers and went home with empty ships. The complaints of London merchants bore out the contentions made by Edward Randolph, the officious Sur-veyor of Customs for the Southern Plantations, in his "An Account of Several Things Whereby Illegal Trade is Encouraged in Virginia, Maryland, and Pennsylvania." In 1696 Parliament passed a compre-hensive trade act, and King William established a permanent Board of Trade.[9]

William's decision to transfer the direction of his government from the so-called "Second Danby Ministry" to the Junto Whigs in 1694 had boded ill for Andros. The vigorous Board of Trade was a crea-tion of the Junto. In the process William Blathwayt, former leader in colonial affairs and patron of Andros, was bypassed and leadership on the Board transferred to the philosopher John Locke whose pa-tron was the Junto leader, John Lord Somers.[10]

Still Andros would not have been in serious trouble had he been able to maintain political peace in Virginia. However, Crown in-volvement created problems for him when the French and Indians put pressure on New York, and the King sent out orders for Virginia to aid her neighbor with money and men. Queen Mary, in her enthu-siasm for the College enterprise had given over to the clergy all the reserves in the royal coffers in Virginia. While the quitrents and the tobacco duties technically belonged to the Crown, these funds had been left in Virginia to pay for royal expenditures. Virginians had come to view these monies as means whereby they could transfer Colony expenses to the Crown. If the royal income went to the clergy, then the Burgesses would have to vote additional taxes for defense expenditures normally loaded on the royal revenues. Eventually the Council got William to suspend Mary's gift but not before Blair had bitter words with his fellow councilors and the Governor. With the royal funds intact the Burgesses were able to slough off William's requests for financial assistance to New York on all but a few occasions.[11]

As the tobacco duties continued to drop amidst the general suppression of trade, Andros could not postpone the political consequences of paying for the clergy, the College, and other local expenditures. From early 1694 when he felt that he must emphasize military expenditures at the expense of the College and the clergy, he had been in some trouble. Andros was backed in his decision by the Council and indirectly by the Burgesses. On the other side Blair, many of the clergymen, and a few dedicated supporters of the College were disturbed. Matters were not helped any when Nicholson arrived in Maryland as governor following the death of Lionel Copley and proceeded to use his position as Rector of William and Mary to keep a hand in Virginia affairs.

A breach in the Council over the College in April 1695 led to a unanimous agreement from the members to ask Andros to suspend Blair from his seat as "not fitt to sitt at the Board." Andros speedily complied. The commissary sailed for England, visited his clerical friends, circulated a scathing attack on the governor entitled "Sir E. Andros no real friend to the Clergy . . . ," and with the aid of timely letters from Nicholson was returned to the Council the following year.

Both the commissary and the Maryland governor undertook a vigorous campaign to get Andros out of and Nicholson into the Virginia governor's chair. Andros' stalwart supporter, Daniel Parke, Jr., strained royal protocol by assaulting Nicholson at a College trustees meeting. Meanwhile the councilors allowed themselves to be maneuvered by Blair into declaring him not eligible for a Council seat under provisions in the Act of 1696 barring Scots from offices in the colonies. Blair had planned for sometime to go to England on College business. Now the councilors gave him a perfect reason to combine religious and political business.[12]

Blair could not have arrived in London at a better time than summer of 1697. Under Locke's aegis the Board of Trade was working its way through an investigation of Colonial governmental operations and had just turned to Virginia. In late August 1697 Locke sought out Blair, plied him with innumerable questions about Virginia, compiled a list of questions for Blair to answer in writing, and sent similar lists to former Virginia residents Henry Hartwell and Edward Chilton. Their composite answer offered to the Board as "The Present State of Virginia" was cogent, informative, and a low-keyed criticism of Andros. Naturally the Commissary during this time was not ignoring his primary contacts, the Archbishop of Canterbury and Bishop Compton.[13]

Although the primary entree into the Junto structure was through Blair to Locke and then to Somers, Nicholson on his own opened contact with the Earl of Bridgewater, president of the Board, by damning Andros as the creature of the detested Nottingham and condemning Blathwayt for soliciting bribes. The Maryland governor with an adeptness necessary in the shifting political tides of the nineties glossed over the fact that Nottingham's blessing had been necessary to gain him his own governorship. And following all possible avenues of approach, he prevailed upon the Maryland Assembly to retain John Povey, Blathwayt's nephew and favorite clerk, as the Maryland agent, and to pay Blathwayt certain necessary "fees." [14]

What finally moved Andros out of Virginia was a general reform of the governor's instructions proposed by Locke and his fellow Whigs over the vehement protests of Blathwayt. These new instructions trimmed the executive powers over the Council, eliminated many of the councilor's special privileges, and altered the land system to prevent the concentration of land in the hands of speculators. The specific recommendations follow closely Blair's comments to Locke; the land reforms bear a striking similarity to Locke's own ideas on property. Obviously Blair and several other Virginians who testified on the instructions hoped it would be Nicholson who would put the new instructions into practice. Still they would not move until Locke was at the Board in the spring of 1698. Andros was virtually without protection. Only Blathwayt could help him. This able minister quickly discerned the drift of things and offered Andros' resignation to head off further and more drastic revisions in the instructions. Nicholson was where he wanted to be—governor of Virginia.[15]

Ironically, by the time Andros was removed and Nicholson's instructions issued, the power behind Somers, Locke, and the Junto was being withdrawn. With the Treaty of Ryswick the New Country members of Parliament turned on the Government, vented their displeasure for the Dutch King and his standing army, and pressed hard at the corrupt methods of the Junto. William for his part had never wanted the Junto and now that peace was at hand and they could no longer carry his business in Parliament he was willing to see them go. Within months after his appointment Blair would find his "friends" out of power and within three years Nicholson would be writing sycophantic notes to Nottingham telling him how wonderful it was to have a "high tory churchman" in office again.[16]

A known and popular leader, Nicholson arrived in Virginia amidst the general expectation of an upsurge in tobacco prices. Politics were put aside as new lands went into cultivation and new counties were formed. Planters literally sailed out to ships to bid on fresh cargoes of African slaves. Even the burning of the Statehouse in Jamestown and the building of the new Capitol in Williamsburg seemed to point toward a new era.

For several years all went well. Then the erosion of political harmony began, starting first among the councilors who objected to Nicholson's implementation of Board restrictions. In a sense Nicholson had a new Council, for death, resignation, and removal to England had changed the membership noticeably. The new councilors, most of them appointed after 1697, were young, eager, ambitious sons of English-born immigrant planters. Whereas their fathers had had to depend closely upon the governors for political and economic survival, they had reached the place where they were no longer dependent economically on royal favor alone. While not admitting it publicly, they discovered that the Board had given them a great deal of freedom to conduct their business in Council without gubernatorial interference. Howard, Nicholson in his early term, and even Andros had had compliant, almost at times, fawning councilors; Nicholson after 1700 and Spotswood in the 1710's faced haughty men, zealous to protect their powers and perquisites.

In quick succession other opponents appeared—large planters who opposed the restrictions on land grants, speculators who fought the rigorous collection of quitrents, fur traders like the Byrds who suspected Nicholson wanted to control the trade, proprietary agents and landholders on the Northern Neck who knew well Nicholson's plans to return the Neck to royal control, and Burgesses who saw behind Nicholson's determined demand for military preparedness and intercolonial cooperation the threat of a standing army, that most volatile of all contemporary issues. Then Nicholson, who usually had a good feel for public appearances, made a fool of himself over young Lucy Burwell, and proceeded to insult her whole family, including six councilors. Nicholson also had a falling-out with Blair, his erstwhile prime minister, over Church affairs. By early 1703 at least half the councilors and a vocal minority of Burgesses, although divided on most issues, were united in their desire to see Nicholson gone.

The councilors drew up a scurrilous bill of particulars against Nicholson and sent it off to England with Blair, while they set out to get the full House of Burgesses behind them. Blair's connections and those of his Virginia associates were with merchants, Junto Whigs, and low-church bishops, factions out of favor following Anne's accession. The Queen's natural alliance was with high churchmen like Nottingham, the Secretary of State, and the loyal Cockpit group of Goldolphin and the Churchills.

Nicholson was not much better off, for his ties too had been into the Junto through the second Duke of Bolton. He deftly shifted positions and wrote ingratiatingly to Nottingham and to several other acquaintances on the Board of Trade. At the year's end he seemed safe. In England the Board of Trade had renewed its confidence in him; in Virginia the dissident councilors could not bring the Burgesses over to their side, and the clergy, tired of Blair's public insults about their incompetency, voted to support the Governor.

The new year brought another twist in English politics. Anne could no more gain full backing for the Marlborough's continental campaigns from Rochester and Nottingham than had William and so was forced at Marlborough's behest to bring back the moderate Whigs and Junto-men. This opened new possibilities for Blair, and with renewed vigor he scurried around reminding everyone how Nicholson had consorted with Nottingham. That same year Daniel Parke, Jr., Nicholson's assailant in 1696, carried the news of Blenheim from Churchill to Anne and asked as his reward the governorship of Virginia. Thus, these two Virginia rivals had brought the Virginia office to renewed attention. Malborough with all opposition to his grand design for British supremacy shattered by his great victory, moved to partially accomplish one element of that scheme, union with Scotland. The Virginia office was a natural reward for his trusted lieutenant, George Hamilton, Earl of Orkney, a member of the powerful Scottish Squadrone, a vital faction in union plans. Parke would have to be content with governing the Leeward Islands, and Nicholson would have to wait for better times. Still there is nothing to indicate that Nicholson would have been displaced automatically to make room for Orkney had not Virginia been called to official attention at this time.[17]

For Orkney the Virginia governorship was a sinecure. As his lieutenant governor he sent out to Virginia in 1705 Major Edward Nott, a colorless career officer with minor administrative experience in the West Indies. Within a year Nott was dead and Colonel Robert Hunter, a veteran of the European wars appointed in his stead. Unfortunately the French captured Hunter on his way to Virginia, and it was 1710 before Colonel Alexander Spotswood, Marlborough's quartermaster, could get to the colony. In the interim the councilors had consolidated themselves in power in such a manner that no governor could again bend them to his wishes.[18]

Spotswood in his first four years as governor set a remarkable record: strict enforcement of land grants and quitrent collections, creation of a central Indian trading company, suppression of a minor revolt and a major Indian uprising in North Carolina, and the establishment of an elaborate tobacco regulation system accompanied by an equally elaborate scheme to bribe nearly every Burgess with a well-paying inspectorship. By 1714 Spotswood thought he could successfully manage the House and was ready to take on the Council by trimming its judicial powers. Unfortunately for him when Queen Anne died, he had to call a new election. In one of the few popular political upheavals in Virginia's history the colonists voted out all but two Burgess-inspectors and demanded an end to tobacco regulation and the Indian trading company. Spotswood lost his poise and tried to browbeat the Assembly. A new Assembly in 1718 was no more tractable and named Councilor William Byrd II as its agent to seek Spotswood's removal.

Conditions in London could not have been less favorable for Byrd.

London merchants had already prevailed upon the Privy Council to recommend repeal of the tobacco and Indian company laws. Whereas a disgruntled Virginia faction might have overturned Spotswood during the dark days of Marlborough's exile or in the confusion attendant to the accession of King George I, there was no hope in 1718. Orkney was a leading Scottish peer in Parliament and a member of the King's Court.

Conversely the Virginians had almost no friends in high places. Blair, disaffected from the governor over ecclesiastical affairs, had outlived all his English connections. In fact, Blair's superior, John Robinson, Bishop of London, was a constant supporter of Spotswood, the governor having thoughtfully named two of the Bishop's nephews to the Council. Two famous sons of powerful fathers, Philip Ludwell II and William Byrd II, quickly found that they carried far less weight in London than had their fathers. Orkney firmly backed Spotswood, the ouster movement failed; Byrd for his part was temporarily removed from the Council by the Board of Trade.

Still Spotswood was uncertain about his own future and in 1720 decided to remain in Virginia. He reached a truce with his Council and sealed the bargain by dividing tens of thousands of rich Piedmont acres with his fellow planters. Word of his actions reached London about the time that Robert Walpole attained power after the South Sea Bubble broke. Walpole needed offices for his cohorts; Orkney and the old Squadrone needed no longer to be placated; Spotswood's land operations made him an easy target for removal.[19] The new lieutenant governor, Major Hugh Drysdale, was a Walpole client. Arriving in 1722, accompanied by the ubiquitous Blair, who still hoped that he might be some governor's "prime minister," the mild-mannered Drysdale spent much of his time seeking to recover his health. He failed, dying in 1726.

So startling is the contrast between the political rivalries in Virginia from 1688–1722 and the calm of the next thirty years that historians have tended to attribute the differences almost wholly to the continuity provided by Walpole and Newcastle in England and to a colonial policy which left the colonies to their own devices. In Virginia this continuity was seen in the long administration of a docile Governor Gooch who was gently led away from royal prerogatives by the General Assembly.

Several factors contributed to political stability in Virginia. There can be no denying that the long peace after the bitter wars from 1689–1714 coupled with the remarkable control of government by Walpole and Newcastle contributed to harmony in the Colony. For one thing, as Walpole stifled effective political opposition to his government, he eliminated any political leverage in England which dissidents in Virginia might use against a governor.[20]

Moreover, whereas Virginians of the late seventeenth century were in intimate contact with royal officials, and influential Englishmen, the Virginians of the postwar period were not. Most of the leading planters of the 1680's and 1690's either had been born in England, educated there, or had brothers and close relatives in English commercial circles; others went "home" periodically to protect their economic interests. Although commercial connections with the mother country were beginning to be regularized just before the Revolution, they were dislocated by the wars and remained on a personal basis. By the 1720's such direct contact was no longer necessary and was disappearing. Planters' ties were less direct than those of their fathers. Most councilors were born in the Colonies; few had been to England. Most members of the House of Burgesses had never been out of the Colony. With the tobacco trade placed on a regular basis, planters conducted business through London and Bristol merchants they never met or with Scots factors who had little political influence. In a measure as the Virginians personally disengaged socially and economically from England, they also disengaged politically. The most important connection the Colony had was Governor William Gooch.

By any standards of the earlier period Gooch had impeccable political credentials. He was a military man and a moderate Whig. His brother Thomas was later Bishop of Norwich and of Ely. A prime patron and friend of both Thomas Gooch and Walpole was Thomas Sherlock, the Bishop of Bangor. At the Board of Trade he was protected by Martin Bladen, and he chose as Virginia agent Peter Leheup, a Walpole political manager.

Quiet and unassuming Gooch was in actuality a strong leader who relied on persuasion not bombast. He fastened his attention on the House of Burgesses, thereby giving recognition to the rising planter gentry, without antagonizing the Council whose members he won over by a generous land policy in 1730. Crotchety old Commissary Blair was smothered with attention and neutralized. International peace and an end to Indian hostilities allowed him to avoid the treacherous issues of military expenditures and reduce taxes to a minimum.

The prime difference between Gooch and Spotswood or Nicholson was his willingness to promote the Colony's interest through his English connections. The primary function of his administration was to stimulate the economy and expand the Colony. He had no desire for personal aggrandizement in Virginia. He expected that should the Colony prosper under his disinterested management he some day would be rewarded with a pension by a grateful monarch. This almost Lockean approach is well illustrated in Gooch's activities on behalf of the most important piece of legislation passed in Virginia during the eighteenth century—The Tobacco Act of 1730.

Periodic depressions had dogged Virginians at least since 1650. Virginians tended to blame their troubles on overproduction of the golden leaves and periodically and without much success they would resort to some form of crop control. Spotswood was the first to suggest that the primary problem was poor distribution and marketing practices caused by the poor reputation the whole Virginia tobacco crop received when trash tobacco was exported. Quality controlled tobacco, certified by government tobacco inspectors, would attract a large and expandable market. When he put his theory to practice, however, he destroyed it with his politically appointed inspectors. In the 1720's a severe tobacco depression threatened ruin for the whole Colony, creating a popular frustration which could be alleviated only by a drastic change in the tobacco economy. Gooch, shortly after his arrival in 1727, turned to the Spotswood theory but insisted that the inspectors would have to be politically neutral.[21]

To secure passage of a comprehensive inspection law required the assent of the Virginia Assembly and at least three groups in England: the Board of Trade, the commissioners of customs, and the tobacco merchants. Gooch procured preliminary approval from the Board before even submitting the bill to the Assembly. Eventually, the Burgesses yielded to Gooch's blandishments, probably for the same reason the merchants came around—no one could imagine how conditions could become worse.

Convincing the commissioners proved impossible. Tobacco, no matter how poor in quality, was always shipped to England where steep duties were charged and delivered to the customs. Since the essence of tobacco inspection was the destruction of trash tobacco, the commissioners argued that this was tantamount to burning the King's money. They recommended rejection.

Warned by Peter Leheup that Crown denial was a possibility, Gooch bombarded the Board, Newcastle, and Attorney General Fane with letters laying bare the fallacies in the commissioners' tabulations and projecting an increase in revenue after inspection. Turning on the customs establishment itself in the style of Edward Randolph in 1695, he charged that the customs service was riddled with fraud, corruption, and gross inefficiency and ought not to be allowed to ruin a perfectly workable law. So devastating were his arguments as presented through Leheup that even when he alone was defending the law after leading merchants and the Board itself wavered before the customs commissioners, he managed to carry the day. In the end the Privy Council allowed the law on a trial basis. So successful was inspection that it remained in force until after the Revolution.[22]

Just at the moment Gooch and the General Assembly thought they had solved the tobacco problems, the British merchants launched an assault upon one of their most vexatious difficulties—collecting Virginia debts. For almost a decade merchants had been seeking some means for bringing the delinquent planter to court. The intransigent colonists, suspecting another mercantile conspiracy to defraud them of their rightful profits, made no concessions for debt collection in the Virginia courts. And so in 1732 the merchants pushed through Parliament an act for the better securing of Colonial debts owed British creditors. The furious reaction of the General Assembly to this act was to dispatch John Randolph with a petition calling for removal of all tobacco duties and the substitution of an excise. Ostensibly an excise would eliminate fraud in the customs system and remove the planters from the grasps of the merchants whom they thought profited excessively by financing tobacco duty payments at high interest rates. From this direct action of the Virginia Assembly came Walpole's Excise Bill and the crisis of 1732–34.

While there can be no obscuring genuine Virginian desire for an excise, John Hemphill has made a good case for the origin of the excise bill and the Virginia petition in Walpole's own offices with Gooch as the agent. The unraveled story is that Walpole in the beginning of his ministry wanted to reform the notoriously corrupt customs service. Should he introduce the same efficiency there that he had at the Treasury, he could increase revenues and reduce or eliminate the wartime land taxes which bore so heavily upon the English gentry. Deciding that reform was probably not possible, he was thinking by 1728 of an excise on certain products and elimination of much of the customs, but he lacked the evidence with which to launch a frontal assault on the entrenched commissioners and their agents. When Gooch in supporting his tobacco act directed his main arguments against the fraudulent customs agents (the law itself was entitled an act to prevent fraud in the customs), Walpole seized upon the opportunity to make the excise appear to arise naturally out of conditions in the tobacco trade. In 1731, before Parliament had passed the debt act, Walpole sent to Gooch a proposal urging the Colony to put forth an excise scheme. The passage of the debt act created the right political climate for the Assembly in June 1732. With Gooch as the manager, the Council the initiator of the petition, and the Burgesses the ostensible petitioner Randolph was sent off bearing "the Case of the Planters of Tobacco of Virginia" and credits of £2,200 for necessary "expenses." Walpole's attachment to Randolph, his procurement of a knighthood for the Virginia agent, his use of the information supplied by Randolph, the vital importance of tobacco revenues, and the ultimate defeat of the excise are well-known episodes in the crisis which followed.[23]

The excise petition was the most direct intervention by an American Colony in eighteenth-century English domestic policy. It was, however, only the most prominent example of the thesis that interaction between England and Virginia was the continuing political pattern between 1690–1735.

Between Scylla and Charybdis: James DeLancey
and Anglo-American Politics in Early Eighteenth-
Century New York

STANLEY NIDER KATZ possesses his A.B., A.M., and Ph.D. from
Harvard University. He has taught at Harvard and is now Associate Professor of History at the University of Wisconsin, Madison. Dr. Katz is the author of *Newcastle's New York: Anglo-
American Politics, 1732–1753* (1968) and various articles, and
he edited James Alexander's *A Brief Narrative of the Case and
Trial of John Peter Zenger* (1963) and (with Stanley L. Kutler)
New Perspectives on the American Past (1969). At present he
is making a study of equity law and chancery courts in England
and America, 1690–1790.

The royal governor's challenge, according to Jonathan Belcher, was
"to steer between Scylla and Charybdis; to please the king's ministers
at home; and a touchy people here; to luff for one and bear away
from another." [1] The notion, if not the metaphor, of a course to be
steered between the English government and a politically self-
conscious American populace has dominated the interpretation of
eighteenth-century American history. Currently, however, many
scholars are applying an interpretation of the period which, on the
contrary, emphasizes that the tone of American politics before the
revolutionary crisis was set by a natural interaction of English and

American politics. On this account, Scylla and Charybdis, the ministry and the Americans, do not appear irreconcilable, and the true challenge was to master them both rather than to skirt their mysterious dangers. Colonial politics in the early eighteenth-century were Anglo-American, and nowhere more so than in the province of New York.

Royal governors and Colonial politicians contended for the tangible rewards of place and power on this continent, but although the stakes in the game were in America, many of the best hands were not. Access to the principal jobs, favors, and policies sought by New York politicians more often than not lay through Whitehall rather than City Hall or Fort George. The powers of appointment and decision-making which were vested in the officers of state and imperial officials in England made a direct impact upon the conduct of politics in America.

Charles Andrews has observed that "the tendency to center colonial patronage in England" was a fundamental factor in "the growing centralization of the entire British system as we advance toward the climax of the Revolution." [2] Certainly this is so, although the process of centralization in itself was not as important as the growing necessity, after about 1750, to make appointments conform to the immediate requirements of the war-torn Empire. During the first half of the century, however, there were many sources of Colonial patronage in England and there were no clearly formulated standards for its use, so that American posts could be distributed according to the pragmatic and self-interested canons of eighteenth-century English political life. Thus, in order to gain or retain their offices, Americans were obliged to enter into the politics of the mother country.

For Englishmen holding Colonial posts and ambitious colonists alike, the challenge of Anglo-American politics was to have "a good stake in the Hedge" [3]—to establish an influential English connection. Colonials and English placemen sought out every avenue of approach to the great officers of state, members of the administrative boards and of Parliament, as well as leaders of the military and the Church. They appealed to formal organizations, such as the Protestant Dissenting Deputies, and informal groups, such as the American merchants resident in London.[4] They sought help in moments of crisis, but, even more urgently, they tried to establish English connections that would spring to action of their own accord when they could be of service. For English placemen, who came to office through the interest of their friends and relatives, connections were already in existence and needed only to be tended and strengthened. For many Americans, however, especially when they were acting in opposition to such placemen, the problem was to establish contacts in an essentially alien ground, which, as a practitioner of the art complained, entailed "a pretty deal of pains." [5]

It was a complex, unsystematic business, which, in the first part of the century, was carried on largely without benefit of a formal Colonial agency. New York employed no agent from 1730 to 1748, but even if it had he would not have solved the problem for most New Yorkers. The agent was, among other things, ill-paid and subject to the vicissitudes of Assembly politics. Often he did act informally in behalf of an individual or faction, as George Bampfield did for the Livingstons and Robert Charles for James DeLancey, but since he was also ostensibly the agent of the whole Colony (or, more accurately, the Assembly) he had to take care whose personal interests he represented. There were, however, more compelling reasons for looking beyond the agent for a means of establishing a continuing personal contact in England. The most important was that it was difficult to find competent agents who were familiar enough with New York and loyal enough to their employers to be trusted with such weighty business. Moreover, the complexities of British politics were such that the formal representations to which an agent was likely to restrict himself were of little practical use. In the words of Lewis Morris, "As to agents, unless the Court is dispos'd to do us service, no agent can do us much." [6]

Imperial placemen and New York politicians, faced with the need to protect or improve their positions in England, had therefore to establish personal channels of communication. Their efforts were of three (frequently concurrent) types: personal missions, the employment of private agents, and the mobilization of English friends and relatives in their behalf.

In moments of political crisis, the first instinct of politicians who were losing their grasp in New York was to set off for London. There, they felt, it was possible to present their case more successfully than any English representative could. One of the first personal trips to England for political purposes was made by Lewis Morris in 1702 in order to wrest the government of New Jersey from the proprietors, although Robert Livingston had gone home as early as 1695 to claim reimbursement for his expenses in provisioning British troops during King William's War. Even well-connected English placemen were sensitive to their political isolation in America. Governor Hunter determined to return home in 1719 when he received word of an organized attempt to secure disallowance of the most recent New York money bill. He was eager "that nothing may be resolved till I am brought Face to Face to answer these or any other men, as to what I Have done in my station," for he felt that only he could conduct an adequate defense:

I know not the objections but I forsee an inevitable necessity of my coming home for that very purpose for it is impossible to answer as one should at this distance or to instruct another.[7]

When in 1725 Governor Burnet unwisely and unsuccessfully attempted to remove Stephen DeLancey from the political scene by questioning the validity of his citizenship, word travelled across the province that DeLancey was "Resolved to go for England if the Chief Justice gives his opinion that he is an alien." [8]

The best known of eighteenth-century New York political missions was of course that made by Lewis and Robert Hunter Morris in 1735, and recorded by the younger Morris in his diary,[9] but for a number of reasons it was also the last of its kind. A pamphleteer of 1714 had long before pointed out the inconvenience and inefficiency of such trips, noting "the great charge, vexation, and loss of time and damage to their Estates [of those] who are forced to take long and dangerous voyages. . . ." Such voyages were seldom successful:

Thus after two or three, sometimes four or five Years excessive charge and trouble, and severall long voyages from the other part of the World, the unhappy American Subjects are forced to bear their oppression.[10]

The irascible Lewis Morris failed in London and became extremely disgruntled when he considered the time, money, and effort he had expended there.[11] Henceforth, New Yorkers turned to methods of communication with England that did not require them to leave their local interests unprotected.

One alternative to private missions to England was the employment of private agents—personal representatives either sent from America or already resident in England. This technique was, of course, employed throughout the century, but it took on an added importance as the stakes of Colonial politics grew higher with the onset of the imperial crisis. William Shirley, the experienced governor of Massachusetts, Robert Hunter Morris, veteran of his father's 1735 adventure, and the ex-soldier John Catherwood, for example, were (among other things) the personal representatives of Governor Clinton when he was hard-pressed by the strong DeLancey connection at mid-century. Costs of transportation and maintenance in England were prohibitive, however, and Colonials could afford representation in London only to a limited extent. It was also generally true that private agents, particularly Americans, stood outside the channels of English political power, and so were less useful as a "stake in the Hedge" than a continuing English connection.

Family connections were the strongest bonds to England a New Yorker could have, since they did not depend upon considerations of business or friendship which required reciprocity. As a leading New York politician put it in a letter to the English cousin who was his firmest supporter, "You will always find in me a gratefull mind, the only return can be made you from this quarter of the world." [12] It might, for instance, be argued that the DeLancey family's domination of New York politics at mid-century was a function of the strength of their family connection in England and a reflection of the failure of the Livingstons to establish such a relationship.[13] During the revolutionary crisis, conversely, when the English political situation became constricted by the requirements of imperial policy and the focus of American politics narrowed to this side of the Atlantic, the Livingstons had their day. Failing family, however, most New Yorkers nurtured any and all contacts they could muster. Cadwallader Colden, for instance, appealed to his old Scottish patron, the Marquis of Lothian, as well as his scientific correspondent, Peter Collinson.[14] The great task was simply to mobilize anyone with the slightest political influence in England.

The American governors generally had the strongest political interests in England, since it was through these connections that they were appointed. The same was true of many of the principal imperial placemen—if their influence in London had been sufficient to put them in office, it often remained strong enough to keep them there. One need only think of Clinton's relation with Newcastle, Cosby's with Halifax and Newcastle or George Clarke's with Blathwayt and Horatio Walpole to understand how hard it was for an opposition to displace them. American politicians had frequently to start from scratch in forming a connection, but it is characteristic of English politics at this time that there was sufficient mobility for even a rank outsider to work his way into the system.

The seeming triviality of the contest for English influence should not, however, obscure the importance of the long-range aims of Anglo-American politics. In contending for immediate objectives such as jobs, political favors, and changes of policy, colonists and imperial officials were really disputing the control of political power in New York. From a broader point of view, Anglo-American politics had two interconnected aspects: the demonstration of American power to impress imperial officials in England, and the display of English influence in order to maintain American political power.

Everyone active in Colonial public life was continually aware of the scrutiny of English officials. Imperial administrators were seldom insistent upon the precise execution of detailed policies, but for a variety of reasons they were strongly committed to the maintenance of stability in Colonial politics. Thus it was vital that the governor, when confronted with a vigorous Colonial opposition, should convince his superiors at home that he was in control of the situation in America. When Lewis Morris was governor in New Jersey, for instance, his daughter warned him from England to maintain an orderly administration at all costs since, if he should "have any difference [he] would find no redress from hence, since they would leave [him] to fight it out" alone in New Jersey.[15] The governor had to restrain the assertive tendencies of the local Assembly and use his domination of the Council to demonstrate that he had local support. At the same time, of course, the opposition attempted to show the governor's incompetence to control the government of the Colony in the hope that the English authorities would lose confidence in him and that he would be replaced, allowing a reallocation of offices and a redistribution of power.

Even more important, however, evidence of political influence in England was the prerequisite for political mastery in America, whether for the administration or for its opponents. For the governor and his adherents, the "ins" of colonial politics, signs of favor with the imperial administration provided a hedge against local political disaffection. So long as the governor's appointees and policies were confirmed in England, New Yorkers looked to him for places and favors. The New York governors were all intensely aware of this phenomenon, and George Clinton was virtually paranoid on the subject. As Cadwallader Colden explained the situation, Clinton decided against returning to England in 1749 since:

The Faction has endeavour'd to persuade the people that the Governors conduct was so blamed that his friends could not support him and that the Chief Justice [James DeLancey] has a better Interest at Court than the Govr and had he gon people would have been confirm'd in this opinion . . . which was exceedingly strengthen'd by the Govrs not having been able to procure any thing directly from the ministry in vindication of his conduct.[16]

New Yorkers were incredibly sensitive to the winds of political favor in England, and when the administration showed signs of having weaker English influence than its challengers (as was the case with Clinton and DeLancey in 1746), it was extremely difficult for the governor to retain control of the political situation in New York. Local families active in politics began to search out alternative sources of favor, the Assembly increased its recalcitrance, and even the Council was likely to waver. Thus the continuing contest for English attention was not simply a series of random private transactions, but a constant test of strength for the indications of imperial favor which were ultimately the determinants of political power in the royal Colonies of America.

Of all eighteenth-century New Yorkers who cultivated transatlantic connections in order to succeed in provincial politics, none managed the task more spectacularly than James DeLancey. A brief consideration of his career reveals the scope and complexity of Anglo-American political life as no abstract analysis can do.

DeLancey's family and education were the base on which his public achievements were built. He was the son of a late seventeenth-century Huguenot immigrant to New York who had amassed a fortune in commerce, specializing in the supply of goods which Albany merchants exchanged with Montrealers for furs. The elder DeLancey had achieved a place in the Anglo-Dutch elite of the province by marrying into the Dutch landholding aristocracy, serving in public office and joining the Church of England. From the very first James DeLancey was groomed to carry on the elevation of the family. He was sent to Corpus Christi, Cambridge, and Lincoln's Inn to be educated in the early 1720's, a time when few New Yorkers had acquired either university education or professional training in the law. DeLancey thus became one of the best educated men in his province, and one of the bare handful of New Yorkers to gain some experience in England. He returned to America in 1725 and soon completed the anglicization of his family by marrying the heiress of Caleb Heathcote, the lord of Scarsdale Manor and New York's receiver general.

DeLancey's career was devoted almost exclusively to law and politics, and was the most remarkable of his generation. He was summoned to the provincial Council in 1729, when he was 26, and in the following year presided over the commission which framed the famous Montgomerie Charter of New York City. He was appointed second justice of the New York Supreme Court in 1731, and was promoted to the chief justiceship in 1733, during the first turbulent years, of Governor William Cosby's administration. In this period DeLancey also began to expand his political horizons. He was one of Cosby's confidantes and an active proponent of the gubernatorial party during the Zenger controversy. He began to recruit adherents in the Assembly during Lieutenant Governor George Clarke's administration, and had gained a position of preeminence by the time George Clinton arrived to govern New York in 1743. Clinton selected DeLancey as his principal advisor, but the ambitious Chief Justice desired the government for himself and soon broke away to form a faction in opposition to the governor. Shortly thereafter he was appointed lieutenant governor of New York, effective upon

Clinton's departure, and in 1753 he assumed the government of the Colony which he held most of the time until his death in 1760.[17]

DeLancey's success is to be explained not only in terms of his unquestionable political genius, but also by his alertness to the opportunities of the Anglo-American situation which he was so well prepared to exploit. He understood English politics, cultivated his London contacts and integrated his activities on both sides of the Atlantic.

James DeLancey's English connections were the most extensive of any native-born New Yorker of the eighteenth century. They were drawn from among acquaintances, relatives, and business associates, and among them they exercised a wide and versatile range of influence. Taken together, they provide an extraordinary instance of the English political power which could be manipulated by an American of good breeding, education, intelligence, and luck. The element of chance cannot be ignored, for it was DeLancey's good fortune that his English associates were extraordinarily successful in their own careers and therefore afforded him constantly improving support.

Consider, for instance, DeLancey's college tutor at Cambridge, Thomas Herring. At the time of DeLancey's matriculation Herring was an obscure fellow at Corpus Christi who was just beginning an ecclesiastical career. He later became a preacher to the King and to Lincoln's Inn, where he met and impressed the Earl of Hardwicke. The Earl became Herring's patron, and the young priest quickly rose from Dean of Rochester (1732), Bishop of Bangor (1742), and Archbishop of York (1743) to become Archbishop of Canterbury in 1747. Herring was an old-style Whig obsessed with thoughts of Jacobite conspiracy who sorely tried the more pragmatic Hardwicke and Newcastle, but he exercised a good deal of influence in the higher reaches of English government by reason of his archbishopric, and throughout his career he maintained his friendship with James DeLancey.[18]

The extensive fur trading interests of the DeLancey family provided another channel of communication to the mother country. The influential London merchants, William and Samuel Baker, were the English commercial correspondents of the DeLancey family and William Baker provided a most effective political connection for them. He was a London alderman, one of the principal financiers of the government, a member of Parliament, and a firm friend of the Duke of Newcastle. The Bakers were deeply involved in American trade and were specialists in American army contracts, and for this reason Newcastle frequently relied upon William (whom he considered "a strong thinker and often a very free speaker") for advice on American problems. Luckily for the DeLanceys, the Bakers traded with them in political influence as well as in Indian goods.[19]

Family relationships, however, provided the most dependable English contacts, and James DeLancey's heredity and prudence served him well in this regard. His marriage turned out to be a brilliant stroke, for it not only contributed substantially to his considerable wealth but it also connected him with the remarkable Heathcote family of London and Lincolnshire. As we have noted, he married the daughter of one of the leading imperial placemen in New York, Caleb Heathcote, whose brother Sir Gilbert, the founder and director of the Bank of England, was a fabulously rich East India merchant and London politician. Various members of the huge Heathcote family were called upon to serve their American cousin in his political quests at one time or another,[20] but Sir Gilbert's son John, the second baronet, was DeLancey's firmest supporter. He was a Lincolnshire member of Parliament for a number of years, with close political ties to Walpole, and he improved his influence by marrying the sister of Newcastle's crony, John White. Sir John Heathcote thus possessed both wealth and access to the leading politicians of the day.[21]

James DeLancey's most powerful family connection, however, was his brother-in-law Peter Warren, a gifted Irish naval officer who married DeLancey's sister while posted to the station ship in New York Harbor. Warren subsequently gained fame and fortune during the war of the Austrian succession by commanding a British fleet which captured the fortress of Louisbourg and hundreds of thousands of pounds sterling in prizes. He was made a Knight of the Bath and promoted to admiral by a grateful ministry. Warren's political influence, which was enhanced by his enormous wealth, derived from his friendship with Admiral George Anson and Anson's patrons, the Duke of Bedford and the Earl of Sandwich,[22] who secured Warren a parliamentary seat for Westminster in the election of 1747. Whereas earlier DeLancey had used his Heathcote relatives to promote Warren's career, at the time of DeLancey's final surge to political power in New York Warren was finally in a position to throw his own weight into the scales in behalf of his in-law. He made such an impression that twenty years after his death a New York merchant cautioned his son "to shew every Mark of gratitude to Lady Warren's Family and its Valuable Connections." [23]

The services of Robert Charles, a professional colonial agent, were a particularly welcome dividend of DeLancey's connection with Peter Warren. Charles, who had learned his trade during the 1730's in the tangled politics of Pennsylvania, was Admiral Warren's private secretary. Warren recommended Charles to the New York Assembly in 1748 when they were seeking an agent who could defend them in London, which, given the New York political situation of the time, meant that Charles was expected to represent the interests of the fur traders generally and the DeLancey family in particular. Since Warren was James DeLancey's principal English ally in 1748, New Yorkers understood the significance of the appointment when it became known that Charles had been ordered by the speaker of the lower house "always to take the advice of Sir Peter Warren if in England." [24] Charles was an effective advocate of the DeLancey point of view during the New York-New Jersey boundary dispute and during the parliamentary discussions of colonial paper currency.

The DeLancey interest was thus promoted in England by a number of well-situated partisans. One of James DeLancey's many talents was to use his connections in the most effective possible manner, and he was particularly successful in combining their efforts. Shortly after his marriage, for instance, DeLancey sent Thomas Herring to call upon Sir Gilbert Heathcote bearing a letter of introduction to his newly-acquired uncle.[25] Once he had cemented his relations with the Heathcotes, he employed their influence to promote Peter Warren's naval career and they were active in the sailor's behalf from 1732–1736.[26] He introduced the Baker brothers to Warren in the early 1730's, and they served as Warren's commercial and political agents in England until his death.[27] Then, during DeLancey's 1735 struggle to achieve English confirmation of his appointment as Chief Justice of New York, Sir John Heathcote and the Bakers joined hands in defense of their common friend.[28] The examples could be multiplied, but the lesson is clear—James DeLancey not only acquired an English connection, but also knew how to use it. His friends "at home" exerted their influence in support of his aims, large and small.

DeLancey was eminently successful in his use of this English connection to solicit jobs and favors. Immediately following DeLancey's August 23, 1733 appointment as Chief Justice, the previous incumbent, Lewis Morris, determined to persuade the English authorities to reinstate him as head of the New York Supreme Court. DeLancey therefore sought a rejection of Morris's pretensions to his new office and, if possible, royal confirmation of the commission tendered him by the governor. On September 3, 1733 he wrote to Sir John Heathcote to explain his situation and asked his cousin "to speak in my behalf to such of your friends as can get the thing done." [29] The following June DeLancey repeated his plea, bearing hard on their relationship:

I am persuaded the recommendation of a gentleman of your Interest and influence will have great weight more especially as your application in this case will be for one who has the honor of being allied to your family.[30]

The Privy Council hearing on the merits of Morris's claim for reinstatement was held in November, 1735. Despite the prodding of Samuel Baker, Heathcote contrived to miss the hearing, but the historian is intrigued to learn that his absence was due to the fact that he was spending the weekend at Houghton with Newcastle and Sir Robert Walpole.[31] The Privy Council's eventual refusal to intervene in New York, which obviated DeLancey's need for a confirmation of his commission, was due to Governor Cosby's powerful influence in England, but it seems fair to conclude that the Heathcote interest must have contributed to it.[32] DeLancey had earlier induced his in-laws to attempt to secure him the surveyor-generalship of New York in 1731 (using Herring as an intermediary once more), but they had failed.[33] By 1735, however, he had found the correct combination of initiative in New York and interest in London.

The Heathcotes and the Bakers helped carry the day in the 1730's, but in the 1740's Peter Warren assumed the responsibility for managing DeLancey affairs in England, as is obvious from the story of DeLancey's solicitation of the lieutenant governorship of New York. After breaking his political ties with Governor George Clinton in 1746, DeLancey sought the government by means of an appointment as lieutenant governor. Clinton, bitterly conscious that DeLancey led an opposition faction in the Council and Assembly, determined to frustrate the Chief Justice by securing the lieutenant governorship for one of his own supporters. Peter Warren undertook the English solicitation for DeLancey, but he faced a formidable obstacle in the fact that the southern secretary, who controlled the appointment, was Clinton's patron, the Duke of Newcastle. The hero of Louisbourg, however, proved equal to the occasion. Warren had earlier won Newcastle's ear on the strength of DeLancey's assistance to Governor Clinton, and he now requested the lieutenant governorship for his brother-in-law as a reward, apparently neglecting to tell Newcastle that the Clinton-DeLancey friendship had already turned into animosity. Clinton was astonished to receive orders from Newcastle in early 1748 directing him to present DeLancey a commission as lieutenant governor before leaving the province for England,[34] and Clinton failed in subsequent efforts to have the appointment revoked.

DeLancey's extraordinary career depended, however, on his ability not only to achieve such immediate goals, but also to play off his influence in New York and England in a long-range campaign which culminated in winning the government of New York in the decade of the 1750's.

He was extremely successful in using his increasing power in New York as an instrument to gain favors from the imperial administration in London.[35] We have already seen how he traded upon his assistance to Clinton and Cosby to obtain tacit confirmation as Chief Justice and to win selection as lieutenant governor, the two posts upon which his political position in New York depended. He also acquired a ruling voice in the Council by inducing Clinton to recommend DeLanceyites to the board of trade for appointment, and he strengthened his hand in England by arranging the appointment of Robert Charles as New York's official agent. In the last half of the 1740's DeLancey achieved an incredibly strong position: he headed the highest court, controlled a majority in the Royal Council, exercised the leading influence in the Assembly and was about to succeed to the government itself.

Even more important than the ability to use American activity to stimulate English action, however, was DeLancey's success in exploiting his English standing to further his ends in New York. Eighteenth-century Americans were extremely sensitive to delicate shifts of favor in the mother country, and DeLancey was continually able to arrange demonstrations of his English influence for the benefit of New Yorkers. The effect was most noticeable from 1747 to 1750, when the news of his appointment as lieutenant governor led many New Yorkers to believe that the Chief Justice had outmaneuvered the governor in the contest for English support. In April 1750, for instance, Clinton complained to Secretary Bedford that DeLancey's "Faction continues still boyed up with the hopes given them by the Interest which their head pretends to have with some of his Majesty's ministers. . . ."[36] DeLancey's prestige in New York during these years was due in large part to Peter Warren's speedy rise to prominence after his spectacular victory at Louisbourg, as well as to the effective lobbying of the Baker brothers.

DeLancey's English influence had two immediate effects in New York. It enabled him to impress voters and politicians in the Colony, strengthening his opposition to Governor Clinton. A decidedly De-Lanceyite Assembly was elected in 1748 and the Governor, somewhat spitefully to be sure, ascribed this setback to "the news of Sir Peter Warrens having obtained the Chief Justice the Lieutenant Governors Commission . . . ."[37] DeLancey's English connection also operated more directly against the governor, however. The Bakers, for instance, organized a group of English merchants in 1750–1751 to testify in Parliament against Clinton's claims for repayment of his military expenditures in New York.[38] This threat from "Alderman Baker and his Creatures" unnerved Clinton and determined him to return to England to settle his finances, just as DeLancey intended.[39] When the governor attempted to cover his retreat by arranging to have Cadwallader Colden or Robert Hunter Morris assume the government when he vacated it, Warren intervened to forestall the scheme.[40]

Clinton thus came to feel trapped in New York, and, even more, deserted by the ministry at home:

Nothing has incouraged the faction so much as this, that I have not been able to obtain any thing to show to them, signifying His Majestys approbation of my conduct, or displeasure of theirs.[41]

Clinton's principal advisor concurred in this assessment, maintaining that as New Yorkers were "prepossest" of DeLancey's "Interest at home":

any thing you have in your power to do cannot be so effectual in curbing the insolence of the Faction as the same things don immediately from the King.[42]

Clinton's isolation was for the most part attributable to the inefficiency of the imperial administration prior to the leadership of Halifax, but it was also due to DeLancey's adroitness in utilizing his English connections.

DeLancey was sensitive to the weaknesses as well as the strengths in his Anglo-American position. From about 1750 until Clinton's departure from New York in 1753, for instance, he found himself on the defensive.[43] Peter Warren fell from Bedford's favor in 1749 and died in 1752,[44] depriving the DeLancey connection in England of its most important member at just the time that Governor Clinton began to reassert his power in New York. Perhaps more important, the ministry became aware of the chaotic state of New York politics and launched a Board of Trade inquiry into the subject, completed in 1751, which resulted in a scorching condemnation of Clinton and DeLancey alike.[45] The Chief Justice's tactic during this period of uncertainty was to call a truce in his war against the governor. "It was therefore expedient," concluded William Smith, Jr., "while Mr. DeLancey's friends were negotiating in England for the gratification of his ambition, to suspend hostilities against Mr. Clinton. . . ."[46] DeLancey hoped to mollify the imperial administration by a display of responsible behavior, but Bedford and Halifax thoroughly distrusted him and sent out Halifax's brother-in-law, Sir Danvers Osborn, to replace Clinton. DeLancey's hopes for the government seemed dashed, when the neurotic Osborn hanged himself by his necktie from a garden fence after three days on the whirligig of New York politics. Lieutenant Governor DeLancey then took over command

and governed New York for most of the remaining seven years of his life.

As an Anglo-American politician, then, DeLancey was a brilliant success. He used his English interest to attract political adherents in New York and to obstruct Clinton's government of the province. At the same time, he relied upon his strong position in America to impress the ministry, and, as a result, obtained important posts and favors. More than anything else, however, the disruption in New York caused by the DeLancey opposition led the ministry to "think it prudent to comply with the humours of the people at this time as the easiest method to quiet matters & make themselves easy from more trouble." [47]

Beverly McAnear, editing the diary of Robert Hunter Morris, has argued that Lewis Morris's unsuccessful English mission of 1735 caused New Yorkers to see that their problems could better be solved in America. "For good reason, therefore," this pilgrimage of the Morrises was the last appeal to be made by a colonial private citizen from New York to the home authorities." McAnear is particularly impressed by James DeLancey's handling of Governor Clinton in the late 1740's and concludes from DeLancey's career that "the colonial politicians might be greater than the vice-roy." [48] The point is, on the contrary, that DeLancey was every bit as involved in English negotiations as Lewis Morris was, but had found better methods of achieving his ends than journeying personally across the Atlantic. Far from rejecting all interest in England, DeLancey had worked out a more efficient method of communication, a continuing English connection, which permitted him to carry on his American activities without interruption. Only by mastering the politics of the metropolis as well as those of its Colony could an American achieve the remarkable control of New York that was DeLancey's from 1745 to 1760. Without a stroke of extraordinary good luck, DeLancey might never have had the chance to become lieutenant governor, but the relevant point is that he had done all that a New Yorker could do to place himself in line for the succession.

In early eighteenth-century New York, then, the complete politician was an Anglo-American politician. Later, when the stringencies of war, debt, imperial reorganization rigidified the structure of the Empire, the American political situation altered violently. Ease of access to English officials and casual interaction between the mother country and its Colonies gave way to a direct opposition of interests between England and America, which minimized the importance of individual politicians on both sides of the Atlantic. Anglo-American politics thus died of strangulation during the 1760's and 1770's, leaving in the lurch those who had practiced the art and favoring those who were more completely identified with American interests. The DeLanceys, one is not surprised to learn, were exiled from New York as Tories.

The Commissaries of the Bishop of London in Colonial Politics

In the two decades before the American Revolution Colonial politicians were irritated by one ecclesiastical issue after another—the "Parson's Cause," other bills affecting clerical salaries, the renewed threat of an Anglican bishop for the Colonies. These issues and other related ones have recently received due attention in a number of studies by historians who have astutely recognized the extensive politicial power and organization of the Anglican Church in the American Colonies.

Such studies are enormously useful—but they must be used with care, for by studying an "Anglican interest" one is tempted to approach the Anglican ministers as a closely knit group of men constituting virtually a branch of imperial authority, and this approach can be seriously misleading. For one thing, in every Colony the Anglican Church was deeply divided in the Colonial period; for another, far from strengthening the imperial authority the Anglican ministers were often—indeed generally—among the most effective opponents of the royal and proprietary governors. One has only to look at the Reverend William Stith's passionately effective opposition to Dinwiddie's Pistole Fee in Virginia,[1] at the untiring—and very nearly successful—efforts of the Reverend William Vesey and his ecclesiastical supporters in New York to bring down the powerful Governor Hunter,[2] or most notoriously, at the decision of the Anglican clergy in Pennsylvania to serve as chaplains to the Constitutional Convention in defiance of the governor and their superiors in England.[3] Time and again the Anglican clergy were leaders of the provincial opposition to the royal and proprietary governors in the Colonies.

Moreover, time and again the clergy were led by the least likely of all individuals—the commissaries of the Bishop of London. On the face of it the commissaries would not appear very promising political figures: few of them were skillful pamphleteers, impressive orators, or even effective college presidents as their colonial opponents often were; few appeared at elections or caucuses to influence the choice of candidates as their English counterparts did.[4] Nevertheless one commissary after another found himself thrust into a position where he had to use his leadership of the Church organization to fight the provincial governor. The governor in turn retaliated by capitalizing on divisions within the Church to undermine the commissaries on their own ground, and from vestries to convocations to councils of the Bishop of London the quarrels between governors and commissaries reverberated and had repercussions for imperial politics.

In 1691 James Blair was appointed the Bishop of London's personal commissary for Virginia. Blair's was apparently the first such appointment [5] and at the time the appointing of a commissary was a unique experiment; at Blair's death half a century later, however, commissaries had been sent to nine Colonies.[6] Only Rhode Island, Connecticut, and Georgia had not received commissaries and even the few Anglican ministers in Rhode Island and Connecticut attended meetings of the New England clergy called by Commissary Price of Massachusetts.

The dates of Blair's career turned out in fact to coincide closely with the heyday of the commissaryship as an institution. Begun by Bishop Compton (1685–1715) the office of commissary reached its high point under Bishop Gibson (1724–1749) and then died out so completely under Gibson's successor, Bishop Sherlock, that within a few years of Sherlock's appointment there was only one commissary left in the Colonies, and by the 1760's the clergy occasionally spoke of "reestablishing" the commissaryship.[7] On the eve of the Revolution prominent Anglicans revived the old agitation for an American bishop, the New York and New Jersey clergy advocated a synodical form of government for the Church in America,[8] and only a few people thought seriously of reviving the commissary's office.

The commissary's job, like so many others in the eighteenth-century Empire, was never clearly defined. Theoretically, of course, the Bishop of London was Bishop for the American Colonies and since he could not live in the Colonies he delegated some, but not all, of his powers to commissaries who resided in the several provinces. In particular the commissaries were expected to handle the discipline of the ever growing numbers of clergy invading the colonies in the "Anglican offensive" of the early eighteenth century. Recent historians have effectively defended the Colonial clergy against charges that drifters and ne'er-do-wells from England sought haven in Colonial parishes. Nevertheless Bishops Gibson and Compton shared a general concern about the uncertain status and behavior of Anglican ministers in the American Colonies; moreover it became clear from the early attempts of the South Carolina and Maryland Assemblies that if the Bishop of London did not take a direct hand in clerical discipline the job would fall to potentially hostile Colonial legislatures.[9]

The commissary was expected, therefore, to call regular meetings of the clergy at which he could check credentials and ascertain that all the clergy in his province had been licensed by the Bishop of London, hold hearings on complaints against any of the clergy, suspend clergy guilty of immoral conduct, and incidentally check regularly on the progress of construction of churches.

In fact, however, the commissaries were never effective disciplinarians. James Blair's failure to handle the Virginia clergy was the most notorious commissarial disaster, but the fact is that none of the commissaries was able to serve as an effective regulator of clerical behavior in his province. Probably the most capable commissary of all, Alexander Garden of the Carolinas, was able to discipline only four offenders in a quarter century of work.[10] All the commissaries complained of the difficulty of getting evidence against offenders; many were reluctant to call meetings or found that when they did call meetings it was difficult to get all the clergy to attend. (This was particularly true in the decade 1725–35, first when Bishop Gibson's authority over the colonies was in question and afterwards when either Gibson, the two secretaries of state, or the proprietary governors neglected to send copies of his commission to the colonies.)[11] After his first few years as Commissary, Blair rarely dared call meetings of the clergy for fear of being outvoted on political questions.[12] In his last twenty-five years in office he called only two meetings;[13] his successors did no better, and for exactly the same reason. In 1757 Commissary Dawson explained that he would have called a meeting but for "some violent heats and animosities I expect." [14] A Boston minister complained that while Commissary Price had investigated occasional cases of misconduct he had held no formal hearings.[15] After Lord Baltimore's break with Bishop Gibson in 1732–33 the Maryland proprietor ceased to recognize even the need for clergy to hold a license from the Bishop and all efforts at ecclesiastical discipline of the clergy broke down.[16] In short, the effort of the commissaries to exercise formal discipline over regular clergy was in sharp contrast with the S.P.G.'s overzealous discipline of American missionaries.[17] Inertia, fear of embarrassing incidents, opposition from secular authorities, and above all lack of real power as individuals to reward service and punish disobedience made the commissaries ineffective within the Church. As Commissary Jenney of Pennsylvania put it:

The patent of ye late Bp did not seem to justify his Commissary in any juridical proceeding, the Laity laughed at it, and ye Clergy seemed to despise it, nor did there appear at home a Disposition to shew any Regard to it.[18]

Ironically, however, while the commissaries failed in their avowed work as purely ecclesiastical leaders they became surprisingly successful as political leaders; although they could not use their powers effectively to create discipline within the ranks of the clergy, they could do considerably better at rallying the ranks against threats from secular authorities. The political activity of the commissaries was particularly striking in view of the fact that English officials from the Bishop of London down did their best to keep the commissaries out of politics. Very early in his administration James Blair was openly rebuffed by the Bishop for his political activities.[19] In 1718 the Bishop warned Commissary Henderson of Maryland against opposing the proprietary governor, arguing that to be effective church leaders, commissaries needed the governor's support.[20] Bishop Gibson instructed the commissaries in 1729 quite explicitly to exhort the clergy to be loyal to the provincial governors,[21] an instruction quite in line with the S.P.G.'s "Instructions for the Clergy Employ'd by the Society. . . . That they take special care to give no offense to the Civil Government, by intermeddling in affairs not relating to their calling and Function."[22]

Yet despite the church officials' concern to keep the American clergy out of provincial politics all but a few of the commissaries became leading opponents of the provincial governors. James Blair's successful efforts to unseat Governors Andros, Nicholson, and Spotswood are best known, but other commissaries, though less well connected at home were equally active in bringing their governors down. Commissary Henderson was a passionate opponent of Governor Hart of Maryland and though Henderson's colleague, Commissary Wilkinson supported Hart, he opposed Hart's successors, most particularly Benedict Leonard Calvert.[23] Commissaries Cummings and Jenney of Pennsylvania consistently opposed the proprietary governor. Jenney told his vestry in Philadelphia that their minister

must not be under prepossession or attachment which may lead him into such an obligation to any great Man as may lay him under a necessity of abetting his political Designs, which may run counter to the Interest of your Church.[24]

Cummings wrote the Bishop,

It would be an advantage to the Crown and the Inhabitants if those parts too were our Government more immediately under its jurisdiction. . . . In Queen Annes reign there was an Agreement made with Penn the first proprietor, which obliges his Successours to surrender up ye govert upon ye payment of 8 or 9000 £. Till yt be done the Church of England will meet with little solid encouragement in this province.[25]

Perhaps it was understandable that commissaries quarreled with proprietary governors, but they also quarreled with governors of royal Colonies. Commissary Bray, who was in Maryland while the Colony was temporarily under royal government, got along with Governor Blakiston of that Colony in 1700 but quarreled violently with Governor Nicholson of Virginia[26] and was in part responsible for developing a quarrel directly between the Bishop of London and Governor Seymour.[27] Commissary Robinson was one of the leading opponents of Governor Fauquier of Virginia; Commissary Price was a vigorous opponent not only of the Dissenter, Governor Belcher of Massachusetts,[28] but also of Belcher's Anglican successor, William Shirley.[29] Commissary Vesey's quarrels with Robert Hunter, though they largely preceded Vesey's actual appointment to office, were among the most bitter in the history of New York.[30]

There were times of uneasy truce between governors and commissaries, and even rare periods of active cooperation. But by and large the story of the commissaries and governors is one of constant turmoil. So much was this true that in the early part of the eighteenth century one of the reasons most frequently put forth to explain the demand for bishops was the need for an arbiter to settle the disputes between governors and clergy.[31]

Why should this have happened? In part the answer is that the ambiguity of the commissaries' instructions and of the governors' own relations to the Bishops of London left real areas of overlapping authority to be contested by governors and commissaries. Governors exercised the ecclesiastical prerogatives of the Crown in their Colonies; commissaries were representatives of the Bishop of London, in whose immediate ecclesiastical jurisdiction the colonies lay. Who, then, had greater authority over the Colonial Church? Who had the right to induct ministers or to call meetings of the clergy? Inevitably these questions came up.[32]

In Virginia particularly the governor's right to induct clergy became an issue. In New York, Maryland, and Virginia Governors Hunter, Hart, and Nicholson themselves called meetings of the clergy without even notifying the commissaries—indeed, often with the hope of eliciting a petition or a vote contrary to the commissary's wishes.[33] In Massachusetts Commissary Price quarreled with Governor Belcher over the governor's right to appoint a chaplain to the Indians.[34] In Virginia, again, Commissary Dawson found himself at odds with Governor Fauquier over the governor's allowing a clergyman complained of by his vestry to be tried out by the provincial Council, rather than by a convocation of the clergy.[35]

In the same Colony Commissary Blair must have been more than a little piqued at Governor Gooch's offer to the Bishop of London to comment directly to the Bishop on the morals and behavior of the Virginia clergy: "If you want, I shall be more open and readily turn Informer in things pertaining unto God." [36] Not a few governors were tempted, in the face of instructions naming them local head of the Church of England and in the face of the obvious weakness of the commissaries to discipline troublesome clergy, to take a hand in such discipline themselves.

But there were other issues not quite so directly connected with ecclesiastical authority, on which the clerical leaders split with the governors. In some Colonies, particularly New York and Massachusetts, the Anglican clergy refused to support the governors' attempts to establish a working relationship with dissenters.[37] Elsewhere clerics whose salaries were dependent upon the issue of paper money quarreled with governors whose instructions forbade their assenting to such issues. In still other Colonies the issue was the establishment and support of denominational schools.[38]

Far more important than these issues in precipitating conflicts between commissaries and Colonial governors was the place of the Church of England in colonial society. In an age when organized opposition to established authority was still considered virtually tantamount to treason it was difficult for Colonial opponents of a governor to find a way of systematically attacking him without seeming disloyal to the Empire. It was at times all too easy for governors to label their opponents "disaffected" to the royal government. This was less easy, however, when the governors' provincial opponents were actively backed by the personal representative of the Bishop of London. Church of England ministers—and the commissaries in particular—became, like the royal officials of the late seventeenth century, the focus for "loyal opposition" to the provincial governors. The very concept of an opposition to the existing government that was nevertheless loyal to the Crown thus became easier to develop in the Colonies with their many representatives of imperial authority than it was in England, where the concept developed only slowly around the Prince of Wales. Around the commissaries of the Bishop of London, men unquestionably loyal to the Crown, flocked parishioners seeking legitimacy in their opposition to the current governors.

The political weapons at the hands of the commissaries were numerous. For one thing commissaries usually held their pulpits in the largest Colonial cities. Their parishes were likely to be the largest and wealthiest of the Colonies and their parishioners among the most influential merchants and planters.[39] The commissary of Pennsylvania held Christ Church, Philadelphia; the commissary of New York was at Trinity Church; the commissary of Virginia held Bruton Parish Church, Williamsburg; and the commissary of Massachusetts had King's Chapel, Boston. So among the commissaries' constituents often were the most powerful men in the Colony, and the commissaries had effective ways of influencing them. Most important, of course, was the sermon directly or indirectly alluding to political subjects. By the mid-eighteenth century there is evidence that the political sermon was beginning to be frowned upon, but in the heyday of the commissaries it was not yet considered in poor taste for ministers to comment directly on political subjects from the pulpit. The Reverend Mr. Vesey, later commissary of New York, spoke openly in favor of his parishioner Nicholas Bayard, at Bayard's trial for treason in 1702.[40] The commissaries of Pennsylvania used the pulpit to attack the proprietors (when Richard Peters was assistant minister to the commissary there he used to follow the Commissary's Sunday morning sermons with his own in the afternoon defending the proprietorship);[41] in Massachusetts Commissary Price forbade the other Boston ministers to preach after they had supported a ministerial candidate recommended by Governor Shirley and opposed by Price.[42] Moreover, the commissary—as indeed any minister—could pointedly leave the governor out of his prayers.

Many leading provincial politicians were also vestrymen in the commissary's Church, and the Colonial vestry could be a powerful political organization, deciding directly matters of local government, circulating petitions among the congregation on larger provincial disputes. Governors themselves and their political protégés were often vestrymen; governors and commissaries at times struggled for domination of the local vestry. The stakes were high: if a governor or a party favorable to the governor won control they could make the commissary's position extremely uncomfortable, by reducing his salary or fees, changing the hours of his sermon, supporting a hostile assistant, or sending back unfavorable reports to England. If on the other hand the commissary secured the upper hand he could on occasion use his friends among the vestrymen to circulate petitions against the governor and use any English connections against him; he could also work to have the governor turned out of the vestry, which did not help him in the eyes of his English superiors.

Serving the central parish in the largest city in the province meant also that during the time that the provincial Assemblies met, commissaries were likely to have a high proportion of assemblymen visiting their congregations. Here was an opportunity to influence Assembly votes that went far beyond the Sunday sermon. For one thing commissaries were likely candidates for chaplain to the Assembly, which gave them the chance to open Assembly sessions with a prayer and a sermon. Commissary Bray, for example, preached before the Maryland Assembly in 1700, just at a time when the Assembly was considering a bill to establish the Anglican Church in that colony.[43] Probably more important, the commissaries could lavishly entertain individual members of the Assemblies—Bray and Henderson[44] were particularly known for their attentions to assemblymen—and to this end there was an unwritten rule that commissaries, unlike ordinary priests, should be men of some means. Commissary Henderson of Maryland, for example, was recommended to the job as a man whose independent income would allow him to undertake generous entertainment.[45]

Beyond this the commissaries derived political power from their authority, however sparingly used, to convene meetings of the clergy. Such meetings were the only opportunity the clergy had for drawing up an address to English authorities and signing it as a group. So important were the regular convocations of the clergy that when the proprietors of Maryland broke with the Bishop of London in 1732 and the clergy of the colony could not meet they considered their political influence at an end.[46] As long as the commissaryship lasted commissaries could usually keep dissident elements within the clergy from calling meetings on their own; when a rare commissary was in league with a governor, as happened in Virginia with the Dawsons, there was little chance for their opponents within the ministry to organize group opposition. But when the commissaryship died out as an institution the ministers in several colonies began meeting together voluntarily, assuming such meetings to be vital to their political influence.

Here the clergy could agree as a group to single out issues to emphasize in their parishes either before elections or before the assemblymen departed for meetings of their Assemblies. In 1718 Commissary Henderson opposed Governor Hart's sponsorship of a bill in the

Maryland Assembly acknowledging the authority of the Bishop of London over the Anglican Church in the province. Henderson's argument, which turned out to be right, was that the bill would surely be defeated because its timing did not give enough opportunity to the clergy to influence the assemblymen from their parishes.[47]

Through addresses drawn up by convocations of the clergy, commissaries could oppose the governors' policies in England. But the commissaries also had their own personal influence with English politicians to match against the governors. The average priest in the Colonies had little if any political influence in England, but the commissaries necessarily had connections with the Bishop of London and his influence counted for something with the Archbishop of Canterbury. Moreover while the governors' patrons might go out of power, leaving the governors without support in the ministry, commissaries had to have their commissions renewed by each new Bishop.

As the Bishop's personal representative the commissary automatically had a friend on the Privy Council; through the Archbishop of Canterbury he often had a patron who would interest himself when ecclesiastical affairs of the Colony came before the Cabinet. Moreover, laws passed by the provincial Assembly regarding religion —laws like the Twopenny Act in Virginia or the Massachusetts act calling a synod of New England clergy—went to the Privy Council, thence to the Board of Trade, and from the Board automatically to the Bishop of London, in his own right and as president of the S.P.G., for recommendation of allowance or disallowance.

In addition, the Bishop and the Archbishops of York and Canterbury were members of the Privy Council to which the commissaries or subordinate clergy could appeal their local grievances. In 1753 the case of the Reverend Mr. Kay of Virginia, supported by Commissary Dawson but turned out of his parish and off his glebe by the powerful Carter family who dominated the vestry, came before the Privy Council. Mr. Kay was suing the vestry of trespassing in turning him off his glebe; so active were the Bishop and his lawyer in rounding up votes on the Privy Council that Mr. Kay not only won his suit but the vestry was assessed the heaviest damages ever recorded for that kind of suit.[48]

But the Bishop's and Archbishop's influence was hardly restricted to purely ecclesiastical affairs. In the early eighteenth century the

Archbishop was still nominally a member of the Cabinet and could affect major policy decisions there—decisions like the sending of extra instructions to Governor Belcher of New Jersey against the land rioters in that colony, which did not affect the clergy directly. Similarly the Bishop of London's recommendations on provincial laws were by no means limited to those directly respecting ecclesiastical affairs. Encouraged by the commissaries, Bishops supported tobacco inspection acts in Virginia because indirectly such acts kept the clergy from being cheated by being paid in inferior tobacco;[49] they opposed fee acts in Maryland which were aimed (by Assemblies hostile to the proprietors) mainly at lawyers and placemen who supported the proprietary interest, but which, incidentally, reduced the salaries of the clergy.[50] In 1723 the clergy of South Carolina wrote the Commissary about paper money in that colony:

We are likewise under no less apprehension and concern in prospect of what our Case will be should all the Bills of Credit be at once sunk, and a final stop put to paper currency in this Province. For then as there would be nothing for a currency but the com(m)odities of the Country which are both precarious and perishing, our Salaries must be paid in them; and not only so, but should they (which we have great Reason to fear) be laid upon our respective parishes by way of tithes, what thru the great trouble, charge, and inconvenience, besides the opposition we should meet with from Dissenters in Collecting them, together with our not knowing how to manage, or make anything of them when collected, we should be in a much worse condition than Ever.[51]

The Bishop accordingly joined in pressing for the allowance of paper money.

On both ecclesiastical and nonecclesiastical matters affecting their Colonies, therefore, the commissaries had potentially powerful political connections in England. Such connections were by no means infallible, however, for the bishops were not uniformly active and they did not always take the commissaries' advice. The three bishops whose tenure of office covered the main period of the commissaryship, Compton, Robinson, and Gibson, were all particularly active in English politics and interested in Colonial affairs. But even these bishops had their periods of prolonged inactivity, Compton's coming from bitterness when he was passed over for Archbishop of Canterbury after 1688,[52] Gibson's coming in the decade after he broke with

Sir Robert Walpole in 1736.[53] Both Compton and Gibson retired from active politics for several years at a time, and though Gibson resumed his activity after Walpole's retirement Governor Glen wrote of Gibson's death "but as his Lordship had for many years kept from the Council Table where the Business of the Plantations is chiefly transacted, the Province of which I have the Honour to be Governour was the less affected thereby." [54] The years when bishops most strongly supported their commissaries were from 1700 to 1733; Gibson's retirement after that date seems to have been one of the early signs that the commissaryship was doomed.

Moreover, even when the bishops and archbishops were active in plantation affairs the commissaries did not have a monopoly on the advice they received. When Colonial issues came up the bishops often sought advice and information wherever they could get it, and there was no reason why the bishops could not get information from the commissaries' enemies.

Colonial agents like Ferdinando Paris considered it part of their jobs to seek help from anyone who would give it, bishops included. Paris was the proprietary agent for Pennsylvania and as such a bitter opponent of Commissary Cummings, but he sought and often obtained the Bishop's ear on provincial matters, much to Cummings' fury. He was particularly active on behalf of Richard Peters, Cummings' assistant minister and chief antagonist at Christ Church. Peters was a proprietary supporter and thus Paris worked actively first to defend Peters against Cummings' attempts to turn him out and later to have Peters appointed Cummings' successor.[55] Ben Franklin, hardly a proprietary supporter but not a friend to the commissary either, felt free to recommend appointments to vacant parishes in Pennsylvania.[56] Moreover, the Bishops frequently sought the recommendations of London merchants and communicated directly with their own political protégés in the Colonies.[57]

Most important, there was nothing to prevent the governors from establishing their own connections with the Bishops of London, and the more enterprising ones were quick to do so in a variety of ways. Undoubtedly the governor who worked hardest was Francis Nicholson, an active member and one-time treasurer of the S.P.G., who spent a good deal of his private fortune in financing ecclesiastical projects in the Colonies. The full extent of Nicholson's activities on behalf of the Church—and indeed his real attitude to the Church—deserves fuller study.[58] Unquestionably he was personally devout; equally certainly he realized more astutely than his contemporaries the uses of the Anglican Church as a political institution in the Colonies. Nicholson personally financed meetings of the clergy,[59] supported indigent clerics, paid the Atlantic passage of his clerical supporters who needed to go to England on business (and denied his clerical enemies the right to make the same trip),[60] and supported leading Anglican vestrymen as candidates for governors in other provinces. Along the way he extracted addresses to the Bishop on his behalf from clerical meetings in Virginia,[61] New England,[62] and South Carolina.[63] The clergy of South Carolina even complained that although they liked Nicholson they were tired of having the governor draw up laudatory addresses on his own behalf which they were expected to support.[64]

Other governors were less obvious, but still quite effective in their attempts to earn the Bishop's support. Governor Gooch of Virginia, noticing that one Mr. Gibson, a close relative of Bishop Gibson's, had moved to Virginia, offered Gibson a tobacco inspectorship and when this was refused finally got him a clerkship.[65] In 1725 Gooch's predecessor, Governor Drysdale, had also worked to get one Mr. Crasby, a friend of the Bishop's, a job in Virginia.[66] In 1736 the proprietor of Pennsylvania got still another relative of Gibson's a job in Pennsylvania. Gooch, Drysdale, and Fauquier[67] had cordial relations with the Bishop; so did Governor Hart of Maryland who even managed to get Bishop Robinson to instruct Commissary Henderson to cease attacking the Governor.[68] Even Jonathan Belcher, a dissenter and the least likely of all colonial governors to attract the Bishop's favor, wooed him with frequent letters on ecclesiastical affairs in Massachusetts, sent personal gifts, and even made recommendations to vacant parishes in the Colony.[69] Often, in fact, the disputes between the commissaries and the governors were carried to the See of London, with both sides seeking the Bishop's support. The Bishop was inclined to support his commissary first, but the decision was by no means automatic.

In their struggles with the commissaries, governors not only appealed to England; they could also make the most of divisions among the clergy in the Colonies. One uncharitable Carolina minister described meetings of the Carolina clergy as being like a bear garden,

What thru ye Folly and Ignorance of some, the insolence and Pride, the ungovernable Passions and implacable Resentments of [   ] towards each other our General meetings for ye Confusion, all language and rude treatment of one another are more like the Bear Garden or Billingsgate than the Assembly of the Clergy of a Province.[70]

This was exaggerated, but it is true that in every Colony there were basic divisions among the clergy. For one thing there were differences of origin among the ministers, Scottish and Irish ministers clashing at times with those of English origin,[71] and more often, especially in New England, the missionaries of the S.P.G., who tended necessarily to be English, being reluctant to associate closely with parish ministers who were provincials who had just gone to England for ordination.[72] More important in the short run, from 1715 to 1725 the clergy in several Colonies were badly split over the nonjuring issue. Commissary Henderson in Maryland was accused of high Tory sympathies after 1714 and the Reverend Messrs. Checkley in Massachusetts, Talbot in New Jersey, and Welton of Philadelphia[73] were all nonjuring clergy, Talbot being consecrated a nonjuring bishop. In each of their respective colonies these clergy were the source of bitter controversy, symptomatic of the more important split between "high" and "low" church clergy.

The governors made the most of these splits and even seem to have fostered divisions among the clergy in order to prevent the Anglican leaders from presenting a united front against them. In some Colonies some of the clergy owed their appointments to the governor who could recommend candidates for ordination to the Bishop and could refuse to induct hostile clergy. Sometimes the commissaries' own congregations were badly split and governors could draw off some of the disaffected parishioners into a church of their own supporting, as Governor Hunter did by setting up a chapel in the fort in New York City.[74] Alternatively, the governors could champion the assistant ministers of the commissaries' church in quarrels with the commissaries themselves in hopes of having the commissary repudiated by his own vestry or congregation. Commissary Cummings of Pennsylvania quarreled bitterly with Richard Peters, his assistant minister, and split the Christ Church congregation badly.[75] Commissary Myles and his assistant, the Reverend Mr. Harris, were perpetually at odds.[76]

At still other times the governors built up their own parties among the clergy by seeking out relatives of the clergy and giving them jobs. For example, the provincial politician Andrew Hamilton of Pennsylvania got the support of some of the Anglican missionaries in favor of Richard Peters to succeed Commissary Cummings by giving their sons jobs in a law office.[77] In other Colonies, where the commissaries were particularly aggressive politicians, governors got support or sympathy from a substantial segment of the clergy who simply objected to being dragged into politics by their ecclesiastical leadership. This was most notably true in Virginia, but in every Colony there were ministers who opposed as unethical the political activities of the commissaries.

Just how effective the commissaries were as political leaders is hard to evaluate. Most of them found politics uncongenial: they slipped into political activity because of divisions within their own congregations or because the position of the Church in provincial life was inseparably linked to certain political issues. Most of the commissaries became disillusioned with Colonial politics in their later years; in Bishop Gibson's later years he, too, was disappointed with the effectiveness of the colonial commissaries and Bishop Sherlock let the job die out.

Nevertheless, in their active years the commissaries did achieve some political successes. Doubtless they contributed substantially toward turning some governors out of office: Governors Belcher of Massachusetts and Keith of Pennsylvania, as well as Governors Andros, Spotswood, and Nicholson of Virginia suffered badly from commissarial opposition. On the other hand, commissaries failed notably in their efforts to turn out Governors Hart of Maryland, Hunter of New York, and Fauquier of Virginia. Doubtless also they succeeded in mobilizing the opposition of English and provincial clergy to acts regulating fees or retiring paper money—acts which would genuinely have hurt the provincial Church. And they did contribute support to important nonecclesiastical measures like the Tobacco Inspection Act in Virginia.

In the reluctance of the American Anglican clergy to take part in politics, in the inverse correlation between the respect commissaries received from other clergy and the extent of their own political ambitions, and in the decline of the political sermon one sees signs of the coming metamorphosis of the Colonial Church into a nonpolitical institution. But in the very circumstances which drove the commissaries into politics one sees the importance of the Colonial Church for future American political development. The commissaries provided, for a while, a chance for colonists politically opposed to their governors to rally around a figure unquestionably loyal to the Empire, to organize opposition within an institution which was itself one of the bulwarks of the Empire. In so doing the commissaryship proved to be an imperial institution encouraging factions and thereby facilitating the later concept of parties operating within an accepted structure of government. The full story of the Anglican Church in colonial politics has yet to be written; when it is, the role of the commissaries will constitute an important chapter.

The Old Colonial System from an English
Point of View

THOMAS C. BARROW received his A.B., A.M., and Ph.D. from Harvard University. He has taught at the University of Missouri and is now Professor of History and Chairman of the History Department at Clark University. Author of *Trade and Empire: The British Customs Service in America, 1660–1775* (1967) and several articles including "A Project for Imperial Reform: 'Hints Respecting the Settlement for our American Provinces,' 1963" and "The American Revolution as a Colonial War for Independence (*William and Mary Quarterly*, 1967, 1968), he is currently at work on the impact of British policy after 1763 on political groups and alignments in Massachusetts.

The one central, unifying theme to English policy after 1763 was the search for adequate Colonial revenues. The motivation behind this search has been explained by historians in various ways. The Seven Years' War had been expensive and England had a large national debt. Defense requirements necessitated the permanent stationing of ten thousand troops in America, and this military force had to be paid for. Or, administration of the newly enlarged Empire was costly and England did not wish to bear the burden alone. Hence the ill-fated Sugar, Stamp, and Townshend Acts.

In the same way, historians have offered a variety of explanations of American resistance to these efforts at taxation. The Americans were spoiled, had been overly pampered, and could not see beyond the confines of their local issues to the general requirements of Empire. They were motivated primarily by principle, objecting not to specific financial contributions to imperial enterprises but rather to taxation without representation. They were businessmen concerned with the burden the new taxes would place on trade and commerce. Or, they were property owners alerted to the threat to private property inherent in the arbitrary taxation measures introduced by Grenville and his successors.

Interesting and provocative as such interpretations are, they overlook one basic item: the English concern with Colonial revenues predated the Seven Years' War by many years and, in fact, the Grenville program was outlined in general terms when that much abused statesman was but a babe-in-arms. The fact is that the heart of the problem lay, not in a temporary situation created by the aftermath of the Seven Years' War, but in the character of the Old Colonial System as it operated *prior* to 1763—and in the English attitude towards that System.

The task of putting the Old Colonial System in its proper perspective is nearly as difficult as that of explaining the motivation behind the changes in English policy after 1763. Rather oddly, considering the enthusiasm of historians for labels and classifications, no one as yet has succeeded in dividing the various writers on the Old Colonial System into separate "schools" of interpretation. Except for a vague grouping of some historians as belonging to the "imperial" school, researchers in this field so far have escaped formal classification.

Perhaps the reason for this is simply that there have been nearly as many varied interpretations of the Old Colonial System as there have been historians. For George Bancroft the English system of commercial regulations was a fundamental cause of colonial discontent: "The commercial liberties of rising states were shackled by paper chains, and the principles of natural justice subjected to the fears and covetousness of English shopkeepers." [1] George Louis Beer, on the other hand, viewed the Colonial System somewhat differently: "The system as a whole was thus based on the idea of the mutual reciprocity of the economic interests of mother country and colony." [2] For Beer, problems of imperial defense, not the commercial restraints, were the basic cause of the division of interests between the Americans and the British.[3] Or, to take yet another example, in the latest major study of the subject, O. M. Dickerson describes the Navigation System as "the cement of empire" and states succinctly that "it worked." For Dickerson the alterations in imperial policies after 1763 were motivated not by a desire for "regulation and development, but regulation for the sake of revenue and political exploitation." [4]

Such diversity of opinion naturally makes it difficult to set up acceptable generalizations, but I suspect that most commentators today probably would agree with Wesley Frank Craven's recent assessment of the current status of research in this area. Craven argues that the pioneer work of George Louis Beer and Charles M. Andrews has "made it difficult to attribute the Revolution to the restrictive influences of mercantilist policy, in part by the clarification they gave to the character of the old colonial system, and in part by the fresh attention they directed to new problems of empire confronted by Britain as a result of the changing character of the empire itself and the great victory won over France." [5]

As Craven's remark suggests, today many surveys of the Colonial Period tend to play down the "restrictive influences of mercantilist policy" and to play up the imperial problems that arose out of the Seven Years' War. This tendency to absolve the Old Colonial System of blame for the existence of tensions between England and her Colonies explains the treatment given to the Grenville program, which now generally is viewed as having originated in response to certain problems of imperial defense or finance arising from the last great War for Empire. A widely accepted theme in such interpretations is the argument that the policies adopted by the British government after 1763 represented a fundamental transformation of both the practice and the theory of the Old Colonial System.[6]

Basic to any such discussion, of course, is the problem of the Old Colonial System itself. Since the Colonial System was, in essence, a mercantilist system,[7] the most obvious question is, quite simply, how effectively did the system of commercial regulation and direction operate prior to 1763? Various attempts have been made to answer that question. Trade figures have been studied, imposts and rebates totaled and weighed one against the other, increases in shipping estimated, and generally a balance sheet of credits and deficits drawn up. Unfortunately, this approach has been unsatisfactory for two basic reasons: first, the statistical information available is too sketchy to support definitive conclusions; and, second, even if more satisfactory statistical materials were available, the answers they would provide would be incomplete. That is, we would be able to estimate the effectiveness of the System for ourselves, but we would not necessarily know how the participants—how the individuals, the people actually affected by the Old Colonial System—viewed its operation. Since the actions of the English government, and the reactions of the American colonists, were based on what they knew and what they thought, the matter of contemporary attitudes and opinions towards the operation of the Old Colonial System is of central importance.

It might be well at this point to clear up one frequently encountered misconception concerning the attitude of the American colonists towards the Colonial System. Some writers, like O. M. Dickerson, have asserted that prior to 1763 "Americans did not oppose the commercial system under which they lived." [8] Dickerson, and other historians such as George Louis Beer, have argued that there is little evidence of colonial opposition to the Navigation System and that consequently there *was* no serious opposition before the introduction of the Grenville program. Unfortunately, this argument is basically unsound, since the lack of evidence of colonial opposition could equally well be taken to show that the Navigation System was ineffective prior to 1763. In other words, the Americans would have had little reason to object to a system which, through its ineffectual operation, left them relatively free to pursue their own interests. So the scarcity of evidence of Colonial opposition is in itself inconclusive.

In any case, the series of events that led to the open rupture between England and her American Colonies originated in London. It was in London that the decisions were made to enact the Sugar Act, to extend the Stamp Act to the colonies, and to place a standing army in America. In short, the initiative lay in England, and consequently the question of the English attitude towards the Colonial System is crucial.

Fortunately, on this point—on the question of the attitude that prevailed in English official circles toward the Colonial System—we are not entirely in the dark. Official policy in the eighteenth century, as in the twentieth, of necessity was based largely on the information made available through the various departments and agencies of government. The central agency concerned with compiling information on the Colonies was the Board of Trade. Through a fortunate coincidence, in 1757, in response to reports of American wartime trade with the French sugar islands, the Board of Trade undertook a major re-examination of the operation of the Colonial System. Instructing their secretary to comb the files of the Board for evidence on the effectiveness of the System, the Commissioners of Trade compiled a collection of twenty-six reports from the Colonies, ranging in date from 1739 to the year of the investigation. This collection gathered together by the secretary represented a useful sampling of the type of information made available to the English authorities over the years. A few quotations from these reports will serve to indicate the nature of the material presented to the Board.

One typical item selected by the secretary was a letter from the lieutenant governor of New York, dated December 1739. The lieutenant governor complained that jury trials had made a mockery of English attempts to enforce the imperial regulations and he added that "if some method be not fallen upon whereby Illicit Trade may be better prevented, I doubt it will be to little purpose to bring any cause . . . to tryall by a Jury, and the Officers of the Customs will from thence be discouraged from exerting themselves in . . . their duty." [9]

Another report, dated February 1742/43, from the popular and able Governor Shirley of Massachusetts observed that "the Illicit Trade, which appears to have been carried on in this Province and some of the neighboring Colonies . . . is such as without the speady Interposition of the Parliament to stop it, must be highly destructive . . . and finally weakening the Dependence which the British Northern Colonies ought to have upon their Mother Country." [10]

A similar letter, dated October 1752, from Governor Clinton of New York, acidly noted that "It is not easy to imagine to what an enormous hight [sic] this transgression of the Laws of Trade goes in North America." Clinton concluded his report by wondering if it might not be discovered that "Holland and Hamburg receive more benefitt from the Trade of the Northern Colonies than Great Britain does, after the expence that Great Britain is at, when their support is deducted." [11]

These few quotations give a fair indication of the general tenor of the reports collected from the files of the Board of Trade. And the reports themselves in turn indicate the type of information on the operation of the Colonial System that was to be found in the possession of the Board. After examining such evidence, it would be difficult to reach any conclusion other than that the Colonial System was both ineffective and dangerously unsatisfactory.

But the information collected by the Board of Trade need not stand by itself as evidence of the attitude of the English government towards the Colonial System. The famous Treasury letter of October 1763 to the Privy Council—the letter that led in the next year to passage of the Sugar Act—was based on the information made available by the Board of Trade, supplemented by further research by the Commissioners of the Customs. In effect, this Treasury letter represented a general policy statement with regard to the Colonies. It began with the oft-quoted words that the revenue in America was "very small and inconsiderable, having in no degree increased with the Commerce of those Countries. . . ." But of more interest are the general remarks in this letter on the effectiveness of the Colonial System. Not only, the letter noted, was the revenue impaired "through Neglect, Connivance and Fraud" but the commerce of the Colonies was "diverted from its natural Course and the Salutary Provisions of many wise Laws to secure it to the Mother Country . . . in a great measure Defeated." These observations were coupled with a warning that the rapid growth of the Colonies made "the proper Regulation of their Trade of immediate Necessity, lest the continuance and extent of the dangerous Evils . . . may render all Attempts to remedy them hereafter infinitely more difficult, if not impracticable." [12]

This letter from the Treasury, coupled with the results of the investigation undertaken by the Board of Trade, suggests that the English government was less than happy with the operation of the Old Colonial System. If this assumption is valid, then logically a further question should be asked: what exactly was thought to be wrong with the System? Again it is possible to suggest an answer to that question by turning to the information—the reports from the colonies—accumulated and studied over the years by the Board of Trade, the Commissioners of the Customs, the Treasury, and the other official agencies involved in the enforcement of imperial policies.

Rather naturally, British officials in the Colonies were led to complain about a variety of problems. Such complaints ranged from irritation with the geography of the American coastline—as one governor commented, the "Sea Coast . . . is so extensive and has so many Commodious harbours, that the small number of Customs House Officers are often complaining that they are not able to do much for preventing illegal trade" [13]—to disgust with the provincialism of the colonists—as a customs officer in Boston wrote, "this is the finest Country and Climate I ever saw, Yet I begin to grow sick of the people." [14]

Basically, however, the complaints of the various Colonial officials centered on one general problem—the weakness of English imperial authority in America. From the point of view of these officials, the Americans paid too little attention to, and had far too little respect for, British regulations and directives. In attempting to explain the reasons for this unfortunate situation, the Colonial officials cited a number of items, not the least of which was the power accumulated over the years by the local Colonial legislatures. As one English agent in America observed, as long as the colonists had "a power (as they imagine) of making laws separate from the Crown, they'll never be wanting to lessen the authority of the King's officers, who by hindering them from a full freedom of illegal trade, are accounted ennemies to the growth and prosperity of their little Commonwealths." [15]

In Colonies that were under charter or proprietary governments complaints against the powers of the legislatures frequently were coupled with recommendations that those Colonies be placed under direct royal control. In fact, the confusion that arose from the coexistence of the various types of colonial governments—proprietary, charter, and royal—often led to such suggestions as that offered by Robert Livingston in 1701 that "one form of government be established in all the neighboring Colonies on this main Continent." [16]

But destruction of the proprietary and charter Colonies obviously was not in itself a final solution, since even in Colonies where royal authority was directly exercised colonial legislative independence was a major source of friction. The struggle over the supply of the treasury in New York, or over the governor's salary in Massachusetts, suggested that the problem lay deeper than in the particular form of government.

Generally speaking, the majority of the English officials who went to America encountered similar difficulties. In most cases they were sent out from London with both general and specific instructions to guide their conduct. They were expected to undertake certain actions, to perform certain assignments, at the direction of the home authorities. They might be told to ensure enforcement of the Acts of Trade in their area. They might be instructed to settle a particular boundary dispute. Or they might, like Governor Belcher of Massachusetts, be instructed to secure an established salary for the governor's office. In any case, whatever their instructions, as Governor Belcher and the other imperial agents discovered over the years, to instruct was one thing and to achieve another. On sensitive issues the Colonial opposition was likely to be so active, so determined, and so effective, as to make success difficult if not impossible.

The reports sent back to London from the Colonies suggested that basically the problem facing the English officials in America was political. Since those officials were forced to operate in a situation in which the Colonial legislatures—and the Colonial courts—played a forceful role in the conduct of government, much depended on their relation to those bodies. In effect, through necessity the English officials had to become active participants in the drama of Colonial political life. Unfortunately this was a role the English officials were ill-equipped to perform. Not only did the rigidity of the instructions provided for them deprive them of some of the maneuverability— the flexibility—so essential to political success, but more seriously they were never given full control of that most basic of political weapons—the power of patronage.

Frequently, when the question of patronage is discussed in relation to Colonial America, emphasis is placed on the quality of the agents sent over by the British government. The argument here is similar to that expressed by one American colonist when he complained that "America has been for many years made the hospital of

Great Britain for her decayed courtiers and abandoned, worn-out dependents." [17] The implication in such a remark is that Colonial offices were made a dumping ground for needy English office seekers who happened to have the right political connections at home. As a result, the argument continues, the quality of the personnel selected for service in America was poor, a fact that helps to explain the lack of respect for English authority in the Colonies.

There is a degree of truth to this line of argument. Unquestionably many of the English agents were not the best possible representatives of imperial authority, and equally unquestionably this fact was noted and exploited by the colonists. But this argument can be over-emphasized. Although it is true that the quality of English official-dom in America may have been poor, it is equally true that the quality of officialdom in London itself was little better. Surely, for example, the Duke of Newcastle was hardly the most suitable person for the high post he occupied for so many years. And yet during his time in office the English government continued to operate not only adequately but rather successfully. The truth would seem to be that in the eighteenth century standards of both political morality and political incompetence were low; and the character of the English agents in America, rather than being exceptional, merely conformed to the general pattern.

In any case, it would seem that the misuse of the patronage powers on the part of the English government involved more than merely the quality of the personnel selected. The simple fact is that, as the Old Colonial System operated prior to 1763, control of patronage over the years was increasingly centered in London. The power of appointment, not just to governorships and other important posts, but to all kinds and varieties of minor offices, was monopolized by the London politicians. This concentration of patronage power in London was, in fact, a double disaster, for it not only restricted the ability of the English agents in the Colonies to build up effective centers of political support within the Colonies themselves but it also accustomed the colonists to look beyond the local English representatives to the source of power in London.

Jonathan Belcher's experiences as governor of Massachusetts illustrate the operation and the effect of this arrangement. Belcher came to the governor's office at a difficult moment. Not only was he faced with a bitter boundary dispute between Massachusetts and New Hampshire but the problem of the governor's salary had for many years undermined the governor's position in Massachusetts. In short, Belcher's assignment was a difficult one, but he soon discovered that his difficulties were compounded by the actions of the politicians in London. Shortly after his arrival Belcher appointed a relative to the lucrative naval office post in Massachusetts. Within a year Belcher learned that his protégé had been thrown out of the office and a candidate selected by the Duke of Newcastle installed in his place. Whatever the merits or demerits of Belcher's appointee, the fact was, as Belcher observed to Newcastle, that such an action tended "to undervalue him to the people of the Country." [18]

To a certain extent, any politician's strength is judged by his control of patronage, and such a slap as that administered to Belcher by Newcastle did indeed damage the governor's prestige and encourage the Colonial opposition to greater activity. Nor was this experience limited to Belcher. When the popular William Shirley succeeded Belcher he too had his difficulties over the question of appointments to the naval office. In fact Shirley himself was driven to complain to Newcastle, much as had Belcher, that loss of control over the naval office lowered his prestige "very much in the eyes of the people." [19]

Another English agent, Lieutenant Governor Gooch of Virginia, went to the heart of the problem when he reported that the patronage system, as it operated, permitted "the most unworthy, if they happen to have friends at Home, to look upon their Superiors with Disdain and bid them Defiance." Noting "how absolutely necessary Rewards as well as Punishments are to maintain Authority in any Government," Governor Gooch commented that to deprive an official of the "Power of rewarding Merit" leaves him only "a Province rather like that of an Executioner to inflict Punishments." [20]

Given this basic situation, it is not surprising that suggestions for strengthening the English position in the Colonies tended to follow one of two possible lines of approach. Some commentators found the only solution to be a total reorganization of the governmental structure in the Colonies. This was the plan that Robert Livingston had in mind when he recommended that "one form of government be established in all the neighboring colonies on this main Continent." [21] Reorganizing the structure of the Colonial governments, strengthening the position of the executive while decreasing or eliminating the authority of the Colonial legislatures and courts, had much to recommend it. A possible model for such a reconstruction might have been the earlier Dominion of New England. But, as the history of the Dominion itself suggested, such a reorganization of the Colonial governments was not only difficult to implement but hard to maintain, since it represented an arbitrary, external imposition on the native Colonial societies. Given the growth and development of the Colonies since the days of James II, with every passing year such a plan became more difficult and less attractive.

However, there was an alternative to total reorganization. It was, simply, to build up English power *within* the Colonial political structure as it already existed. The problem here was to increase the political effectiveness of the English officials and agents in the Colonies to the point at which they would be able to alter the political balance of power in their favor. And, as Governor Gooch pointed out in the remarks quoted above, the problem of control of patronage was intimately connected to the problem of political effectiveness.

But patronage, of course, involves more than the mere assignment of offices. Inseparably coupled with patronage is the question of money. Not only must the disposable jobs be reasonably profitable and desirable, but there also must be available enough job openings to satisfy a substantial number of applicants. In short, the amount of patronage available to a government is related to the size of the revenues at its disposal. If the English government wished to increase both the attractiveness and the number of official appointments in the Colonies, an augmented revenue of some kind was a necessity.

In fact, in many ways the idea of using a colonial revenue to create an American civil list, on the English model, was very attractive from the British point of view. The creation of Colonial offices, with established incomes which were in no way dependent on the generosity of the colonists, would give greater freedom of action of the English officials in the Colonies, and the multiplication of such offices would increase the number of desirable assignments available to the English government. Properly used, such augmented patronage openings could create a substantial proadministration party or faction within any given Colony.

It should not be surprising, then, to discover that recommenda-

tions for the establishment of the Colonial civil list and for the creation of additional Colonial revenues were frequently forwarded to
London. In 1716, for example, the surveyor general of the customs
for the northern Colonies suggested the raising of a revenue "by a
customs and excise on the whole continent, upon an English foot-
ing." Nothing, this Colonial official argued, could be "more reasonable than that all the plantations and dominions abroad should . . .
be made to bear the expence they occasion and not remain a dead
weight on the nation that severely groans under the debts of which
they have been in large measure the cause. . . ." [22]

In 1722 another Colonial customs official outlined a plan by which
the English government could raise a sizeable revenue in America.
Through duties on rum, molasses, sugar, and other items, and
through the extension to the colonies of the Stamp Act that already
was in existence in England, this official thought that the British government could raise a fund which could be used to provide both for
the defense of the Colonies and also "for the better support of Gov-
ernours and officers of the Crown, in the Plantations." [23] Interest-
ingly, as Edward Channing pointed out, this suggestion outlined in
1722 "anticipated Grenville's plan in almost every particular." [24]

Besides this suggestion in 1722 other recommendations for extension of the Stamp Act, and for creation of a Colonial civil list, were
offered over the years.[25] And it is worth noting that, as Sir Lewis
Namier has shown, Charles Townshend, so crucial a figure in later
events, had formulated his plans to strengthen English authority in
America by raising a revenue and establishing a Colonial civil list as
early as the year 1754, well before the beginning of the great Seven
Years' War, which is so often credited with bringing up the question
of a Colonial revenue.[26]

Analysis of the operation of the Old Colonial System prior to 1763
suggests that the English attitude might be summarized in this way:
First, whatever the objective truth may be about the effectiveness of
the System prior to 1763, it seems clear that the information made
available to the English government by their agents in the Colonies
gave the impression that the System was ineffective and highly unsatisfactory; second, the one common thread that seems to run
through many or most of the complaints about the ineffective opera-

tion of the System was the inherent weakness of English political authority in the Colonies; and third, recommendations for reform tended to center on the creation of a Colonial civil list and the more effective use of patronage opportunities, both of which involved an increase in the available Colonial revenues.

If these propositions are valid, then the English attitude towards the Old Colonial System might best be characterized as one of increasing impatience both with the attitude of the colonists and with the ineffectiveness of the System itself. Given the existence of such an attitude, it would not be surprising if impatience should eventually result in a movement for reform. Nor, indeed—again if these propositions are valid—should it be surprising that reform, when it came, should be centered on the problem of a Colonial revenue. In fact, to carry the point a step further, if it is argued—as it frequently is—that the major innovation introduced by the Grenville ministry after 1763 was the attempt to procure an adequate Colonial revenue, then perhaps it may be that Grenville and his associates acted after 1763 not to violate but to fulfill the spirit of the Old Colonial System. In any case, whatever the specifics of the Grenville program, the evidence does seem to indicate that over the years the English government found the operation of the Old Colonial System inadequate and unsatisfactory and that after 1763—whether or not the Seven Years' War had ever been fought or George Grenville had ever become Prime Minister—still reform, of one form or another, was not only possible but probable.[27]

Nor do the implications of this line of reasoning end with the matter of the motivation behind the English policies adopted after 1763. It is possible that historians have been unduly naïve in their approach to the problem of understanding the nature and intensity of the American resistance to English efforts at taxation. The establishment of a Colonial civil list—or, more basically, of an independent revenue—involved a threat to the very structure of government in the Colonies. If today an effort should be made by any official in any given town, or state, or in Washington itself, to establish an independent revenue—a revenue beyond the control of the people's representatives, a revenue freeing the hands of the executive branch of the government from the necessity of consulting the people generally or their representatives specifically—no one would be surprised at the consequent uproar. If to this picture was added the fact that those executives who were to be given such power and freedom of action were not elected but appointed officials, representatives indeed of alien power and interests, it would be the height of foolishness not to expect an explosion of great intensity. Yet such, of course, was the exact nature of the threat to American self-government inherent in the taxation policies followed by the English government after 1763.

Historians may have been naïve, but the evidence suggests that the American colonists were not. According to John Adams, it was exactly his awareness of this threat that determined the course of action followed by Oxenbridge Thacher from 1763 until his death:

His favorite subject was politics, and the impending, threathening system of parliamentary taxation and universal government over the colonies. . . . From the time when he argued the question of writs of assistance to his death, he considered the king, ministry, and nation of Great Britain as determined to new-model the colonies from the foundation, to annul all their charters, to constitute them all royal governments, to raise a revenue in America by parliamentary taxation, to apply that revenue to pay the salaries of governors, judges, and all other crown officers.[28]

John Adams himself put the case more succinctly. Reminiscing later about the threat inherent in the passage of the original Molasses Act, Adams observed that had it been collected it would have provided a "fund amply sufficient . . . to pay all the salaries of all the governors upon the continent, and all the judges of admiralty too." With the steady growth of the molasses and sugar trade, the receipts would have increased until they were "sufficient to bribe any nation less knowing and less virtuous than the people of America, to the voluntary surrender of all their liberties." [29]

In effect, the struggle between 1763 and 1774 was not over abstract principles, however important rhetoric may have been in communicating the danger.[30] Nor was the dispute simply over such peripheral issues as standing armies or unnecessary burdens on Colonial trade and commerce. The ineffectual operation of the Old Colonial System, as seen in London, suggested the need for the more effective exercise of English authority in America. For the Americans, the efforts at taxation represented a threat to the very self-government that had made their Colonial status tolerable. The consequence was a dispute which ended in revolution.

British and Imperial Interests in the Age of the American Revolution*

MICHAEL G. KAMMEN holds his A.B. from The George Washington University and his M.A. and Ph.D. degrees from Harvard University. Among his publications are *A Rope of Sand: The Colonial Agents, British Politics, and the American Revolution* (1968), *Deputyes & Libertyes: The Origins of Representative Government in Colonial America* (1969), and *Empire and Interest: The Politics of Mercantilism and the First British Empire, 1660–1800* (1970). He has edited *Politics and Society in Colonial America: Democracy or Deference?* (1967), and co-edited *The Glorious Revolution in America* (1964), and is presently writing an interpretative study of Europe and the origins of American civilization. He is Professor of History at Cornell University.

Interest groups have had a rather shadowy existence in histories of British and imperial politics in the eighteenth century. We know a good deal about certain individual interests; and many of them as well as the term "interest"—used in a variety of ways—appear in the literature repeatedly yet casually.[1] Nonetheless their cumulative significance for eighteenth-century public life remains ill-defined, their

* An earlier version of this paper was read before the College of Social Studies, Wesleyan University, Middletown, Conn., on April 18, 1966. I am grateful to Richard V. W. Buel, Jr. (History) and Edward J. Nell (Economics) for their helpful suggestions.

collective phasing as part of the "system of politicks" is still unclear, and their relation to major events—such as the American Revolution —is undetermined. In brief, we lack a comprehensive estimate of the role played by interest groups in the Anglo-American world.[2]

Sir Lewis Namier's emphasis upon family connections and parliamentary interests is perhaps confusing in this context, because Namier's recognition of "the absence of organized parties" led him to a fragmented view of the essential units competing for favor and power. In reacting against traditional interpretations of eighteenth-century politics, he reduced the dynamic elements in public life to individuals, families, and "circles which are primarily concerned with the nation's political business and form therefore the political nation."[3] In his own work and in that of scholars who have been closely associated with him, these circles are referred to as interests.[4] Although such terminology is unexceptionable, it has created something of a false cognate because these family-oriented, electoral, and parliamentary interests correspond neither with our own understanding of interest groups,[5] nor with the very considerable numbers of such groups that were active in eighteenth-century politics.

Between 1675 and 1775 there was a viable party system during certain periods and a factionalized one during others. (In the past thirty-five years, especially, we have had their checkered history charted in staggering detail.) But there were *constantly* interest groups: some manifest and some latent, some articulate and some inarticulate, some formally organized whereas others were merely "a condition of like-mindedness and informal communication about issues." As Gabriel Almond has pointed out, the kinds of interest groups present in a society, the specificity or diffuseness of their demands, their conceptions of the political arena and of the "rules of the game," the ethos they bring with them into the political process —these are the "raw materials" of politics—the unaggregated demands which some set of mechanisms must transform into public policy.[6]

Such functional groupings, broadly defined as interests, were strategic units in British and imperial politics to be sure. Yet definitional caution is necessary, for as we have noted, in the eighteenth century there were both the local, familiar parliamentary connections, called interests, and the broader, regional, national and imperial extraparliamentary groupings also referred to in this way. The former type was inextricably part of and usually subsumed by *one* of the latter, known as the landed interest. Our concern here is with the larger groupings, for although they were simultaneously less ephemeral and greater determinants of national and foreign policy, they have received less notice from historians.[7]

Even these complex aggregations, however, and their commonly competitive components—the real interest groups in the eyes of a political scientist—were far from similar in purpose, function and importance. The Bank of England, the iron manufacturers, and the Protestant Dissenting Deputies were as unlike as General Motors, the National Rifle, and National Education Associations. Yet they all participated in the same political system, were affected by the same instability, sought influence, paid dearly for it, and maintained at least skeletal organizations to sustain their concerns. In the eighteenth century, moreover, two factors tended to augment the number and intensity of interest groups active in public life: the vagueness of the distinction then held between public and private sectors, especially in financial matters and in parliamentary acts; and the fact that many elements in Georgian society, especially the newer urban areas, were unrepresented in Parliament. Understandably then, as a contributor wrote in the *Gentleman's Magazine*, "to recite the different struggles between these contending interests . . . would require a volume." [8]

In attempting to generalize about these groups and their political role,[9] it is exceedingly important to note that they were by no means monolithic—at least not consistently. The "mercantile interest" comprised a variety of dissimilar components, some of which, for example, thrived on political stability while others did not.[10] The planters and merchants known as the West Indian interest did not always share common objectives, especially with respect to monopoly prices and the direct trade to Europe.[11] The landed interest included both aristocracy and gentry, country gentlemen and larger farmers whose aims did not always coincide.[12] The East India Company's internal divisiveness has become notorious.[13] The iron merchants and shippers often differed with forge owners.[14] The City of London's "monied interest" was not consistently a harmonious whole,[15] nor were the clothing and textile interests.[16] Moreover, there were times and circumstances when an interest was a greater force in politics when internally divided than when cohesive and tranquil! The East India interest's role in the famous election of 1701 provides a case in point.[17]

Nevertheless, many of these bodies enjoyed or developed considerable stability and cohesion through long stretches of the eighteenth century; and in general they were more forceful and influential when stable and cohesive. One should not, however, regard them as fully discrete entities, for their memberships commonly overlapped and interlocked with governmental personnel as well as with each other. Many individuals among the landed groups, for example, were involved in the woollen industry, which led to alliances with textile manufacturers as against trading and commercial interests.[18] Even so, their identities were sufficiently distinct to be recognized by contemporaries, who singled out and discussed one or another interest in responding to the dynamics of public life. Unlike a party or faction, the interests were not themselves prepared to undertake the responsibility of government. Yet their configuration and interaction provide a continuum, leading to and including the state and its policy-making organs. Consequently these phenomena deserve closer scrutiny, for their history taken collectively lends a broader dimension to our knowledge of Georgian Britain and its imperial possessions.[19]

Before the middle of the eighteenth century there had been no lack of British and imperial interest groups focused in London. But viewed in broad perspective, an equilibrium had prevailed between them and government. On occasion, as in 1720 or 1733, for example, the balance might temporarily go askew. For the most part, however, a combination of political discipline and mutual understanding obtained. Following the age of Walpole, roughly between 1748 and 1762, a transformation occurred. Incredibly rapid economic growth in Britain, coupled with Henry Pelham's permissive attitude toward interests (1749–1754) and the political instability following his death, provided a matrix in which virtually every significant interest group underwent alterations of major proportions: internal changes, changes in relation to each other, in relation to politics and to the state. The attendant metamorphosis in British and imperial politics was far-reaching in its implications, and belies Professor Gipson's picture of a calm, untroubled system at mid-century.[20]

The implications for the American Colonies had already become apparent to a few by the close of the 1750's. Facets of Colonial trade, Benjamin Franklin wrote from London in 1759, offended "the Trading and Manufacturing Interest; and the Landed Interest begin to be jealous of us as a Corn Country, that may interfere with them in the Markets to which they export that commodity." A reading of David Hume's essay, "of the Jealousy of Trade" (1758), prompted Franklin to write the author in 1760 that free trade would have "a good Effect in promoting a certain Interest too little thought of by selfish Man, and scarce ever mention'd; so that we hardly have a Name for it; I mean the *Interest of Humanity*." [21]

Fundamental changes in the position and influence of various interest groups during the 1750's, as well as altered attitudes toward them, formed a prelude to the wild, general instability of the 1760's. The process of fragmentation, realignment, and aggressive emergence, complete well before the formal close of the Seven Years' War, set the stage for the political deterioration that followed it. In consequence, perhaps, the immediate origins of the Age of the American Revolution may lie not in 1763, or 1760, or 1759, but in the years directly following the Peace of Aix-la-Chapelle.[22]

The two decades after 1763 may properly be called an age of interests, for the groups so came to dominate politics that men were prompted to observe that mercantilism had changed from the control of trade in the interest of national policy, to the control of national policy in the interest of trade. As Professor Guttridge has noted, the increasing importance of Parliament seemed to encourage the efforts of powerful groups seeking to influence legislation by political pressure.[23] Spokesmen for the Old Whigs believed it their function while in office to reconcile the "jarring and dissonant" interests, to serve as arbiters among them. In 1774, when Shelburne sent his analysis of the deepening colonial crisis to Chatham, he first discussed the positions of the various interests, and only as an afterthought turned to "parties and particular men." When the war had dragged its course longer than most groups were willing to indulge, it was a combination of interests "that influenced Parliament to reorganize the government and end the war." The contours of settlement in 1782–83, as Professor Morris has shown, were molded by a variety of groups.[24]

In almost every conceivable sphere, these were years of major dislocation: domestic, imperial, and international politics, economic theory, and social cohesiveness were all sharply tested and shaken. "Our Government has become an absolute Chimera," David Hume remarked in 1769; "So much Liberty is incompatible with human Society. . . ." In his troubled view, control of the ship of state had slipped out of the grasp of "the King, Nobility, and Gentry of this Realm." [25] The government was susceptible as never before to pressures from the interests, whose success depended largely on their influence and financial strength, the administration's particular weakness at a given moment, and what other groups were then active and aggressive.

In a period of such dangerous instability, interest groups had the power to force or help force ministerial resignations. More important, the search for a new equilibrium led administrations to seek every available prop to steady the system. Hence the special support given to certain traditional interests regarded as bulwarks of government, such as the East India Company.[26] The quest for allies and stability caused administrations to become absorbed into the world of interest politics, and Parliament no less so. A factionalized and undisciplined party system opened the legislative process as never before to covert interest group domination of committees and agencies, as well as propagandistic maneuvers. Private bills passing through nineteen stages in the House of Commons left most Members with little notion of what was about. Committees were the effective and instrumental organ in the legislative process, and they were invariably occupied by the very M.P.'s with personal stakes in the legislation being considered.[27]

A party system is capable of mediating between interest groups and the authoritative policy-making bodies by screening them from the particularistic and disintegrative impact of special interests. When parties are strong, they tend to inhibit the capacity of private groups to formulate specific demands into programs with wider appeal. Since no cohesive interest group is large enough to gain a majority, and the factionalized party system cannot aggregate diverse interests into a stable majority and a coherent opposition, the result is commonly, and was in the age of the American Revolution, a splintered legislature permeated by relatively narrow interests and uncompromising tendencies, a legislature which could be used as an arena for propaganda, or for the protection of special interests, but not for the effective and timely formulation and support of major policy decisions.

Moreover, with the party system in Parliament unable to perform the function of interest articulation and regulation, that process gravitated more than ordinarily to the bureaucracy, whose capacity for responsible administration was diminished. Under these circumstances the bureaucracy, especially the imperial civil servants, tended to become multifunctional: it responded to and coordinated interest groups, making policy for them and helping to administer it. When the bureaucracy became weak, as with the American Department after 1772, the result was a system in which agencies of political choice failed to function, and in which basic policy decisions could not be made. Government became a task of protection and maintenance in which the effective bodies were special interests and parts of the bureaucracy. The latter was "colonized" by interest groups, and penetrated by incompatible demands.[28]

Rapid economic growth of the sort that occurred in Britain after mid-century is likely to be a source of political instability of itself.[29] When that condition occurs for other reasons as well, as it did during the 1760's, the combination can be volatile in the extreme. Accelerated economic growth and the quest for political equilibrium both involve and are attended by changes in the way policy is made, where it is made, and in the distribution of power and prestige. All these interrelated characteristics were in motion during the seventh decade of the eighteenth century.[30]

The years between the two Peaces of Paris, then, did not constitute an age of interests in the sense that special groups *controlled* government, for they were not always in a position to do so. Some of the groups themselves were unstable. Yet the dominant characteristic in public life was governmental and general political absorption in the affairs of these groups. The decision-making process became intimately tied to their concerns, and the major events of these years seemed to be shaped by the needs of or crises created by the leading intcrests. Observers, both foreign and British, stand as witnesses to this trend. During the 1760's and 1770's, for example, liberal French intellectuals sketched out their picture of a republic of virtue. For men like Mably, Holbach, Diderot and Rousseau, that republic had no room for conflicting interests. Hence their conviction that England, which had fallen victim to such interests, could never approximate the good society.[31]

In Britain a broad range of observers brought their notions of political behavior into consonance with reality. Hence the recognition by the Scottish historical school "that a commercial organization of society had rendered obsolete much that had been believed about society before it." [32] Hence Sir William Mildmay's quest for a special department of commerce: "These difficulties in guiding *the separate interest of each Trade* to the general interest of the Whole, make it necessary for a government to appoint a particular department . . . to superintend the affairs of commerce, and examine all proposals. . . ." [33]

When Edmund Burke was first elected an M.P. in 1765, he found it necessary to distinguish and analyze the various British and imperial interests. His sensitivity to their importance grew in succeeding years, so that by 1770 he argued against any man's achieving public office without first gaining experience and distinction among the major interests. Otherwise "such a man *has no connection with the interest of the people.*" [34] In addition to the established groups of economic or commercial orientation, he noted that "a great official, a great professional, a great military and naval interest, all necessarily comprehending many people of the first weight, ability, wealth, and spirit, has been gradually formed in the kingdom . . . [and] must be let into a share of representation. . . ." Although recognizing that the structure of British political society was closely rooted in these diverse interests, Burke nevertheless believed that Parliament must not be regarded as a microcosm of them. Speaking in 1774, he offered his most extended thoughts on the place of interest groups in public life:

Parliament is not a *congress* of ambassadors from different and hostile interests, which interests each must maintain, as an agent and advocate, against other agents and advocates; but Parliament is a *deliberative* assembly of *one* nation, with *one* interest, that of the whole—where not local purposes, not local prejudices, ought to guide, but the general good, resulting from the general reason of the whole. . . . We are now members for a rich commercial *city* [Bristol]; this city, however, is but a part of a rich commercial *nation*, the interests of which are various, multiform and intricate. We are members for that great nation, which however, is itself but part of a great *empire*, extended by our virtue and our fortune to the farthest limits of the East and of the West. All these widespread interests must be considered,—must be compared,—must be reconciled, if possible.[35]

For Adam Smith, writing at the same time, interest groups exerted a truly pernicious influence. Throughout *The Wealth of Nations* a recurrent theme laments their influence, especially in extorting monopolistic privileges from Parliament. The result was a vast array of corporation laws, duties, bounties, prohibitions, drawbacks, commercial treaties, and Colonial monopolies.[36] And in Smith's view the crisis of Anglo-American relations was deeply imbedded in the fierce competition among interest groups that characterized the 1760's and 1770's. On this point Smith and Josiah Tucker, otherwise poles apart on matters of political economy, were agreed. Prior to 1763 "the interest of our American colonies was regarded as the same with that of the mother country." Since then, however, a process of fragmentation and discrimination had occurred, distributing the burdens and privileges of Empire unequally. In search of responsibility for these changes, Smith by-passed the politicians, believing instead that the "merchants and manufacturers have been by far the principal architects."[37]

Smith's sentiments mirrored a mounting concern of the colonists ever since the early 1760's, when the Sugar Act "was procured by the interest of the West India planters, with no other view than to enrich themselves, by obliging the northern Colonies to take their whole supply from them." In the Middle Colonies, as well as New England, observers noted that Americans "always looked with an evil eye on the West Indian interest as clashing with and opposing their own." To John Watts, a New York merchant, it seemed that "the West India and North American interest is always jarring." Even the imperial bureaucrats in the Colonies, such as Nathaniel Weare, Comptroller of Customs in Massachusetts, felt "there is not a man on the continent of America, who does not consider the Sugar Act . . . as a sacrifice made of the northern Colonies, to the superior interest in

Parliament of the West Indies. . . . How the apprehension of so imperious a preference, of one Colony to another, operates upon the affections of those northern people towards the mother country, may be easily imagined." [38]

By 1765 a sense of discrimination was commonly voiced. "The Statutes made to restrain the trade of the Continent in favour of the islands," wrote John Dickinson, "seem to tend rather towards promoting *partial* than *general* interests." Daniel Dulany echoed these sentiments, for "the commercial interests of Great Britain are preferred to every other consideration. . . ." Americans on the scene in London became more explicit in blaming rival interests for the precarious political situation. "Most of our acts of Parliament," Franklin wrote in 1769, "for regulating [trade, manufacturers, and taxes] are, in my opinion, little better than political blunders, owing to ignorance of the science, or to the designs of crafty men, who mislead the legislature, proposing something under the specious appearance of public good, while the real aim is, to sacrifice that to their own private interest." [39] By the mid-1760's Franklin and other North American agents were reporting to their employers the dangers inherent in new parliamentary legislation, "notwithstanding all the Opposition that could be given . . . by the American Interest." [40] By the early 1770's, the London façade of that interest seemed to be crumbling.

Compared with its competitors the North American interest suffered from strategic disadvantages. There was the problem of distance. James Roebuck, an authority on lobbying in Georgian England, noted that "it is much more easy to speak to Members than write to them." Consequently almost the entire burden of presenting the Colonial case was placed upon the agents, whereas the strength and leverage of other lobbies was more broadly distributed, as for example the West Indian, African, iron, monied, naval stores, and even the Irish interest.[41] Many of the American agents, moreover, were only part-time employees, whereas their analogues devoted full attention to the affairs of their employers.

To compound the difficulty, after 1768 the agents' institutional and political roles became highly ambiguous, while their employers became the only interest looked upon unfavorably for intellectual and constitutional reasons. When Lord North announced that Parliament would "not consent to go into the question [repealing the Townshend duties], on account of the combinations going on in America against the mother country," he essentially declared that in an age of government sensitivity to group pressure, one in particular was beyond the pale.[42]

Its isolation was compounded by several factors. First, there was the loss of identification between Colonial groups and their traditional counterparts in Britain. What had once in many cases been transatlantic interests became separated into distinct and even antithetical groups. Relations between merchants and dissenters on both sides of the ocean deteriorated.[43] Pitt had remarked to the House of Commons in 1759 "that he did not know but the landed gentlemen seemed to consider themselves in a separate interest from the colonies, that he should ever consider the colonies as [part of] the landed interest of this Kingdom and it was a barbarism to consider them otherwise." His remarks were not well received. By 1767 a major objection to Colonial concessions was that "the landed interest of the Colonies, will be promoted; while the . . . landed interest of Great Britain will be depressed to its utter ruin and destruction; and, consequently, the balance of the power of government . . . will be *locally* transferred from Great Britain to the colonies." Franklin insisted that "the contrary had always been the fact," i.e., assistance to American agriculture had benefited the entire Empire.[44]

The isolation of North America's London interest became more obvious thereafter. Repeal of the Stamp Act had been facilitated in part because, as Richard Jackson observed: "however the Colonies have friends, I shd say, the British Empire has friends." After 1769 it was no longer possible to "consider the Merchants here [Philadelphia] and in England as the Links of the Chain that binds both Countries together." Bristol's Society of Merchant Venturers had petitioned for repeal in 1766; after 1770 it ceased as a body to support the North American cause. The iron industry had also sought repeal; but in 1775 Birmingham's iron manufacturers hoped for stringent enforcement of Parliament's punitive colonial legislation. The prospect of war meant a tremendous boom for the industry. In petitioning against the Coercives during the spring of 1774, William Bollan "had considerable expectation that the honorable India merchants would assist and strengthen your defence; afterwards that the manufacturers in the principal towns, who, according to my information, were alarmed and stirring, would make their opposition to the Bill for shutting up the port; but all failed, even the London merchants declining their opposition to it." [45]

By the early 1770's, practically the only sphere in which the North American interest did not stand isolated involved the intellectual sympathies of British radicals. Ironically, that transatlantic connection was destined to hasten rather than impede the imperial breach, by stimulating and encouraging antiauthoritarian impulses. In 1769 John Horne Tooke and others founded the Society of the Supporters of the Bill of Rights. The organization acquired a national reputation and excited enthusiasm in the Colonies where Sam Adams became an overseas member. His efforts led to the creation of similar units which would help foment revolutionary unrest in the early 1770's. [46]

Until the Stamp Act crisis, North America's interest at the seat of Empire had been advocated by a coalition of agents, merchants, religious societies, and others. By the later 1760's, the agents' supporting cast had been partially stripped away, so that their isolation was intensified by group disintegration. Before that time the colonial land companies and their London lobbyists had not been incompatible with the colonial agents. In the eight years or so before independence, however, the wildly increased tempo of land company politicking by Americans undermined the integrity and single-mindedness of some agents. Virginia and Edward Montagu were pitted against the Grand Ohio Company and Benjamin Franklin by 1770, while Arthur Lee and the Mississippi Company (a Virginia group) aroused the hostility of Pennsylvania's proprietors. [47] Competition between exponents of the land companies had always existed; but after 1768 a mad scramble was under way among London representatives of the Ohio, Indiana, Mississippi, Grand Ohio, and Vandalia Companies to secure or obstruct vast grants of American real estate. [48]

One response to the deterioration of North America's London interest (as well as to local, provincial pressures and circumstances) was an increase in political activity and organization in the New World. News of such goings-on, however, was not at all well received in England, where there was deep skepticism of "such mixt interests as the Colonys are compos'd of." Political consciousness quickened in Boston, New York, Philadelphia, and Charleston during these years, leading, for example, to the formation of the Society for Encouraging Trade and Commerce within the Province of Massachusetts Bay, and New York's Chamber of Commerce in 1768, which actively promoted the cause of New York's commercial groups. Yet compared with the simultaneous organization and impact of London, Bristol, Liverpool, and even Manchester, Birmingham, and Lancaster on British politics, the Colonial cities were a marginal force.[49]

In summary, at a time when pressure groups constituted much of the matrix of British and imperial politics, the North American interest was a relative weak sister, especially within Parliament. As Isaac Barré commented, "there are gentlemen in this House from the West Indies, but there are very few who know the circumstances of North America." [50] Advocates of the mainland Colonies were less well connected and organized, less well financed and informed, less committed, and in several cases less capable than their rivals,[51] who knew precisely what they sought, and how far they might go in achieving it. North America's political influence in no way equaled its economic importance. Too often the Colonies were on the defensive because some other, more aggressive interest, took the offensive against them. More and better agents, a more cohesive and purposeful lobby in London, and greater political advantage of economic leverage were required.[52]

Instead the North American agents became less of an interest group and more of a constitutional protagonist, thereby violating the political conventions of an age. In consequence, the group's isolation and fragmentation, as well as its employers' alienation, met with deep hostility, not only from North's administration, but from the other interest groups as well. In 1767 Charles Townshend decided that if the government pressed its "right" to certain East India Company revenues, endless complications would ensue. The sensible policy therefore, involved an amicable arrangement with the Company, avoiding the question of right altogether. Similarly Lord North might have worked out an accommodation with the Colonial agents, just as he did with Thomas Allan, Ireland's agent, in the difficult circumstances of 1770–71. The attitudes and pressures of the other major groups helped serve as a preventive of sorts.[53]

Food and price riots, as well as machine-smashing, in England during the 1760's and 1770's brought significant governmental redress to working classes there. In the Colonies a tea party that also wilfully damaged private property brought rapid retribution. In direct clashes with the African interest the North American agents came off badly, as they lamented to their friends at home.[54] As 1775 opened the alignment was overwhelming. Provincial merchants and manufacturers were activated, as Matthew Boulton wrote, "to prevent, if possible, some of my neighbours from running into unwise measures, [initiated] by the intrigues of American and minority agents, who I have reason to believe have been busy . . . in most of the other manufacturing towns in England." Simultaneously the fisheries interest welcomed the administration's program to restrict colonial trade and fishing opportunities.[55]

Edmund Burke summarized the impasse in January:

. . . if the Merchants had thought fit to interfere last winter [1773–74], the distresses of this might certainly have been prevented; conciliatory Measures would have taken place; and they would have come with more dignity, and with far better effect, before the Trial of our Strength than after it. . . . By means of this reserve, the authority of the Mercantile Interest, which ought to have supported, with efficacy and power, the opposition to the fatal Cause of all this Mischief, was pleaded against us; *and we were obliged to stoop under the accumulated Weight of all the Interests in this Kingdom.* . . .[56]

By September these conditions had only worsened. Stirrings on the part of a few British merchants for reconciliation were meaningless. The North American interest had ceased to exist; its transformation inaugurated a new era.[57]

During the first half of the eighteenth century, then, British and imperial interest groups, along with the formal political alignments and rate of economic growth remained *comparatively* stable. Immediately after mid-century, almost simultaneously, a period of accelerated economic activity was accompanied by dramatic changes in the configuration of interest groups; and both were quickly followed by a sustained period of pronounced political instability. Given the total picture of competitive demands being made upon the imperial government, the nature of the decision-making process at that time, and the limited "seasons of business,"[58] a delicate balance existed quite susceptible to violation. Under these circumstances the North American interest played the maverick's role. It had until 1766 possessed real influence, if only nominal power.[59] When it lost its influence as well, and became ideologically entangled, even the most cautious colonial observers felt a sense of helplessness. As Thomas Hutchinson remarked:

Not one tenth part of the people of Great Britain have a voice in the elections to Parliament; and therefore, the colonies can have no claim to it; but every man of property in England may have his voice, if he will; Besides, acts of Parliament do not generally affect individuals, *and every interest is represented.* But the colonies have an interest distinct from the interest of the nation; and shall the Parliament be at once party and judge? [60]

All of these factors and apprehensions helped to destroy the equilibrium; for as John Stuart Mill later wrote, "one person with a belief is a social power equal to ninety-nine who have only interest."

Thomas Pownall, Henry Ellis, and the Spectrum of Possibilities, 1763–1775

JOHN SHY received his B.S. from the United States Military Academy, his M.A. from the University of Vermont, and his Ph.D. from Princeton University. He has taught at Princeton and is now Associate Professor of History at the University of Michigan. His book, *Toward Lexington: The Role of the British Army in the Coming of the American Revolution* (1965), won the American Historical Association's John H. Dunning Prize. Other publications include sketches on Charles Lee in *George Washington's Generals* (ed. George A. Billias, 1964) and Thomas Gage in *George Washington's Opponents* (ed. George A. Billias, 1969) as well as (with Peter Paret) *Guerrillas in the 1960's* (1962). He is presently making a military, social, and political study of the Continental Army officer corps.

Little more than a year after Great Britain had given up the fight to hold her North American Colonies, a remarkable meeting took place at Marseilles, where ancient ruins, the winter's sun, and fate brought Thomas Pownall and Henry Ellis southward to the same supper table. A generation earlier, during the critical years of The Great War for Empire, each man had governed one of the American provinces: Ellis in Georgia, Pownall in Massachusetts. After their coincidental return to England in 1760, their careers had diverged. Ellis had soon withdrawn from politics altogether; Pownall only lately had taken the same course. They were wealthy, cultivated men—both were Fellows of the Royal Society—and they would appear to have been finding solace for the recent wreck of Empire in the study of classical Greece and Rome. But there is no evidence that they ever spent an evening together before, or after, their meeting in Marseilles.

The meeting was remarkable, if more ironic than historic in its significance, because Ellis and Pownall are a matched pair for those who would relate British politics to the American Revolution. Their careers are full of parallels: Both were born just as Robert Walpole was climbing to the top of British government; both lived on into their eighties and saw Napoleon at his zenith; they died almost at the same time, in the years of Trafalgar, Austerlitz, and the death of the younger Pitt. Brilliant and leisured dilettantes, yet serious enough about antiquity, natural science, and political theory to write and publish, they are almost caricatures of the Enlightenment. Patronized as young men by the Earl of Halifax, reform-minded president of the Board of Trade, they were two of the ablest governors ever to serve in the old Empire, although neither was willing to bury himself for more than a few years in the remote and primitive cities of North America.

The differences between the two are equally striking, however. Even their host was moved to record the contrast between them:[1]

Governor Pownall was splendid and magnificent in his dress; Governor Ellis was covered with a Scotch plaid cloak, and the cut of his coat beneath, had not been changed for the last thirty years; and though abundantly rich, he would not visit in a carriage, but left his wooden clogs at the door.

Differences went deeper than mere appearance: Ellis was a great wit, an idiosyncratic bachelor who ran off to sea as a boy, begot numerous natural progeny, regularly visited Voltaire, gave parties that were legends, and followed the seasons through Europe "like certain birds." In his twenties he had spent a winter camped on Hudson's Bay looking for the Northwest Passage and then had written a book about it; in his forties he was content simply to enjoy life as far as money, uncertain health, and the eighteenth century would allow.[2] Pownall, on the other hand, had matriculated at Trinity College, Cambridge, and then followed his elder brother John to a clerkship at the Board of Trade. He became known for his pursuit of rich women—marrying two of them—and otherwise spent much of his health, and their wealth, "making a figure" in the House of Commons, the bookstalls of the City, and the drawing rooms of Mayfair.[3] No one ever accused Pownall of being a great wit, but some thought he was a great pedant; one especially unkind contemporary used Shakespeare to describe the former governor of Massachusetts:[4]

> . . . and in his brain,
> Which is as dry as the remainder biscuit
> After a voyage, he hath strange place cramm'd
> With observation, the which he vents
> In mangled forms.

Their host at Marseilles was more sympathetic: "Pownall and Ellis, both men of deep erudition, kept the uninitiated at an awful distance; they were both excellent when separate, but as they rarely agreed on any learned topic, I never wished them to meet . . ."[5]

The evening when they did meet was a protracted and contentious dialogue between the "two great dictators," as they were branded for their behavior. Evidently the question in dispute concerned the ancient ruins at Arles, but beneath the surface of an antiquarian argument lay a less remote, more painful question. That question: Who lost America?

Pownall and Ellis are sufficiently important figures in the coming of the American Revolution to deserve study, but they are also interesting because they were in some ways typical. Both men were consulted by government on major points of Colonial policy; both exerted influence in other, less direct ways; each came to stand for what appeared to be opposed approaches to the problem of America. Ellis was associated with those who took a hard line: he was the most influential adviser to the Grenville ministry 1762–63; he was asked in vain by the notoriously "firm" Earl of Hillsborough to serve as Undersecretary of State for the Colonies in late 1767; and in 1774, on the eve of war, he urged the government to take coercive measures.[6] In short, Henry Ellis would seem to be the kind of "Tory" who filled the fantasies of John and Samuel Adams. In contrast to Ellis, Pownall was one of the most outspoken advocates of a conciliatory approach to America. For a decade, in his writings on the Colonies and in his speeches to a rudely inattentive House of Commons, he hammered on the urgent need to listen sympathetically to Colonial grievances and demands. Not only were his gloomiest predictions soon realized, but his mind played with the possibilities of a radically different basis for Empire, one similar to that which developed in the nineteenth century and would be called Commonwealth. If any British politician saw the way to prevent an imperial revolution, it would seem to have been Thomas Pownall.

Considered together, then, Ellis and Pownall offer a new way of looking at an old subject—the limits of historical possibility from 1763 to 1775, and in particular the range of policies for America actually perceived by informed, influential, and typical men in London before war brought an end to negotiation. It is hardly surprising that the evening at Marseilles was an unpleasant memory to their host, for each of his "great dictators" must have loathed not merely the sight of the other but even more the reminder of what the other's kind of thinking had produced. Each surely knew the answer to the question, Who lost America? Ellis knew that it had been lost by ill-advised appeasement and the seditious promise of further concessions. Pownall knew that it had been lost by foolish rigidity and the tyrannical propensity to use force. The lucky record of their meeting invites us to consider how neatly these two men stood at the poles of possibility, and to look once again, closely, at the distance between those poles.

Henry Ellis does not require extensive analysis. His position was fairly clear, consistently maintained, and the one usually assumed by successive British governments in the period between the end of the Great War for Empire and the outbreak of the American Revolution. Compared to Pownall, he wrote and said little about America. He was concerned, but not obsessed, with the Colonies—a sense of proportion characteristic of all except a few of his contemporaries in the British political community. Equally characteristic was his belief in the military weakness of the colonists and the absurdity of their grievances. That Ellis helped William Knox, perhaps as anti-American as any British minister in history, to become Undersecretary of State for the Colonies in 1770 is also worth remembering.

Ellis may have been variously bored and irritated by American affairs, but his whole attitude toward them was more complex. He had been an exceptionally able and successful governor of Georgia at a time of crisis, and the political skill with which he got what he wanted from an elective Assembly argues for something better than mere dislike of obstreperous colonials.[7]

There may be a clue to his earliest thinking in his book on the Northwest Passage, published in 1748. His hostility toward some of the policies of the Hudson's Bay Company led him to contrast "public utility" with "private interest," to call for a truly "national" approach to the subject under consideration, and (after rehearsing the mercantilist arguments for further exploration of Hudson's Bay) to write of the need to "awaken us from that slothful and drowsy State into which, through Indolence and too great Fondness for Pleasure, we are visibly fallen." [8] Eight years later, as wartime governor of Georgia, he was most impressed by the terrible defenselessness of unsupported Colonies, and by the urgent need to find some way of adequately securing the Empire. And then for two years, from mid-1761 to mid-1763, he was in a position to make his views on imperial policy felt. As principal but unofficial adviser to the Earl of Egremont, Secretary of State for the Southern Department, his specialized talents, as well as Egremont's acute need for such assistance, gave Ellis more weight than anyone else in the transaction of American business.

The single most prominent theme running through his correspondence and memoranda for Egremont is the need for imperial security. Attack either Havana or St. Augustine, he argued in early 1762, despite all the objections being raised, in order to acquire permanent control of the Florida Strait, thus pulling the teeth of the Spanish threat in any future war. Placate and win over the Indians by concessions and the military enforcement of fair dealing, he argued on the eve of peace, because they are too strong and elusive to be held down by force, and they must never again become the tools of Britain's enemies. The peace treaty itself he defended as providing the territorial contiguity, the buffer areas, the strategic positions, and the clear and defensible boundaries which had long been needed to secure the North American continent. His opinions found their most authoritative expression in the Proclamation of 1763, which he was later accused of having written, and in the deployment and direction of the peacetime military establishment in the Colonies.[9]

Throughout his career as governor and adviser Ellis had grown ever more certain that the traditional makeshift arrangements for defending the Colonies were wasteful and dangerous. Vulnerable frontiers, mismanaged Indians, unregulated trade and settlement, and a hopelessly inefficient militia had cost an enormous amount of Anglo-American blood and money. The Great War in its early years had been all but lost, and it would be madness by any standard to return to the old system, so cheap and comfortable in peacetime, so disastrous in war. A little more military effort now, and a little more attention and expense in the postwar years, would literally secure the imperial future. One may disagree with Ellis, but it is difficult not to see and sympathize with the realism and rationality of his argument.

Though appointed Governor of Nova Scotia and to several minor but lucrative sinecures at the end of the war, indolence and illness soon drew Ellis out of Colonial administration and away from England itself. He could not stand London: "The Smoak, the foggs, and the cold humid air of that City, never agreed with me, even when I was a young man," he wrote to Knox.[10] But correspondence with Knox, whose star rose through the years of the developing imperial crisis, was an influential channel through which he occasionally expressed himself on American affairs, and his letters leave little doubt about his views. It may be safely inferred that Ellis had no sympathy with American complaints. Never, in his opinion, had British government so carefully and responsibly dealt with the vexed and bloody problem of Colonial security as had government during and after the Great War; how then could Americans expect to be taken seriously when they refused even a small share of the burden which the solution to the problem required? Letters from Knox, who vehemently felt the same way, surely reinforced this opinion, as did occasional contact with Hillsborough and his friend Lord Barrington, Secretary at War.[11] Such, after all, was the opinion of the King himself. A year before the battle of Lexington, Ellis stated his position to Knox with clarity and vigor:[12]

We know the real inability of the Americans to make any effectual resistance to any coercive method which might be employed to compel their obedience. They are conscious of it themselves, but may well give a

scope to their insolent licentiousness when they have so long been suffered to practice it with impunity. What is decided upon [i.e., to crack
down on Boston] appears judicious. . . .

Perhaps it is sufficient to note that Henry Ellis was entitled to his
opinion; it had its roots neither in ignorance nor in lack of feeling.
On the contrary, he seems to have known almost as much as anyone
about America, and his own writing indicates that from his youth he
had seen the Empire as something more noble and demanding than
mere commercial venture. His success as a Colonial governor was
surely related to his evident concern for the need to protect colonists
as well as Colonies. He neither offered nor supported any sweeping
program of imperial reform, but merely believed that certain unde-
niably acute problems demanded limited, reasonable changes. His
later position—on the "hard line"—grew naturally from earlier experience and belief.

The symmetry suggested by the meeting at Marseilles must at last
be sacrificed when we consider Thomas Pownall, for not only do his
ideas require extensive analysis, but his position is in one sense not
comparable to that of Ellis, because Pownall seems to stand for all
those decisions not taken, and thus for events which did not occur.
Ellis should be regarded as no more than a convenient foil, representing typicality and historical reality, against which to test Pownall's
perception of what might have happened.

Caroline Robbins, in her original and influential book on British
radical thought in the eighteenth century, has inducted Pownall into
the company of "Commonwealthmen." "His ideas," she tells us, bas-
ing her judgment largely on a study of his more general political and
historical writings, "show more originality than those of almost any
of his contemporaries." [13] Others, who have examined primarily his
ideas on Colonial policy, agree. His biographer thinks that "it is
probable that no one understood the total situation more completely" than Pownall, and Leonard Labaree, whose extensive investigation of imperial government gives his conclusions unusual
weight, calls Pownall's *Administration of the Colonies*

. . . the ablest and most discerning treatise on the major colonial problems written by an Englishman in the years of conflict before the Revo-

lution. Though speaking as Englishman, Pownall showed a broader understanding of the colonial point of view than almost any other British public man could display.[14]

John Adams, at 81, may be given the last word: "Pownall was a whig, a friend of liberty . . . the most constitutional Governor, in my opinion, who ever represented the crown in this province." [15]

This essay is concerned with his mind, and only incidentally with his personality, but it is impossible to ignore Pownall's enormous energy. From 1752, when he published his first book, *The Principles of Polity*, until his retirement from the House of Commons in 1780, he wrote extensively on archealogy, linguistics, the East India Company, Adam Smith's *Wealth of Nations*, American geography, as well as Colonial policy. One finds Governor Pownall, at a time when British fortunes in the Great War were ebbing, badgering Cadwallader Colden of New York about obscure points of Iroquois etymology. His engraved sketches of American scenes were sold in London. His lengthy proposals to the government for the conduct of military operations in America are remarkably similar to what Pitt actually decided to do in carrying on the war. In the House after 1767, he spoke often, at length, and then polished his speeches for publication by his friend John Almon. Though his views on Colonial policy went largely unheeded, he was able to draft and see enacted an important reform of the Corn Laws. After his retirement, the political tracts, archeological treatises, and other miscellaneous writings continued to appear. In 1782, he offered a prospectus for the scientific study of history; at the turn of the century he was drawing up plans for a revolution in Spanish America; and, shortly before his death, he produced a curious book—half psychology, half theology—called *Intellectual Physicks*, which aimed to treat the human mind scientifically, and to prove the immortality of the human soul. At times in his life such energy and omnicompetence had struck unfriendly observers as pomposity or naked ambition. But whatever drove him to these intellectual efforts, they are nonetheless impressive.[16]

The concern here is with his ideas on Colonial policy. These are most fully developed in *The Administration of the Colonies*, to which his speeches and few extant letters provide a gloss. Aside from its intrinsic interest, this book is peculiarly valuable because of its literally dynamic quality: there are five editions, distributed over the course of a decade of mounting crisis; Pownall tried to keep the book abreast of a changing situation. He wrote the first edition soon after the end of the Great War, before any tangible signs of crisis had appeared; the second when trouble over the Stamp Act was evident; the third after the repeal of that Act; the fourth as resistance to the Townshend Acts was growing; and the fifth just before the outbreak of the Revolutionary War. Through these successive editions it becomes possible to trace the relation between events in America and avowedly liberal ideas in Britain.

The opening words of the first, anonymous edition of *Administration of the Colonies* bear quotation, because they convey, however turgidly, the almost mystical sense of great change and new possibilities which was an important part of the postwar mood in England, and in all Europe. The prospect was thrilling, a little frightening, and more readily felt than easily defined:[17]

The several changes in interests and territories, which have taken place in the colonies of the European world on the Event of Peace, have created a general impression of some new state of things arising . . . some general idea of some revolution of events, beyond the ordinary course of things; some general apprehension, of something new arising in the world; of some new channel of business, applicable to new powers; —something that is to be guarded against on the one hand, or that is to be carried to advantage on the other.

. . . yet one does not find any where . . . any one precise comprehensive idea of this great crisis. . . .

I have seen and mark'd . . . this nascent crisis at the beginning of this war. . . .

Of course Pownall himself had worked out the "precise comprehensive idea of this great crisis": it was the need to formulate imperial policy measures that were systematically related to "the interest of all as a One Whole" (p. 2).

Pownall's belief in the "wholeness" of imperial society, by which he meant the natural harmony of interests created primarily by economic interdependence, had been set forth at length in his *Principles of Polity* (1752), a book cast in the form of a classical dialogue, and heavily dependent on the political thought of James Harrington. The distribution and exchange of property, the "scite" and circumstances of individual lives, were for Pownall real, natural, and the origin of society and government, whereas the administration of government was epiphenomenal, becoming more artificial and "impractical" as it diverged from basic social and economic reality. European history had now entered its third phase, leaving the ages when first naked violence, then religious superstition, had controlled the affairs of men. In this third phase,

. . . the spirit of *commerce* will become that predominant power, which will form the general policy, and rule the powers of Europe: and hence a grand commercial interest, under the present scite and circumstances of the world, will be formed and arise. The rise and forming of the commercial dominion is what precisely constitutes the present crisis [p. 4].

Within the Empire, commerce was immutably real, and British government could do no better than perceive and conform to commercial reality. "It is not men that form great events, but the crisis of events duly possessed and actuated that form great men" (p. 5).

The outcome of the Great War had clearly put the chance to lead in the hands of Englishmen. They must, however, cease regarding their kingdom as a mere island with many provinces, but see it "as a grand marine dominion, consisting of our possessions in the Atlantic and America." This idea, repeated throughout the book, has since been treated as if it prescribed a decentralised Empire, and even accepted a shift of power westward across the Atlantic. In 1764, at least, the idea was nothing of the sort: "Forming all these Atlantic and American possessions into a one dominion, of which Great Britain should be the commercial center, to which it should be the spring of power, is the *precise* duty of government at this crisis" (p. 6).

Mercantilist principles were, to Pownall, not artificial, but basic. All profits of Colonial agriculture and manufacturing ought to center in the mother country, and the Colonies were her "sole and special" customers. Some of the present navigation laws in fact misapplied these principles, and therefore ought to be amended. But there was nothing wrong, illiberal, or unrealistic in the principles themselves: they were "mutually coeval and coincident with the interests, rights and welfare of the colonies." Interests, properly understood, naturally harmonized (p. 25; also pp. 7–9, 22–24).

The most important reason for the occasional perversion of mercantilist principles (as in the Molasses Act of 1733), as well as the main source of trouble in colonial administration generally, was faulty organization. The first step in meeting the present crisis, then, was to create a single center of Colonial government in England, an agency with the powers of a Secretary of State, the expertise of the Board of Trade, and all the various strings of patronage and direction (which currently led to the Treasury, Admiralty, War Office, Board of Ordnance, and so on) firmly in its grasp. This was an old idea, finally implemented half-heartedly and with disappointing results in 1768; the novelty lay in the emphasis, indeed precedence, given to it by Pownall. Nothing was wanted more in Colonial administration, he said, than greater efficiency (pp. 10, 15, and especially 21).

The harmony of interests, the primacy of commerce, the need for efficiency—these were the premises from which Pownall moved to a discussion of specific administrative problems. There were current, he admitted, two views of the imperial constitution: the one prevalent in America emphasized the equal rights of all Englishmen, whereas the other, held widely in Britain, stressed the necessary subordination of Colonies. Pownall saw these as conflicting claims, but not as contradictory beliefs. The conflict could, and should, be resolved, not by a tarnished royal prerogative, but by Parliament. By the enactment of "a general bill of rights, and establishment of government on a great plan of union" for the Colonies, Parliament could "regulate and define their privileges; . . . establish and order their administration; and . . . direct the channels of their commerce." Until constitutional uncertainty was removed once and for all, "there can be no government, properly so called, but merely the predominance of one faction or the other, acting under the mask of government" (pp. 28–32).[18] The cardinal point was to clarify and strengthen the tie between each Colony and Whitehall, but to do nothing that would unify the colonies among themselves. Using one of the Newtonian metaphors he found so compelling, Pownall saw danger in united Colonies acquiring an "equal force, which might recoil back on the first mover," Great Britain. But the danger itself was remote, because the Colonies were so inherently disunited that "nothing but a tampering activity of wrongheaded inexperience misled to be meddling, can ever do mischief here" (p. 34). This strong language may have been directed at his successor in Massachusetts, Francis Bernard, who was just then urging on government a thorough alteration of the whole imperial system. Only in Rhode Island, where flagrant abuses had occurred, might an exception be made, Pownall believed, to the rule of not carrying out drastic constitutional changes.

He was certain that the acute problems could be solved within the existing legal framework of Empire. The Colonial claim to possess "the right of representation and legislation" was valid and ought to be respected; only some of its abuses and encroachments should be prevented. This would mean, above all, guaranteeing to the executive and judicial officers of provincial government an income free from legislative manipulation. Perhaps it would also be well to separate the provincial council into quite distinct bodies for the performance of executive and judicial functions, respectively, and to create several regional supreme courts of appeal which would further the cause of justice and produce greater legal "conformity." The legal and judicial systems were critical, for Pownall emphasized "how little the crown, or the rights of government, when opposed to the spirit of democracy, or even to the passion of the populace," could expect from colonial courts in the way of protection (pp. 56–57; also 61 and 63). These minor improvements would create an administration "that shall firmly, uniformly, and constitutionally govern the colonies" (p. 65).

The payment by the Crown of its Colonial appointees raised the question of revenue. On this important question, Pownall's words deserve a most careful reading. Because the government already had

the colony revenue under its consideration, I must, for the present, think myself precluded from entering into a discussion of those points. . . . However, I will just venture to suggest,—that the best and surest funds of such revenue, will be, first, the customs arising from the trade *regulated as hereafter to be mentioned*: secondly a stamp-duty . . . [p. 66].

which he thought would raise a third more per capita than it did in England; and, finally, "the quit rents, if duly laid and collected" (p. 66).[19] To be sure, he expressed some doubts about taxation, and these also require scrutiny. With respect to any form of tax on real property, he said it is a point that ought very deliberately and dispassionately to be weighed, how far even the supreme government of the mother country can, consistently with general liberty, proceed in laying taxes on its colonists, where the consent of the people cannot be, in any constitutional way taken [p. 67].

A different doubt, however, would arise in connection with customs, excise, and stamp duties; and that doubt was

how far these colonies, who, for the necessities of government, and the emergencies of service, have already, by their proper powers, laid these duties on the people, and granted the revenue arising therefrom to the crown, by acts which have received the consent of the crown [p. 67].

In short, a land tax would raise the question of right, whereas customs, excise, and stamp duties would raise only a question of equity: taxes on real property might be unconstitutional, but taxes on legal and commercial transactions, in which there was inherent an element of consent, must only be kept commensurate with the legitimate needs of government. Subsequent editions make clear that this distinction is neither a slip of Pownall's pen nor a perverse interpretation of his words.

The rest of the first edition is taken up with discussion of the new military establishment, the Colonial money supply, and the reform of the navigation system. Pownall seems to take a liberal position: he is critical of the military, and favorable to paper currency and to relaxation of trade restrictions. But there are limits to his liberalism: his brief attack on the military is confined to the office of Commander in Chief, which encroaches on the power of royal governors and threatens to create that ever-dangerous union of the Colonies. He supports paper currency, but not as legal tender. He favors extension of trade, but mainly through resident British "factories" and with precautions against foreign re-export of British goods. In Pownall's view, the desideratum of imperial economic policy is to discourage the growth of manufacturing in the Colonies (pp. 129–131).

If prolixity, and reiterated calls to greatness and expressions of good will, are not allowed to obscure the author's more specific ideas, then the first edition of *The Administration of the Colonies* is seen to adumbrate much of what the government actually did or tried to do during the decade after the Great War. No sweeping changes are proposed, only what might be called "economical reform." Raise a modest revenue, being careful to be both legal and equitable in doing it. Use the money raised primarily to give Crown officials the independence no reasonable man would deny them, and what is left will help to pay for the new military establishment, essential to Colonial security. Do not suppress paper money altogether, but curb the abuse of it passing as legal tender. Rationalize the laws of trade, putting national interest above vested interests. Centralize administration, but only in London. Perhaps reorganize provincial Councils, but certainly ensure that Colonial courts do justice. All of this to be effected by Act of Parliament.

The Sugar Act, the Currency Act, the Stamp Act, the Townshend Acts, the extension of vice-admiralty jurisdiction, the creation of West Indian free ports and a Secretary of State for the Colonies, even threats to the Rhode Island charter, the alteration of the Massachusetts Council, and adamant opposition to intercolonial congresses —every one was at least suggested, none was clearly warned against, by Thomas Pownall in 1764. Of course this is not a fair indictment; his analysis is often perceptive and always knowledgable though it is seldom lucid. His proposals for some form of regulated paper currency, greater freedom of trade, and perhaps even a colonial bill of rights, if enacted in time and with an informed benevolence, would have reduced American discontent to a significant degree. Nevertheless, the strongest impression created by the book is of an innocent, well-meaning articulation of the very attitudes that would soon lead to serious trouble; of a nearly total failure to anticipate that trouble; and of a dearth of other ideas sufficiently concrete to guide policy makers.

Judged in the harsh light of the coming Revolution, this first edition can be made to seem ridiculous, but it must also be regarded in another way. Pownall began his book with a passion for the imperial future that only his leaden prose had kept from soaring; yet he consistently rejected any program of reform that would have matched the grandeur of his emotion. Instead, he had tried to analyze the existing situation, problem by problem, and he had produced a set of truly modest solutions. In each case, his appeal had been to fact and reason; every argument had been anchored to the assumption that more explicit and rational practices and institutions would lead, not only to greater efficiency, but to a heightened awareness of mutual self-interest, the basic premise of all politics.

The second edition, which appeared as rioters against the Stamp Act roamed the streets of Boston and New York, reinforces the impression. Although he wrote to William Pitt for permission to publish a wartime document in an appendix, he dedicated the new version of the book to George Grenville.[20] This may seem a strange thing for a liberal on Colonial policy to do, unless he did not yet perceive the polarization of opinion which is the subject of this essay. Grenville, according to the dedication, would "lead the people of the colonies, by the spirit of laws and equity to that true and constitutional obedience, which is their real liberty." Pownall's only expressed fear was that "false and mistaken patriots" in the Colonies might create "undue impressions to their disadvantage."

There are many minor revisions of the text, which indicate that he had carefully reconsidered every sentence, and some of these little changes are interesting. The early section asserting the interdependence of the parts of the Empire is expanded by factual evidence, as if to refute any hint that economic tension or competition was inherent or natural (1765 ed., pp. 5–9; cf. 1764 ed., pp. 4–6). American and British interests, however, though they remain "coincident," have ceased in the second edition to be "coeval" (p. 27). Friction between royal officials in the Colonies emerges as a new argument for a centralized administration in London, but the need to keep the colonies themselves disunited is now italicized (pp. 21–22, 36). The suggestion of 1764 that administrative reform would itself create the conditions for a new American spirit of obedience and cooperation disappears in 1765 (p. 87; cf. 1764 ed., p. 65).

Major additions concern taxation, Indian affairs, and military policy. On taxation, Pownall argues from logic, and his tone is huffy:

I do suppose it will not bear a doubt, but that the supreme legislature of Great Britain is the true and perfect representative of Great Britain, and all its dependencies: and as it is not in the power of the House of Lords or Commons to exempt any community from the jurisdiction of the King, as supreme magistrate, so that it is not, nor ever was, or could be in the power of the crown, to exempt any persons or communities within the dominions of Great Britain, from being subject and liable to be taxed by parliament [p. 89].

He cannot seriously entertain the idea that the King in Parliament is anything less than sovereign. There are, however, different "objects" of taxation; some are properly British, others provincial. Polls and estates are "the special internal private property" of the colonies, and ought to be left to them. "Duties," on the other hand, may be freely levied by Parliament so long as the principle of equalization of real obligations within the Empire is maintained. On this last point, he adds, the stamp duties may have been set too high through faulty information (pp. 90–96). But by conservative calculation, which he makes for the reader, a revenue of about £ 100,000 can easily be raised in America (pp. 97ff.).

A new, long section on Indian affairs is especially interesting because it clarifies part of the conclusion to the first edition (pp. 154–181; cf. 1764 ed., pp. 127–131). In the latter, he had said that the danger of Colonial manufacturing would not become serious as long as Colonial settlement was not restricted, whether by policy or by Indian pressure. Without the second edition, this passage might be interpreted as oblique criticism of the Proclamation of 1763, of the so-called Plan of 1764 to regulate trade with the Indians, and of the kind of thinking, which we have previously ascribed to Henry Ellis, that lay behind both measures. On the contrary: given space in which to deploy his ideas on this question, Pownall expresses sympathy for the Indians and hostility toward the traders and frontiersmen who goad them to violence; he recognizes the practical impossibility of controlling the Indians by force or even of building effective military defenses against them; security lies, he believes, only in dealing fairly with them on matters of land and trade—"honesty" toward the Indians is "the best policy." He says nothing explicit about westward migration, but implies that it—like the Indian trade—will require some kind of imperial regulation. In short, this section might have been written by Henry Ellis himself.

His attack on the office of Commander in Chief is now longer and more vehement (pp. 54–70). The source of his animus was undoubtedly his own humiliating controversy as governor of Massachusetts with Lord Loudoun, the Commander in Chief 1756–1757, but his arguments against having a supreme military commander with no civil counterpart are not frivolous or unreasonable, and they would later provide the text for more than one speech in the House of Commons. He does, however, recognize that a regular military establishment as such is "in the same manner and degree necessary in North America as in Britain or Ireland"; he simply wants to put that establishment under the control of the royal governors, who by their commissions are "Captains-General" of their provinces. In fact, a decade earlier he had argued for a more efficient and presumably more centralized system of Colonial military administration (p. 69).[21] The appendix added to the 1765 edition deals exclusively with defense policy and its wartime background, which suggests the importance Pownall attached to that aspect of American policy in general. His long attack on the Commander in Chief concludes with the hope that the office will be weakened by the newly-instituted brigadier-generals, regional commanders in Canada and Florida first proposed, it seems, in 1763 by Henry Ellis.[22]

The third edition, which appeared in 1766 after the repeal of the Stamp Act, was struck from the old plates, but contains a new appendix: "Considerations on the Points Lately Brought Into Question as to The Parliament's Right of Taxing the Colonies and of the Measures necessary to be taken at this Crisis." There is simply no question about the sovereignty of Parliament, Pownall asserts, nor is there any way to distinguish between taxation and legislation (Appendix pp. 3–5). But he now shows a grudging willingness to move from legal and logical arguments toward one that is historical:

I do not believe that there ever was an instance when this principle of the supreme Legislature's power to raise monies by taxes throughout the realm of Great Britain, was ever called in question. . . .

The whole controversy, as he sees it, has been stirred up by ignorant demagogues in America; nevertheless, expediency and history require that the claim of right should not be forced by the British government, but rather taught. But it is also obvious that the present situation, if permitted to drift, will eventually produce astronomical change:

The center of power, instead of remaining fixed as it is now in Great Britain, will, as the magnitude of power and interest of the Colonies encreases, be drawn out from the island, by the same laws of nature analogous in all cases, by which the centre of gravity of the solar system, now near the surface of the sun, would, by an encrease of the quantity of matter in the planets, be drawn out beyond that surface.

What, then, is to be done?

Form one general system of dominion by an union of Great Britain and her Colonies, fixing, while it may be so fixed, the common center in Great Britain [Appendix, pp. 17–18].

The way to fix the center in Britain is to grant the Colonies representation in Parliament, which measure is to be prepared by the dispatch to America of some *"very considerable person"* with full powers and an advisory council. Pownall refuses to elaborate on this proposal because, he says, even at that moment the government is considering it (Appendix, p. 33; also pp. 18, 48ff.).[23]

At this point, we may usefully consider the political atmosphere within which Pownall was thinking, writing, and publishing. Except for James Otis and Benjamin Franklin, the most important American spokesmen had already made it clear that Colonial representation in Parliament was not an acceptable solution to the current crisis. Pownall hints as much in the 1766 edition, but somewhat lamely opines that the measure would still be effective if British government can act with great prudence, good temper, and "spirited council." As for his other proposals, the Rockingham government, allegedly receptive to all liberal ideas, was indeed considering them. William Dowdeswell, whose judgment was highly respected within and outside his party, discussed Pownall's plan in a letter to Rockingham. His tone was one of barely concealed contempt for the idea of sending the Duke of York (Pownall's *"very considerable person"*) as a viceroy to patch things up in America, and Rockingham's endorsement on the letter dismissed the idea of parliamentary representation as "Shirley's scheme." [24] Obviously, the political atmosphere was not congenial, and it is hardly surprising that these proposals did not flourish.

Pownall had bought himself a seat in the House of Commons by the time the fourth edition appeared in 1768. The book is now more than twice the length of the first edition, and its ideas have become far more qualified and convoluted. From the original sense of restrained excitement and programmatic zeal, the mood has shifted in four years to an unhappy mixture of alarm and resignation, with an occasional note of utter despair. Some bits of the newly composed preface are pathetic. He tries to weasel out of having dedicated the second and third editions to Grenville. He says he wants to end his days in America as an humble citizen (in one of his private letters he says that only his wife is holding him back).[25] Perhaps saddest of all is to hear him say: "It is a great pity that questions of this nature were ever raised. . . ."

But it is also in this edition that he is at his best, and the book as a whole is a richer, if less confident, analysis of Empire and its problems than earlier versions. The treatment of the nature of parliamentary power and colonial liberty becomes seriously and extensively historical; no longer satisfied with the easy answers he had been giving himself, Pownall obviously had done some research. Through a hundred pages of new material worked into the text, he wrestles with simple but baffling questions: Can a man separate himself from his political community? Can sovereign power be reconciled with restrictions on that power? After canvassing the law of emigration and the history of Colonial charters, he finds an ingenious answer to the first question:

. . . how much so ever the colonies, at their first migration, may be supposed to have been, or were in fact, without the Realm, and separated from it: Yet, from the very nature of that union of the community, by which all civil society must subsist, they could not have migrated, and been absolved of their communion and connection to the Realm, without leave or license; they had such leave [as his study of the charters has previously demonstrated], according to the then forms of the constitution, and the terms [on which permission to emigrate was granted] were, that the society, community, or government which they should form, should neither act nor become anything repugnant or contrary to the laws of the Mother Country [pp. 119–120].

"Here then," as he moves toward an answer to the second question, "is an express subordination to a certain degree." But he falters, because his research had taught him that the seventeenth-century constitution could not have incorporated colonies of the kind that had actually developed, and his mind is still caught on the hook of sovereignty:

There is no doubt, but that in the nature, reason, justice and necessity of the thing, there must be somewhere, *within* the body politic of every government, an absolute power [p. 130].

But in the end it is necessary to choose. Either America is within the Realm, or it is outside. As matters now stand, Pownall admits, he cannot be certain of the correct answer, in which case one must act as if one or the other were correct. If America is outside the Realm, then the relationship is contractual—an alliance; and only request and requisition by the Crown to an American union are possible. History, however, points to the long-term consequences of such an arrangement:

If we keep the basis of this realm confined to this island, while we extend the superstructure, by extending our dominions: we shall invert the pyramid (as Sir William Temple expresses it) and must in time subvert government itself. If we chuse to follow the example of the Romans, we must expect to follow their fate [pp. 162–163].

This would be an "artificial" system, and he clearly prefers the alternative: to consider the Americans as within the Realm. In that case, there is only one course: to grant them—force upon them if necessary—Parliamentary representation. "There is no other practicable or rational measure" (p. 152).

The problem, which Pownall now sees as a problem, is that representative government, "the very spirit of this country," trades recognition of equal rights for the acceptance of equal obligations. The precedents argue well enough that the extension of representation is right and can work—the annexation of the counties palatine of Chester and Durham, and the union with Scotland. But Americans must accept their obligations; the British debt is theirs as well, for the last two wars had been fought "solely in defence, and for the protection of the trade and actual existence of the colonies" (p. 167). Yet Pownall as much as admits that he knows they will not accept representation, even if government has the nerve to offer it. "One has only to hope, that the ruin is not inevitable, and that heaven may avert it" (p. 177).

Otherwise most of the original ideas are still there, tucked somewhere into the book. A few are trimmed or refurbished. The plan to pay the salaries of royal officials, which was just then being tried under the Townshend Acts, is dropped for reasons not made explicit, and a pension fund for ex-governors is suggested to perform roughly the same function. Pownall gives up his objections to legal tender currency, and now presents a detailed plan to create a colonial money supply by Act of Parliament. The proposal to send a viceroy remains, but he knows that it will not be adopted. At this and a few other points in the fourth edition, one begins to feel that Pownall is writing for the record.

Not until war was only months away, late in 1774, did the fifth edition appear. Pownall was able to retain most of his original analysis of Colonial problems by the device of changing verb tenses from present to past, but he finally felt compelled to recast the introductory paragraphs. The original sense of mystery, ambivalence, and high challenge disappears; in their place is put a flat assertion that the Great War created a new pattern of interests and a consequent shift of power, and that the government should have made the corresponding adjustments in policy. Pownall's feeling, more than his meaning, has changed in the course of a decade. Aside from these opening words, perhaps the most interesting revision is a note in which the author explains why his proposal for a unified Colonial department, when adopted in 1768, had not produced the results he had predicted:

It was sown in jealousy; so, in proportion as it arose in power, the resistance of cabinet faction obstructed it at home, and nursed up opposition to it abroad. To this an impracticable line of conduct, mistaken for system, and an unhappy tone of government misunderstood for firmness, gave ample scope; so that the last state of this unfortunate department became worse than the first [p. 16n.].

The main cause of failure is obviously "faction."

Appearing first in 1764, growing sharply in 1768, echoing through his parliamentary speeches and private letters to friends in Massachusetts, and rising to become a major theme in 1774, is this concern with the damage done by party politics and the spirit of faction. In 1768, he had gloomily predicted that

the colonies will for some time *belong to some faction* here, and be the tool of it, until they become powerful enough to hold a party for themselves, and make *some faction their tool*. The latter stage of this miserable connection will be one continued struggle . . . until some event shall happen that will totally break all union between us [1768 ed., pp. 29–30].

He had hoped for a reform of Empire in 1763, "but from the moment that American affairs became an object of politics, they became the tools and instruments of faction" (p. 45). In speeches and lectures afterward, he had proudly advertised his own independence of any party or group, and had repeatedly advised his friends in America to keep themselves and their problems free of British factions, by which of course he meant the Opposition splinters led by Chatham and Rockingham. In 1774 he still believed that the "*consensus obedientium* which is alone the bond and tie of practical and efficient government" was, by definition, incompatible with the existence of political parties, but he also had reluctantly come to modify his view that political conflict is wholly unnatural: "Nature knows no such distraction and separation of interests as the practices and powers of men have introduced"; yet "the very attraction which naturally draws them together—creates in their spirit, when they are thus drawn together, a principle of repulsion, that is too hard for nature, truth, and right" (1774 ed., II, pp. 8–9). Conflict may be ineradicable, but Pownall could not imagine that it was anything but a destructive force, a perversion of reason.

The illegitimacy of party politics in the eighteenth century is familiar, and it is not surprising to find an author resorting to this contemporary cliché as an explanation for political failure. In this particular context, however, one expects to find the argument being used exclusively by "conservatives"—the Henry Ellises, friends of the King and supporters of government—in order to blunt and confuse the Opposition "party" attack. Edmund Burke read the fourth edition of *The Administration of the Colonies*, or at least part of it, and Pownall's strictures on "party" drove Burke to make furious marginal comments, and perhaps even to adopt a hostile attitude toward the book as a whole. Burke's *Thoughts on the Causes of the Present Discontents* (1770), especially the latter pages where he makes his celebrated defense of political parties, when read in conjunction with some of Pownall's speeches and the 1768 edition of the book, seems almost a dialogue with Thomas Pownall. We will return to Burke's position with respect to Pownall later; here it is sufficient to note that Pownall's attack on "party" comes, like Thomas Jefferson's, not from the putative Right, but from the Left. Moreover, the attack is not merely the use of a handy weapon, for Pownall's earliest writing, *The Principles of Polity*, is largely taken up with the rejection of conflict as an acceptable premise for political theory. J. G. A. Pocock has recently written that the work of James Harrington, twisted into several shapes by his interpreters, did much to create the "mood" of eighteenth-century British politics; nowhere can Harrington's influence, with its attendant confusion of "Right" with "Left," be seen more plainly than in the views of Thomas Pownall on "party." [26] And, finally, it may be noted that Pownall rather than Burke reflected the feelings of almost all their contemporaries on this matter.

On the current American crisis Pownall added another long essay, as he had in 1766, "Wherein a Line of Government Between the Supreme Jurisdiction of Great Britain, and the Rights of the Colonies is Drawn, and a Plan of Pacification is Suggested." He had no illusions about the likelihood of its acceptance, but he hoped that his "line" would provide a basis for negotiations wherever they once again became feasible. Although he still thinks that the best solution for all concerned is Colonial representation in Parliament, he at last admits that this is not possible "since America as well as Great Britain will have it so." He accepts the possibility of an American Union "incapable of being admitted to a perfect participation in the legislature, the soul of the British dominions," but instead *"subject to the King as to their own head"* (II, pp. 11-12; italics mine). Here, it seems, is recognition of James Wilson's argument for colonial autonomy within a royal empire. But is it?

Pownall no sooner makes the concession than he begins to analyze, qualify, and finally come near to withdrawing it. Using the very words of James Harrington, he distinguishes between "internal" or "national" government and "external" or "provincial" government.[27] Internal government relies on free will and is essentially active; external government relies on coercion and is essentially passive. A mixed form of government, appropriate to the present case, is "Colonial Government." It is "national" when operating on its own body, but the *supreme sovereign power*" may act as "provincial government" whenever any British subject or his property moves outside the jurisdiction of the "national" government of his Colony. In particular, any attempt to resist or reject Colonial government, or to redefine its composition, will have to be met with force, which is the essential characteristic of provincial, or external, government. This, says Pownall, is all that was meant by the Declaratory Act of 1766. At four different places in the essay he argues that the analogy of an omnipotent God giving man complete freedom of will is applicable —indeed is the solution—to the problem of Empire. The supreme power of Parliament, by which he means the King-in-Parliament, may be used only when the very existence of Empire is threatened.

Precisely what Pownall had in mind becomes steadily less clear in the course of the essay. But when he implies, after eighty pages, that the impossibility of an imperial relationship on the model of the union with Scotland means that the relationship must be modeled on the existing connection with Ireland, the reader may feel that he has drifted a long way from any vision of a modern Commonwealth. This feeling is strengthened by a "Postscript," in which the author rejects, one after another, the demands made by the Pennsylvania provincial congress that Britain give up her powers to punish treason in the colonies, to interfere with internal legislation, to lay taxes, and to regulate trade except by consent, as well as demands for repeal of the Quartering Act and other laws supporting the regular military establishment, for the abolition of vice-admiralty courts, and for the relinquishment of any right to alter Colonial charters and constitutions. "The Colonies," Pownall had written truly in the introduction of his latest essay, "have so often shifted and advanced the ground of their claim of rights, that the best reasoning of their truest friends, even the most active zeal of their warmest partisans, have fallen short in the course" (1774 ed., II, p. 3). Pownall is in fact prepared to concede almost nothing, and his movement into Lord North's camp in the election of 1774 bears out this interpretation of the fifth edition of his book.[28]

How, it may be reasonably asked, could Thomas Pownall ever have been seen as a liberal on the American question, as "a true friend of the colonies"? The answer is simple: because he thought he was, and spoke and wrote in a way that persuaded himself and others that he was. Through ten years of mounting controversy, he had increasingly defended specific American actions and attacked specific British policies. His demolition of the government's case against Boston in 1769 was perhaps the high point of his Parliamentary career, and his explanation of the Boston Massacre as the inevitable result of irresponsible military power may have reduced the desire of the government to take any new, vigorous steps against Massachusetts in 1770. His speeches, like the later editions of the book, were suffused with sympathy for the Americans, and with dismay at those who held power in London. It is only when his ideas are disentangled from his feelings that Pownall's real position becomes evident.

To return briefly to Edmund Burke permits us to reconsider our premise in studying Pownall. It may be that the premise is wrong, that Pownall did not stand at the Left end of the political spectrum on the American question, and that he was somewhere to the Right of those other critics of the government, Burke and Shelburne. The results of the scholarly attention given to Shelburne's conduct in office would make it very difficult to sustain any such claim for him and for the Chathamites as a whole,[29] but what about Burke? Fortunately, Burke's marginalia in the 1768 edition of *Administration of the Colonies* make it possible to locate him, and presumably the whole Rockingham group, with some exactness on our spectrum.

When Pownall proposes a general inquiry into American grievances on the spot, Burke says it can be done as well in England, and besides "it is against the sound principles of government, to go about on officious and voluntary collection of grievances" (pp. 32–33)[33]. When Pownall contrasts the unnecessary restrictions of the navigation system as it actually existed with the two basic principles of a commercial empire, and argues for investigation and liberalization, Burke simply—and ignorantly—notes "that all our plantation Laws have these two points certainly in their view, and that nothing is less necessary than *general* information on that subject" (p. 40). When Pownall refers to the dependence of American merchants on British credit, Burke dissents, again through ignorance: "Not the case of the Northern colonies, if I am rightly informed" (p. 41). And when Pownall tries to find some historical basis for the American claim to inalienable legislative rights, Burke will not even listen:

These charters differed in no respect from those then and since given to all Trading corporations. They were forfeitable in Westminster Hall by process in *Quo Warranto*—might by the same process be carried into the House of Lords in *Error*, were ever subject to the Privy Council as a *Tribunal*—and it seems extremely absurd, that the Colonies should be *subject* to the *Judicial*, but free from the *Legislative* authority of their mother Country [pp. 52–53].

In the end there may have been little substantive difference between the two men on the American question, but in the spectrum of attitudes Burke stands plainly to Pownall's Right.[31]

Finally we may come back to Caroline Robbins to test our premise in another way, by asking if her own praise of Pownall's originality and radicalism is mistaken. Could she have been deceived by rhetorical flourishes and political opportunism? The answer is certainly No. When his ideas on American policy are set in the context of his political career and his thought in general, two things stand out: one is that his ideas on the American question fit with everything else known about him, and the other is that he consistently and—as far as it is possible to judge—disinterestedly took what must be recognized for mid-eighteenth-century Britain as a fairly radical political position. His support of the government in 1774 ought not to count too heavily against him, because it followed from premises stated much earlier, and he was one of the first in the House of Commons to say flatly during the Revolutionary War that Britain had better recognize American independence. His ideas on reform of the navigation system were liberal, comprehensive, and—for his time—extreme. He publicly praised *Wealth of Nations* when it appeared, but politely argued in *A Letter to Adam Smith* (1776) that the farmer and wage-earner must be protected even though the cause of their suffering is the salutary and ineluctable operation of the "unseen hand." Otherwise, he said, developing a critique of classical economic theory that would be repeated and elaborated by the Left through the next two centuries, "we shall, in the triumph of our general prosperity, be the constant oppressors of those who have the best title to share in this prosperity" (pp. 6–7). His support for revolution in the Spanish Empire has already been mentioned, and his sympathy for the United States after the Revolutionary War could hardly have been stronger. His refusal, following Harrington, to find the guarantee of political liberty in a balanced mixture of monarchy, aristocracy, and commons, freed his mind from the kind of conservative paranoia that pervaded both British and American politics at the time, and his emphasis instead on *communitas* as the proper basis of all just and effective government is reminiscent of Rousseau (who, as far as I have been able to tell, was not directly influential in Pownall's political thought). A second look, then, shows that his credentials as a "Commonwealthman" are in good order; by any test, he stood near the Left edge of the British political community.

The main argument of this essay must now be clear: if Thomas Pownall and Henry Ellis are taken to represent the limits of what was conceivable in American policy between 1763 and 1775, then the range of historical possibilities was very narrow indeed. The argument is not new, but its opposite is more frequently encountered. A great deal of historical writing on the American Revolution contains at least the suggestion that there were available alternatives for British policy, and that what actually happened may be seen as a sad story of accident, ignorance, misunderstanding, and perhaps a little malevolence.[32] George Grenville is narrow-minded, Charles Townshend is brilliant but silly, Hillsborough is stupid and tyrannical, Chatham is tragically ill, Dartmouth is unusually weak, and the King himself is very stubborn and not very bright. But if politics had not been in quite such a chaotic phase, perhaps the Old Whigs or an effective Chathamite ministry would have held power, been able to shape and sustain a truly liberal policy toward the Colonies, and avoided the disruption of the Empire. So the story seems to run.

Closely related to this view of might-have-been is the common assertion that the need for imperial reform in 1763 was real and urgent, but that British leaders—Grenville especially—had no master plans which threatened American liberty; on the contrary, they were merely practical politicians, trying to solve immediate problems with limited measures.[33] A little more knowledge, a little more tact, a little more political sensitivity, and it all might have turned out differently. As this bogey of a master plan for Empire is exorcised, historical possibility seems to widen out before us.

Though historians tend to dismiss speculation about what might have happened as a futile exercise, their understanding of any event is bound to be affected by what they think *could*, and could *not*, have happened. Today the focus of attention in the historiography of the Revolution seems to have shifted away from the British side toward a preoccupation with events in America. But before we leave what one historian has recently called "the dustbowl of English history," we ought to ask the unfashionable question—what could have happened in London?—if only to get some better measure of the American side of the dispute. Of course such a question can only be answered in terms of probabilities; nothing can be proved, or even demonstrated beyond reasonable doubt. And certainly the study of one or two men cannot be conclusive for a question involving the politics of a whole society. Yet if one accepts the proposition that men seldom do what they cannot imagine doing, then the mind of Thomas Pownall provides a prima facie case that British colonial policy in this period was neither fortuitous nor susceptible of change.

On this issue, as on so many others in early American history, Edmund Morgan has expressed some stimulating and influential thoughts. In his seminal essay on the historiography of the American Revolution, he finds a basic incompatibility between the so-called imperial and Namierist contributions to our understanding, and he therefore suggests the inadequacy, perhaps the unreliability, of both.[34] The imperial school, associated most readily with the name and work of Charles M. Andrews, seems to sympathize with those men who administered the Empire, to appreciate their difficulties, and especially to find in their efforts a body of ideas and principles that command respect. Andrews agreed with George Louis Beer that there was a basic shift by 1763 in their concept of the colonial relationship—from "mercantile" to "imperial"—and that this shift was a major factor in the coming of the American Revolution. The Namier school, on the other hand, appears to have taken "mind out of politics," to have reduced the historical importance of consciously held ideas and principles to nearly zero, at least for the explanation of British politics in the age of the American Revolution. Consequently, British politicians appear as petty, selfish, narrow men, with even the most able and serious of them absorbed in the complexities of a purely domestic game. Professor Morgan has asked how both schools —or either—can possibly be right.

This essay is meant to suggest an answer. Everything of interest about Thomas Pownall and Henry Ellis can not only be reconciled with the insights of Andrews and Namier, but a comparison of these two eighteenth-century lives sharpens our perception of what these two twentieth-century historians were trying to tell us about the British background of the American Revolution.

Pownall and Ellis, especially when considered together, offer support for the view that basic assumptions about empire, and the imperatives which followed from them, were undergoing a major change which was at first retarded, then accelerated and sustained by the Great War, 1755–1763.[35] The center of change appears to have been the obscure Earl of Halifax, though the roots of change can be traced back for decades; but the main point is its growing importance after mid-century. Whatever the explanation for it may be, the fact is that the Colonies were coming to be regarded, even by the less informed and interested British politician, in a new way and with a new concern by about 1750. Perhaps Charles Townshend was brilliant and silly, but even his behavior is best explained in terms of an attitude—more highly developed and strongly held than one would expect in such a man—toward the Empire.[36] This new attitude can hardly be characterized as either "liberal" or "conservative"; it may more aptly be described as "enlightened." It was, or purported to be, factually better informed than previously held opinions about the Colonies, and it took a broader view of relationships, a deeper view of value, and a longer view of time. Above all, it sought rationality.

"Rationality" is of course a treacherous abstraction, and a reader may hardly be blamed if he has not so far found either Thomas Pownall or Henry Ellis, or their British contemporaries, to be notably rational in attitude and argument. But surely Pownall and Ellis, like Shelburne and Burke, like Grenville and George III, saw themselves separated from earlier generations by their own readiness to subject government, in its political as well as its administrative dimensions, to rational analysis. As never before, chronic problems of government were to be first clearly formulated and then vigorously solved. Men might disagree about particular solutions, as differences of intellect and information might cause them to analyze particular problems in various ways, but the problem-solving approach to government was becoming universal, and it was new. There had always been those who sought to change Colonial policies and procedures, and they had always tried to make reasonable arguments for change; but by 1763 there was something altogether different: a general dread of arrangements and practices that defied logical explanation, and a growing desire to rationalize them. Both the dread and the desire were themselves beyond reason: one simply knew that mysteries were dangerous, and that future happiness in some way required the elimination, or at least clarification, of the many mysteries of the colonial relationship.

Pownall, like Ellis, was moved to attack absurd and slovenly aspects of imperial government wherever he encountered them, and to call for policies that could pass the test of reason. They might stress different aspects of reform: to Ellis a more rational defense policy was the basic need, while Pownall argued that only a more rational administrative organization at the top could produce more rational policy. But they were very alike in believing that the time had come to rid the Empire of contradiction. When Ellis and Pownall attacked the Hudson's Bay and East India Companies, respectively, they both subordinated private interest, and even property rights, to public interest and the common weal. When they examined the related problems of American security and Indian affairs, they both saw the long-run public interest, not to mention national honor, in a humane and fairly expensive plan of defense and Indian pacification. The essence of their thought on Empire—the same essence which had begun to percolate into the mind of the most blasé courtier or sleepiest country gentleman by 1763—was that equity and efficiency were the keys to a policy based on reason, and that a more reasonable policy was the key to a British greatness exceeding that of the empires of Rome and Alexander. The difficulty of course would come in deciding just what "equity" and "efficiency" should mean in practice, but the desire, often the passion, for the attainment of these ideals is clearly visible. It is what Andrews meant by a new view of Empire.

As important as the newness of the view is its remarkable unity, and it is this latter quality that is more relevant to the influence on historical understanding of Sir Lewis Namier.[37] Namier shattered old, instinctive, and anachronistic notions about the popularity of British politics in the mid-eighteenth century. By analyzing away Whigs and Tories, he is often said to have atomized our picture of what was happening. But he also, though less explicitly, enabled us to see the deep consensus which gave politics its peculiar quality, and which provided his own frame of reference. Political disagreement and controversy, by getting all the publicity then and later, have obscured the unconscious agreement on standards of behavior, on the objectives of politics, and on the goals of life itself. Pownall and Ellis offer a footnote to Namier's insight. Their mutual dislike in 1784 mattered very much to them, apparently, but it should matter less to us than the remarkable, and not accidental, agreement of their views of Empire in and after 1763. If Pownall's mind was the broader and more flexible of the two, it was no less bound by the same canons of unthinkability. That "equity" could absolve the Americans from any share in the burden of Empire, that "efficiency" did not require in some way the recognition of Parliamentary sovereignty—both ideas were unthinkable, to Pownall as to Ellis. No trauma had yet shattered the controlling consensus in British political life, and this consensus channeled imperial policy as surely as it did other forms of thought and action.

There is nothing really wrong with the insights of Andrews and Namier on British politics in the American Revolution. Each looked at the evidence from a different perspective, but what they saw was mutually illuminating, not contradictory. If Namier stressed the complicated scurrying of politicians for places and prestige, Andrews saw that all were more or less afflicted by mounting anxiety for the future of the stage on which they scurried. America made enemies of Pownall and Ellis, but their antagonism seems to have had more to do with chance and perhaps temperament than with opposed principles. We must not be deceived by the rhetoric of the debate on America; disagreement follows, and does not precede, the event. The conventional categories of historical analysis, "liberal," and "conservative," are even more misleading than the largely discredited "Whig" and "Tory" for politics generally. The impulse that swept the British Empire toward civil war was powerful, and did not admit of any real choice.

III ───────────────────────────

BIBLIOGRAPHICAL ESSAY

Recent Scholarship Concerning Anglo-American Relations, 1675–1775

Joseph E. Illick, a graduate of Princeton with his M.A. and Ph.D. from the University of Pennsylvania, is Associate Professor of History at San Francisco State College and book editor of *The American West*. His publications include *William Penn the Politician* (1965), *America & England: A Book of Readings on the Background to Colonization and Development, 1558–1776* (1970), and "The Pennsylvania Grant: A Re-evaluation" (*Pennsylvania Magazine of History and Biography*, 1962). He is currently at work on a history of colonial Pennsylvania.

As recently as 1959, a distinguished American historian bemoaned the homogenization of our history by conservative writers who depicted our past as "placid, unexciting." Unlike the radical historians of an earlier generation, who had "an eye for the convulsive moments in history," contemporary scholars were "carrying out a massive grading operation to smooth over America's social convulsions." However, when these conservative historians sought an ideology to justify their point of view, none could be found in the Colonial period. Consequently, they turned to experience, rather than thought, as the root of conservatism. This frame of reference created "a paralyzing incapacity to deal with the elements of spontaneity, effervescence, and violence in American history" because the new writing celebrated not action in itself, but only constructive action—that which preserved the *status quo* in order to build on it toward a stable future. Who could deny that such an experience-oriented perspective had "a deadening effect on the historian's ability to take the conflict of ideas seriously?" [1]

This prognosis reckoned without the convulsions of the 1960's, which have spawned a new school of radical historians.[2] More striking, however, is the resurgence of interest in intellectual history. This revival, sparked by scholars whose competence lies in seventeenth- and eighteenth-century England as well as America, suggests that the conflict-consensus dichotomy is not always an illuminating approach to an understanding of current writing about the Colonial period. If, as in the case of this essay, the focus is on the transatlantic community rather than the thirteen Colonies, new alignments of historians occur. Frederick Jackson Turner, an "old radical," and Daniel J. Boorstin, a "new conservative," quite obviously belong together, united by their insistence on the determinative effect of the American environment. Louis Hartz, another member of the consensus school, has criticized historians who consider America in isolation from Europe. Such an approach obscures their vision of the uniqueness of the New World experience—the absence of a feudal past.[3] More recently, Hartz has viewed America as a liberal bourgeois "fragment" of the Old World, traditionalist or conservative since a fragment "loses the stimulus to change that the whole provides." [4] This point of view is almost antithetical to Boorstin's theme of American adaption and pragmatism.

The recent voluminous literature on Puritanism has often been set in a transatlantic context and, insofar as the American Puritans are concerned, has focused on the history of ideas. Howard Mumford Jones, also fastening on the European ideological background of the New World, has assigned less weight to the effect of the Reformation and the Age of Reason and more to the Renaissance.[5] Studies by Richard M. Gummere and Robert Middlekauff also show the endurance of the classical tradition brought to America from England, although this does not necessarily argue for a stronger Anglo-American relationship. Apparently there were many colonials who knew more of Rome than of London.[6] Without doubt the most original and, in our day, relevant account of the transatlantic voyage of ideas is Winthrop D. Jordan's *White Over Black: American Attitudes Toward the Negro, 1550–1812*, which traces to England the origins of prejudice against color.[7] Colonials anxious about the apparent chaos of life in America fell back on this prejudice to reaffirm their identity as Englishmen, thereby giving tacit approval to the debasement of African blacks and, ultimately, institutionalizing slavery.

The transit of English political ideas has received more attention that any other ideological traffic. Probably the most influential and certainly the most comprehensive work on this topic is Caroline Robbins' *The Eighteenth-Century Commonwealthman: Studies in the Transmission, Development, and Circumstance of English Liberal Thought from the Restoration of Charles II until the War with the Thirteen Colonies.* Miss Robbins' theme is the passage of the ideas of such republicans as Milton, Harrington, Sydney, and Locke to later generations by Real Whigs, or Commonwealthmen, whose existence in conservative England was marginal. The implications for America are stated clearly: the Commonwealthmen for over a century "kept alive political ideas which proved suitable and useful for a great new republic. The American Founding Fathers were influenced by the whole body of this tradition . . . and gained as much from the moderators and commentators as from the Whig classics themselves."[8] Quite a few Commonwealthmen reappear in H. Trevor Colbourn's *The Lamp of Experience: Whig History and the Intellectual Origins of the American Revolution,* though the emphasis is on history rather than political theory. Both Englishmen and Americans held a mythical view of a golden age in the Saxon period, terminated by the freedom posed by the Hanoverians. The Founding Fathers viewed their revolution as an effort to conserve this pristine, libertarian state.[9]

The view of the Revolution as an intellectual movement, essentially conservative, had already been suggested—though with less documentation—by Bernard Bailyn and Edmund S. Morgan.[10] Nor was Colbourn the first to note parallels, or analogies, between Old-World thought and New. A number of scholars had applied this method to eighteenth-century events, documents and policies.[11] The point is that Colbourn underlined an irony not immediately apparent: the ideological traffic between England and America served ultimately to sever rather than savor the imperial nexus. Indeed, Richard S.

Dunn has noted that by the late seventeenth century "the transatlantic difference in outlook was steadily widening, while the regional colonial difference was not." British historians had an imperial viewpoint, whereas Colonial writers were establishing a local tradition, the first step in the direction of an American identification.[12] By the eighteenth century Englishmen and Americans could ride the same ideas to separate conclusions.

This point is drawn clearly in Bernard Bailyn's *The Origins of American Politics,* where it is noted that the "political culture of colonial America" was British, "but British with a peculiar emphasis." [13] The pattern of this culture was shaped by ideas which came from the government opposition, or country group, in England. Their arguments were accentuated in America, which diverged from the mother country in that government existed on two levels, local and imperial, and the franchise was decidedly broader.[14] Bailyn sees the legacy of these deviations from the English model in the immoderation of American politics. In a comparative study which includes both ideology and practice, *Political Representation in England and the Origins of the American Republic,* J. R. Pole concludes that the House of Commons represented different interests from those associated with the Assemblies in Massachusetts, Virginia, and Pennsylvania.[15]

Accepting the Revolution as undeniable evidence of divergence between mother country and Colonies, historians run the danger of seeing Colonial America from the vantage point of ruptured relations.[16] The alternative, other than purely descriptive history, is to start from the beginning and deal with the vagaries of ideals, intentions, setbacks, and failures.[17] Yet from the perspective of Anglo-American relations, this approach has the drawback of excessive concentration on internal development. The dilemma is seen between the lines of Clarence Ver Steeg's *The Formative Years, 1607–1763,* the most imaginative textbook in the Colonial field:

Although the seminal theme during the seventeenth century continued to be the transmission of English civilization to the colonies, the New World environment often influenced the direction of colonial expansion and the development of colonial society. Subtle forces, impossible to measure with precision, operated to create a colonial Englishman who did not live and who did not think as his English counterparts. . . .[18]

Ver Steeg's major contribution is his interpretation of American coming-of-age, the transition from Colony to province which took place in the late seventeenth and early eighteenth centuries. It was a time of personal anxiety and social instability, which accounted for such upheavals as Bacon's, Leisler's, and Coode's Rebellions, as well as the Salem witch trials. That society could withstand these strains was testimony to the strength of local government, a theory not far removed from Dunn's concept of an emergent local tradition as the first step toward an American identity.

Jack P. Greene's *The Quest For Power: The Lower Houses of Assembly in the Southern Royal Colonies, 1689–1776*, published almost simultaneously with Ver Steeg's study, puts the same thesis into institutional terms.[19] Within each Colony the emergence of an economic and social elite (symbolic of the movement from amorphous colony to structured province) brought in its wake a quest for commensurate political status within the lower house of the legislature; within each provincial government there was a spontaneous but inexorable trend toward predominance by the assembly in emulation of the House of Commons' achievement in the seventeenth century. Although Greene has illustrated his theme by reference to the four southern royal Colonies, he claims the same process could be traced in any of the former plantations after 1689, though the rate varied considerably. As an explanation of the American Revolution, institutional momentum is seen to be as important as constitutional principle.[20] As an explanation of the Colonial metamorphosis, mimicry of England is the most concrete explanation put forward thus far.

Treating an earlier period, Bernard Bailyn focuses on the new economic elite in Massachusetts as it contested with the original Puritan leaders and their descendants for political power in Massachusetts.[21] Many of these merchants had come to the Colony from England in the 1650's. Not only did they bring with them a transatlantic viewpoint (as did the first Puritans), but their livelihood depended on the maintenance of good relations with the home government (unlike the Puritans). Yet when the merchants' loyalty was tested by the Dominion of New England, they cast their lot with their Puritan antagonists. This alignment of American interests against English control is carefully described in Richard S. Dunn's *Puritans and Yankees: The Winthrop Dynasty of New England, 1630–1771*, which nicely complements Bailyn's study.[22] The succession from John to John, Jr., to Fitz and Wait Winthrop shows the declining quality of Puritan leadership, the secularization of New England, and the increasingly selfish motives for protecting the "city upon a hill" from the inroads of the home government.

Dunn's focus on failure and Bailyn's portrait of success both serve to substantiate the finding of Ver Steeg and Greene concerning the emergence of a new society and a new elite whose interests represented contemporary economic and social realities.[23] Additionally, Dunn and Bailyn show a transatlantic awareness which has been characteristic of writing about the late seventeenth and early eighteenth century ever since C. M. Andrews made his famous remark about the neglected period in Colonial American history. But although the interest in institutions and policy shown by the imperial historians of Andrews' generation almost dictated an emphasis on gradual development and continuity, the concentration of today's scholars on politics and the economic and social underpinnings of politics leads to an emphasis on rapid change and conflict.[24] A bridge between these two approaches has been provided by W. F. Craven's *The Colonies in Transition, 1600–1713* which, in emphasizing the importance of the English connection, gives equal attention to institutional and political matters.[25]

The eclectic but sophisticated quality of present scholarship may best be illustrated by reference to writing on the American aspects of the Glorious Revolution.[26] The analogy to the mother country and the attention paid to the determinative effect of Colonial policy on the success or failure of the various provincial upheavals would gain the approval of the imperial historians. Their contemporaries but opposite numbers—the Progressive historians of the Beardian school, who saw the past in terms of internal social and economic convulsions—would applaud the focus on conflict and recognition of the local causes of revolt. Yet the present view does not represent a simple coalescence of two earlier interpretations. The concern with both policy and politics has led not only to a more imaginative reconstruction of the well springs of both but also to an emphasis on connections between the two.

Michael G. Hall, in tracing the transatlantic career of Edward Randolph, has shown how the indefatigable efforts of a civil servant almost brought the private Colonies under Crown control.[27] In England, William Blathwayt was pursuing a similar policy, according to Stephen S. Webb. Webb has also used the public life of that ubiquitous royal official, Francis Nicholson, to illustrate the Crown's efforts to tighten control over the Colonies "through imperial administrators who conceived of government as army duty. . . ." [28] Delineating the short career of Governor Benjamin Fletcher, James S. Leamon has portrayed the affairs of New York as "exceedingly sensitive to political developments in England," a point of view substantiated by John D. Runcie's study of the governorship of the Earl of Bellomont.[29]

Philip S. Haffenden has argued that the formulation and execution of Colonial policy was virtually determined by Restoration politics, although there is not full agreement on this point.[30] Alison G. Olson points out that from 1701 to 1706 the Tories shielded the proprietaries from Parliamentary attack for reasons "in part personal, in part political." [31] William Penn, who not only protected his Colony during his lifetime but led the resistance to increasing English control in the decade following 1696 as well, has been depicted as a skillful politician whose success stemmed from his utilization of wide-ranging personal contacts among English statesmen and civil servants.[32] In *Politics of Colonial Policy: The Board of Trade in Colonial Administration, 1696–1720,* I. K. Steele has demonstrated that the Board's influence, and therefore Colonial policy, was closely related to domestic politics, as well as the international situation.[33]

There is a dearth of writing on the relation between English domestic politics and Colonial policy in the decades after the death of Queen Anne.[34] In contrast to the age of the later Stuarts, virtually unaffected by historical revision in the past several decades, the era of the early Hanoverians has recently been a field of major reinterpretation.[35] Apparently, Colonial American historians are awaiting the calm after the storm before writing. Whether the timeworn concept of "salutary neglect" can serve as further explanation of the deficiency in scholarly endeavor, based on the assumption that there is little to write about in this period, seems at least debatable. John W. Wilkes has asserted that "the generally accepted theory that the ministers from 1690 to 1763 were uninterested in colonial matters cannot be sustained." Yet interest did not necessarily lead to action. As Wilkes demonstrates, the central political problem in England during the century after the Glorious Revolution was the search for balance—sufficient power to administer laws without endangering liberties—in the executive office. This quest for capable ministries, complicated by the disintegration of parties, was the focus of political energy. Next came Continental affairs, leaving politicians little if any time for America. And, as Wilkes shows, "some leaders used colonial problems to strengthen their own positions within a government," much to the detriment of American affairs.[36]

Approaching the same period in greater detail in *Newcastle's New York: Anglo-American Politics, 1732–1753,* Stanley N. Katz has labeled the years when Newcastle was a secretary of state as the "golden age of imperial politics in New York." He attributes more flexibility to the imperial system than Wilkes does, and he demonstrates that New Yorkers were dependent on connections in England, just as politics in the province responded to transatlantic pressures.[37]

Both Katz and Wilkes have shown how to utilize the recent scholarship of Sir Lewis Namier and his followers in a consideration of the colonial scene. Certainly the starting point for a study of the relation of English domestic politics to America is an understanding of Namier.[38] An examination of the way England lost her North American colonies was Sir Lewis's original purpose, but he became so absorbed with his study of Parliament in the eighteenth century that he virtually abandoned his initial intentions. His thorough and intense scholarship led him to the conclusion that men were less moved by abstract principles than by personal motives, a judgment not intended as a denigration of public life in eighteenth-century England but, if anything, a tribute to the ascendency of action over theory.[39] Not national but local interests were primary, the structure of politics having to be understood by reference to family and the "connections" among families' political parties did not exist. The new findings brought to bear on older scholarship by the Namierites can be observed in C. H. Stuart's revision of Basil Williams' *The Whig Supremacy, 1714–1760.*[40] The text is not changed, but bracketed in the footnotes are interpretations postdating Williams.

Not only has the weight of recent scholarship on mid-eighteenth-century politics begun to be felt in writing on Anglo-American relations, but work in administrative history has been applied here as well.[41] F. B. Wickwire, in *British Subministers and Colonial America,*

1763–1783, describes the influence of these men on imperial policy.[42] Dora Mae Clark, in *The Rise of the British Treasury: Colonial Administration in the Eighteenth Century*, traces the increasing involvement of the Treasury in colonial affairs under the first two Hanoverians until, at the accession of George III, it had the dominant voice in these matters.[43] "In the years between 1766 and 1776," according to Miss Clark, "the Treasury bore the major responsibility for measures inciting to revolution." But its policies were built on foundations laid by earlier generations. In *Trade and Empire; the British Customs Service in Colonial America, 1660–1775*, Thomas C. Barrow relates mercantile theory to the actual operation of the Empire as seen in the functioning of the customs service.[44]

Above all the work being done on the transatlantic community in the middle of the eighteenth century towers the imperial history of Lawrence Henry Gipson.[45] Describing the British Isles and the Northern and Southern Plantations (his use of the word is significant) in the first three volumes of *The British Empire Before the American Revolution*; then devoting five volumes to the war between England and France for the control of the North American continent; and finally discussing the effect of England's victory on her relations with the colonies down to 1776, Gipson "crosses and recrosses the Atlantic and seems as much at home on either side of it." [46] Yet his vantage point is the center, not the periphery, of Empire. He has no real sympathy with the view that the colonial legislatures had powers co-ordinate with Parliament, and his institutional framework does not admit a discussion of colonial development to maturity, though he is by no means unaware of this change. The caprice of politics, English or American, does not affect Gipson's writing. His emphasis is economic, as befits a work concerned with an Empire built on a theory of mercantilism.

This theory itself has been the subject of a number of recent studies.[47] One of these has raised many scholarly eyebrows: William A. Williams' *Contours of American History*.[48] The contrast between the writings, both style and content, of Williams and Gipson is striking. Gipson's institutional approach and his indifference to speculation bespeak an innate conservatism entirely foreign to the panoramic view of Williams, with its concern for the temperament of the past and the past's grip on the present. It would be difficult to point to another recent work in economic history or theory which matches Williams' in imagination; in fact, scholarship in this area is apparently moving in quite another direction, that of quantification.[49] Yet Stuart Bruchey, in *The Roots of American Economic Growth, 1607– 1861. An Essay in Social Causation,* has demonstrated that statistics and literacy are not incompatible, nor does an understanding of numbers preclude a discussion of nonmeasurable phenomena.[50]

There is a wealth of writing on the economic history of England and the colonies in the late seventeenth and early eighteenth centuries. Predictably, most of it concerns ocean-going commerce. The logical starting point is the center of Empire and Ralph Davis' work on shipping and trade,[51] supplemented by the more synthetic approach of D. A. Farnie.[52] Davis points out that until the late seventeenth century, the export of wool or woolen cloth was the central feature of English commerce. By that time the re-export trade was most vigorous, and the colonies played a large part in it. In the eighteenth century the export of manufactured goods to America was of primary importance. He finds the Navigation Acts, because they were preventive, hard to assess, but he observes that "the force of habit was, by the mid-eighteenth century, even stronger than the force of law in maintaining the Anglo-American commercial connexion."

Seldom does Davis venture so far beyond his statistics. Jacob M. Price, however, plunges into the three decades following the Glorious Revolution with the observation that few writers have conveyed "the tone of the age, its atmosphere of expectation, its ponderous consideration of the possible, its achievement of the next to the impossible."[53] And he suggests that the merchant community of London played a role in the political as well as the economic history of the times. That the East India Company was active in politics has been proved beyond a doubt.[54] J. H. Plumb has argued that by the time Walpole entered politics, London's commercial life was dominated by a small group of wealthy financiers (including members of the East India Company), whose new watchword was caution, at least in political life. "They were willing to forego the passions of party strife and throw in their lot with any group of politicians who could give security to an administration."[55]

Of the merchants in London and the smaller commercial cities,

Plumb says that "their significance for eighteenth-century politics has been overlooked by recent historians." The same statement cannot be made with regard to the colonies, perhaps because the nexus between economics and politics is more obvious. Provincial legislatures often held the key to fortunes to be made in land speculation. But political power was not only economically lucrative, it was psychologically necessary. Successful merchants, and some not so successful, were familiar figures in the Assemblies. A roll call of recent writings on such men would include the Pepperells of Massachusetts; Jonathan Trumbull of Connecticut; the Browns of Rhode Island; Robert Livingston of New York, his son-in-law Samuel Vetch and the Beekman family; the Dulanys of Maryland; and the Blounts of North Carolina.[56]

Bernard Bailyn has written that in the seventeenth century New England merchants very much valued the imperial nexus. By the eighteenth century, contrary to Ralph Davis' observation on the binding force of habit, it is difficult to generalize. The Pepperells, who maintained agents and investments in England, and whose political activities were partially dependent upon royal appointment, were faithful to the Empire. And later, at Newburyport, merchants endorsed the Revolutionary movement for political rather than economic reasons, having no quarrel with the mercantile system.[57] The Browns in Providence, unlike so many of their counterparts in Newport who became loyalists, felt they had a greater stake in Rhode Island than in the Empire. Robert Livingston, working in the interior of New York, was virtually unaffected by mercantilist restrictions; his son-in-law simply disregarded them and traded illegally. The Beekmans, initially more active in provincial politics than the Livingstons, were also more involved in imperial commerce. Diversity of activities, a high degree of mobility, regional variety and, of course, personal peculiarity make it impossible to put forward "a colonial merchant viewpoint" on mercantilism.

Not only was consensus lacking but, according to Bernard Bailyn, "the colonial merchants never were a 'class,' "[58] Having earlier shown that the capriciousness of overseas trade in the seventeenth century forced merchants to "follow pre-existent ties of blood and long acquaintance," but denying that commerce was ever a way of life in America as it was in England, Bailyn has more recently declared that "the analogy to the situation of the English aristocracy is a false one." Families, in the Namierite sense, did not exist in the New World.[59] Neither the economic nor the political life of eighteenth-century America was a copy of England.

The question of whether the mercantilist system tended to unite or divide the colonies and the mother country remains a pertinent one, though there appears to be no answer that covers all situations. Recent studies of Pennsylvania and the southern royal colonies show that the axioms of mercantilism were pervasive and accepted, although destructive forces were at work in the Quaker province.[60] In Maryland and New England there was notable animosity toward imperial policy.[61] A hitherto neglected area of policy, the often-ineffective attempts at control of colonial currency, has recently come under the scrutiny of several scholars.[62] The generally accepted opinion is that both the government and the merchants in England were grappling with the problem as best they could.[63] Apparently imperial policy regarding currency was not a grievance in the colonies until the passage of the Act of 1764.[64]

Forces less tangible than economic theory and practice may be seen in terms of their cohesive or divisive effect on the Empire.[65] The field of science, for example, has been used by some historians to illustrate the growing divergence between England, populated by theoreticians, and America, the land of experiment. Recent writing indicates that this is an erroneous oversimplification. Even in areas such as medicine, where the pragmatic Americans should have excelled, scientific influence was consistently one way—from the Old World to the New, largely because of American indifference to investigation.[66] The greatest of the colonial scientists, Benjamin Franklin, carried on his work in the Newtonian tradition of Europe.[67] There was a small transatlantic scientific community, and some of its members were summoned into the political arena with the coming of the Revolution.[68] But even such an irony was testimony to the positive effect of this community on Angloamerican relations.

Not all personal contacts between mother country and colonies led to increased mutual regard. Americans visiting England, most of whom returned, found the mother country immediately attractive. However, sometime around the middle of the eighteenth century this Anglophilia waned, due largely to "a growing belief that Britain was decadent, and would continue to decline because of apparent indifference to her social and political ailments; and with this came a consciousness that American society was sounder and better ordered, and had the future on its side." [69] Emigrants from the British Isles, virtually all of whom remained in America, sought economic solace rather than political freedom in the New World (contrary to the opinion of the Earl of Bristol and Bishop of Derry, who wrote to the Earl of Dartmouth in 1775 that "the rebellious spirit in the central provinces in America" was due "to the exportation of nearly 33,000 fanatical & hungry republicans from Ireland in the course of a few years").[70] There is little literature on the reaction of Englishmen to visiting provincials and of visiting Britons to the colonies.[71]

There is no lack of documentation, however, for the universal fear and abhorrence in the colonies toward the migration of one Englishman: an Anglican bishop. The most heralded new study in this field has been Carl Bridenbaugh's *Mitre and Sceptre. Transatlantic Faiths, Ideas, Personalities, and Politics, 1689–1775*.[72] According to Bridenbaugh, the Church of England, working persistently and highhandedly through its colonial agency, the Society for the Propagation of the Gospel, battled with New England Congregationalists (and, later, Presbyterians from the middle colonies) for social prestige and the political power necessary for the establishment of an episcopate in America. In defense, colonial Dissenters allied with their English counterparts against the Anglicans, drew upon the arguments used earlier by these Nonconformists and made the issue a matter of public debate. Bridenbaugh sees the consequent airing of grievances as crucial to the coming of the Revolution, of which religion was "a fundamental cause."

The year before Bridenbaugh deplored "the tendency of modern historians to omit any consideration of the significance of religion at all" when discussing the Revolution, Perry Miller had written: "Though by now the Revolution has been voluminously, and one might suppose exhaustively, studied, we still do not realize how effective were generations of Protestant preaching in evoking patriotic enthusiasm."[73] In a book dedicated to Miller, Alan Heimert argues that it was not eighteenth-century liberalism but resuscitated Calvinism that "provided pre-Revolutionary America with a radical, even democratic, social and political ideology, and evangelical religion embodied, and inspired, a thrust toward American national-ism." [74] Edmund S. Morgan, a former student of Miller's, doubts that the evidence supports Heimert's position. Earlier, Morgan had em-phasized "the substitution of political for clerical leadership" with the coming of the Revolution, the shift in interest from religion to politics being attributed to Parliament's attempt to tax the colonies. More recently, he has made it clear that he believes the Revolution-ary politicians were unable to shed their religious past: "the move-ment in all its phases, from the resistance against Parliamentary taxa-tion in the 1760's to the establishment of a national government and national policies in the 1790's was affected, not to say guided, by a set of values inherited from the age of Puritanism." [75]

Studies concentrating on the English side of this issue give a rather different cast to the picture. Philip Haffenden has noted the failure of Restoration statesmen to develop, much less implement, a policy wherein the Anglican Church would act in tandem with the Crown toward centralization in the plantations.[76] J. Harry Bennett has shown that in the same period the Bishop of London did, in fact, assert himself, but his power existed largely in theory; when a later Bishop demanded commensurate practice, the London See's author-ity in America was immediately reduced.[77] Norman Sykes and Spen-cer Ervin have made it clear that monarchs and ministries hindered the Bishops of London and hampered attempts to establish an Ameri-can episcopate.[78] Ervin has also pointed out, and his argument is sup-ported by Glenn Weaver, that the Society for the Propagation of the Gospel may have been vigorous but it was not powerful.[79]

If the Anglican offensive was weaker than Bridenbaugh has de-picted it, there is no evidence that he has exaggerated the virulence of the counteroffensive. William Kellaway, in *The New England Company, 1649–1776*, has shown that the S.P.G. had a Puritan coun-terpart; indeed, before 1660 the Company was known as the Corpo-ration for the Propagation of the Gospel in New England. The Prot-estant Dissenting Deputies, representing churches in the vicinity of London in their dealings with Parliament, kept close lines of com-munication across the Atlantic, according to Maurice W. Arm-strong.[80] Charles W. Akers' biography of Jonathan Mayhew con-firms Bridenbaugh's estimate of the Boston minister's role in attack-ing the idea of an American episcopate, as well as transmitting liberal English ideas to the colonies.[81] And the controversy which raged in New England and the middle colonies was also present farther south.[82]

In addition to seeing religion as a basic cause of the Revolution, Bridenbaugh views it as the foundation of nationalism. Howard H. Peckham has pointed to more secular origins of American self-awareness: military experience.[83] The difference in tactics between the British regulars and themselves made colonials feel they were a breed apart, not simply transplanted Englishmen. John A. Schutz has shown how conflicting strategies—indecision in London and aggressiveness in the provinces—could reinforce this opinion.[84] The same misunderstanding has been explored in depth by John Shy, who describes British policies and military activities during the years immediately preceding the Revolution. In another context Shy has dealt with the colonists' reaction, arguing that "quartering a standing army provided, not a basic grievance, but a convenient weapon, in the fight for self-government." [85]

Religious and military approaches to the coming of the Revolution are suggestive of the many-sided treatment that event is now receiving.[86] The literature is not only variegated but voluminous. This was not the case when imperial historians dominated the colonial field. Their focus was on the late seventeenth and early eighteenth centuries, when the institutions of Empire were created and slowly developing, not when the structure was falling apart. The contemporary revival of interest in the revolutionary period does not necessarily connote a radical point of view. As John Higham has pointed out, the emphasis on consensus and the denial of internal conflict is indicative of a point of view as conservative as that of the imperial historians. (Ironically, the late seventeenth and early eighteenth centuries, all but ignored by writers of a radical persuasion until recently, are now being viewed in terms of conflict and turmoil, when colonies struggled to provincial status by way of local rebellions and witch trials conducted by anxiety-ridden Americans.)

The classification of historians as conservative or radical always runs the danger of confusing the past with the present. The political terminology used is contemporary; applied to a colonial situation, it can be misleading. Yet the practice persists as a by-product of national introspection, which explains the logic of concentrating on the colonies at the expense of England. This bias is evident in recent historiographical essays on the coming of the Revolution. The quantity of writing and the rapidity with which these essays have revised their predecessors suggests not only scholarly vitality but American self-consciousness.

The best known of these reformulations is Edmund Morgan's, appropriately titled "The American Revolution: Revisions in Need of Revising." [87] Reviewing the past half century of scholarship, Morgan sees three major schools: the economic and social interpretation, put forward by Beard and Becker; the imperial approach of Andrews and Beer; and the concentration on personal and local politics to the exclusion of principles, as advocated by Sir Lewis Namier. All these schools of thought have discredited—"indirectly, almost surreptitiously"—the older Whig view, the gospel according to Bancroft and Trevelyan. Morgan examines the three newer interpretations, finds each of them wanting, and suggests that the Whig approach "may not be as dead as some historians would have us believe." The important but still unanswered questions, according to Morgan, are: "How did the Americans, living on the edge of Empire, develop the breadth of vision and the attachment to principle which they displayed in the remarkable period from 1763 to 1789? While English politics remained parochial and the Empire was dissolving for lack of vision, how did the Americans generate the forces that carried them into a new nationality and a new human liberty?" He suggests that the answer may be found in a study of the local institutions that spawned the Patriots.

Although Morgan, through his novel synthesis of older interpretations and especially his attempt to link motivation with principle, had laid down the lines for a new perspective, most historians noticed his American focus and equation of the Patriot cause with virtue, a view usually associated with such nineteenth-century figures as George Bancroft. Meanwhile Page Smith came forward with the claim that eighteenth-century historian David Ramsay demonstrated the best understanding of the upheaval.[88] According to Smith, no one writing after Ramsay recognized the decisive nature of the American reaction to the Stamp Act. From that time until the Revolution the colonists were united on constitutional principle; There was no distinction made between internal and external taxation. Only in 1953, with the publication of Edmund S. and Helen Morgan's *The Stamp Act Crisis: Prologue to Revolution*,[89] was the essential correctness of Ramsay's view recognized. Smith finds the Morgans' point of view quite acceptable. Mutual misunderstanding after 1765 led ultimately to the Revolutionary War; from the Stamp Act crisis to 1775 the English were inflexible and the Americans acted on principle. (The pejorative connotation of inflexibility, as opposed to the virtue of acting on principle, may suggest something about the historian's sympathies.)

The emphasis on the American side of the Atlantic is evident again in Wesley F. Craven's essay, published two years after Smith's.[90]

Noting that most scholars now agree that the Revolution was both conservative and liberal, since liberal principles were preserved, Craven wisely suggests a search for the origins of these principles (as Morgan had called for five years previously): "The 'silent and peaceful revolution,' . . . which presumably preceded *the* Revolution, lacks anything approaching full documentation. . . . Daniel Boorstin's *The Colonial Experience* (1958), however suggestive, can provide no substitute for the required monographic study. We know all too little even of the history of the legislative assemblies during the great period of their development, from 1689 to 1783."

A year later Jack P. Greene's study of this very subject, *The Quest for Power,* was issued. Greene prepared the way for his book with a statement about historians of the Morgan school, whom he labeled neo-Whig: "Their emphasis has been upon immediate issues and individual actions rather than long-range determinants or underlying conditions."[91] This definition would exclude historians such as Daniel Boorstin, who see in America the gradual emergence of a new society. Although Greene should fall into the latter category, he gives the neo-Whigs his blessing.

Greene's explicit concern was not the insularity of the new history. When he noted that the neo-Whig's "primary focus has been upon American grievances against Britain, the central question being why Americans were angry in the fateful years after 1763, his emphasis was not on the words "American" and "Britain," but "grievances" and "angry." These were symptomatic of the psychological nature of inquiry being carried on by today's writers, underscoring the "flight from determinism." Several years passed before this theme was taken up by Gordon S. Wood, who noted that the "preoccupation with men's purposes was what restricted the perspectives of the contemporaneous Whig and Tory interpretations; it is still the weakness of the neo-Whig histories. . . ." [92] Seeking to justify the Revolution, the new historians have sought also to justify the writings and actions of the Patriots. Thus, they have ignored "the exaggerated and fanatical rhetoric uncovered by the Progressive historians," such as Becker and Beard, who denigrated the role of ideas in the Revolution rather than exalting the Americans' devotion to principle.[93]

Wood's essay comes in the wake of Bernard Bailyn's first volume of *Pamphlets of the American Revolution, 1750–1776*,[94] containing fourteen reprints (mainly from the Sugar Act and Stamp Act controversies) and prefaced by the author's own interpretation of the coming of the Revolution. This involves a detailed analysis of political theory—Bailyn clings to his "rather old-fashioned view that the American Revolution was above all else an ideological-constitutional struggle"—but Wood will not call him a neo-Whig.[95] Rather, by arguing that men became the victims of ideas, Bailyn makes devotion to principle less praiseworthy. If this appears to be a step backward toward determinism, his concern with the "dynamism and emotionalism" of ideas, according to Wood, represents a step forward—toward a behaviorist's understanding of the Revolution. Taking Namier at his word, that ideas and principles had little relevance in eighteenth-century England, Wood suggests that a new conception of their meaning in America is necessary. It is in "a relatively unsettled, disordered society" that "ideas become truly vital and creative." The thirteen colonies, caught in a "revolutionary syndrome" after 1763, suffered severe social strain—the product not only of "alienation" from British authority but of local anxieties as well. These strains were the source of the bombastic rhetoric which is now reprinted in Bailyn's *Pamphlets*. Wood concludes:

By working through the ideas—by reading them imaginatively and relating them to objective social reality—we may be able to eliminate the unrewarding distinction between conscious and unconscious motives, and eventually thereby to combine a Whig with a Tory, an idealist with a behaviorist, interpretation.

To follow Wood's prescription would be to underwrite the American emphasis in recent scholarship concerning the Revolution. The publication of the papers of the Founding Fathers, now taking place, is an eloquent testimony to the merits of this vantage point.[96] But it may be wondered whether biographers will be able to bring the called-for imagination to bear, and if they do, whether the results may not be more subjective than heretofore. [97] Although Wood has raised honest and provocative questions about earlier interpretations, his essay and those of his predecessors should be considered in the light of this caution by Wesley F. Craven: "The revisionist has, of course, a vital function to perform, but the very character of the function encourages overstatement, which in turn can invite new revisionist efforts." [98]

Indeed, the historiographers appear to have moved ahead of the historians of the Revolution who, plodding from article to monograph, have not yet reached agreement on some of the more prosaic and factual aspects of the period. A case in point is the economic interpretation of the coming of the Revolution. Though out of vogue, it is neither forgotten nor entirely rejected, as demonstrated by the debate on the relation between planter indebtedness in Virginia and the break with England.[99] The class conflict approach to the American Revolution has not been revived,[100] though Jackson Turner Main has made some pertinent observations in *The Social Structure of Revolutionary America*.[101] As Gordon Wood has drawn upon psychology to enrich history, Main has used the methods of sociology, quantifying the economic and social classes in the years 1763 to 1788. Whereas Wood sees evidence of social strain, Main's findings—an accepted class structure which did not hinder mobility, an absence of extreme wealth or poverty—suggest the opposite, unless the "alienation" from England was a great deal more significant than local anxieties.

Other studies, more political in nature, reinforce Main's point of view. David S. Lovejoy has shown that the heated controversies in prerevolutionary Rhode Island were not symbolic of a social upheaval or even concerned with representation; the colony was democratic in that regard. Local and personal issues were the matters at stake, as in Namier's England, and when Parliament threatened these interests after 1763, both factions reacted against the mother country (and both tried to stigmatize the other as British sympathizers).[102] A similar conclusion, explicitly contradicting Carl Becker's long-accepted class interpretation, emerges from the new look at New York, where contending aristocratic groups dominated the political scene.[103] In Virginia, according to Thad W. Tate, a united gentry talked of the violation of constitutional rights and feared a loss of power [104] Whether the upheaval in South Carolina was issue or class-oriented is a matter of debate.[105] Georgia followed the lead of other colonies, especially South Carolina, rather than generating indigenous revolutionary fervor, and Marylanders moved into the fray with real reluctance.[106] Both Merrill Jensen and Jackson Turner Main have made the generalization that prior to the Revolution, Americans "were content to be ruled by local elites," that colonial society was not democratic in operation. The theoretical and practical shift took place after 1776; "the American Revolution was a democratic movement, not in origin, but in result." [107] Recent scholarship, in de-emphasizing internal threats to the provincial ruling elites, points to the primacy of an external menace. The recommendation of historiographers, that scholars scrutinize local institutions and provincial psyches, if followed, will provide only partial explanations for the rupture in Anglo-American relations.

Additionally, what is needed is an understanding of British policy and its formulation. Obvious as this may sound, it is not easily achieved. The scholarship in this area is vast, but the divergent sympathies and intentions of writers, the array of manuscripts, and the complexity of the subject, have not been conducive to general agreement.[108]

Lawrence H. Gipson has viewed the coming of the Revolution in terms of the impact of the Peace of Paris.[109] The territorial gains and consequent need to administer a larger Empire while saddled with enormous war debts gave England a perspective quite different from that of the carefree colonies, now rid of a hostile France to the north. Jack M. Sosin is at least as sympathetic to the British point of view as Gipson, though he traces the origins of England's policy toward the west to the experience of the Seven Years' War (rather than the fruits of its Peace), pays more attention to English politics, and is less understanding of the colonial point of view.[110] Bernard Knollenberg also sees the changes in British colonial policy antedating 1763, explicitly rejecting the Stamp Act crisis as the major turning point of the prerevolutionary period, but he is highly critical of the home government.[111] O. M. Dickerson agrees with Gipson that 1763 was the turning point in Anglo-American relations; up to that time the Navigation Acts had brought prosperity to the colonies, but the revenue and restrictive acts which followed the Peace of Paris caused revolution. Dickerson describes the British government, and particularly the Commissioners of Customs sent to the colonies after 1767, in terms of spying, conspiracy, and arbitrary power.[112]

Thomas C. Barrow, arguing that "in undertaking its program of imperial taxation and reorganization the Grenville ministry (1763–1765) was motivated by something of more fundamental importance than a temporary concern over defense or finance," finds the real reason in "dissatisfaction with the effectiveness of the colonial commercial restrictions" stemming from investigations conducted by the Board of Trade as early as 1757.[113] More traditional interpretations of the Sugar and Stamp Acts, though equally sympathetic to Whitehall, can be found in articles by Allen S. Johnson and C. R. Ritcheson, the latter labeling Grenville's ministry the only one between 1763 and 1775 to offer "a comprehensive, statesmanlike, and, on the basis of the eighteenth-century British Constitution, an unimpeachable plan of imperial organization."[114] As pointed out earlier, the Morgans (whom Ritcheson accuses of lack of sympathy for Grenville) have done the major work on the Stamp Act crisis in America; W. E. Minchinton has demonstrated the influence of colonial reaction on British opinion.[115] Not public pressure, however effective, but the powerlessness of the mother country to subdue colonial rebellion and the weakness of the Rockingham administration (1765–1766) have been held responsible for the repeal of the Stamp Act.[116]

Jack M. Sosin, defending the Grenville regime, notes that it issued "definite instructions to ensure that money raised in the colonies by the new revenue measures would not leave America."[117] Indeed, since E. James Ferguson's explorative essay in 1953, in which the lack of scholarship on British policy concerning colonial currency was lamented, there have been several substantial efforts to fill this gap.[118] The most ambitious is Joseph A. Ernst's explanation of the Currency Act of 1764 in terms of "the close of the French and Indian War, the long-standing 'hard money' bias of the Board of Trade,

Virginia's paper money practices, and the response of the British merchants concerned with the security of their investments in Virginia during periods of depression." Glasgow mercantile houses also became involved, the result being a compromise which by 1765 pleased no one.[119] Jack P. Greene and Richard M. Jellison have traced the long-range effect of the Act, concluding that all colonies save Delaware considered it a major grievance.[120] Richard B. Sheridan sets the currency problem in the framework of British capital investment. With the collapse of an economic boom in 1772, the colonies, especially those raising tobacco, faced the problem of balance of payments. Almost everyone was affected, making them "more responsive to anti-British propaganda." [121]

Concerning another imperial reform, the strengthening of the vice-admiralty courts through the Sugar Act, there is agreement that it originated in reports of unpunished smuggling during the Seven Years' War, but some debate exists as to whether it was the innovation itself or the association of the courts with the new revenue laws that provoked colonial resistance.[122] As with the currency problem, the vice-admiralty courts were a source of irritation but not a major cause of the Revolution. In fact, no one has attempted to give relative weights to the various factors which precipitated revolt, and for good reason: it cannot be done.

Assigning responsibility for the formulation of colonial policy should be more easily accomplished, but again recent scholarship points in no certain direction. B. D. Barger defends Lord Dartmouth's role as American Secretary, while F. B. Wickwire argues that Dartmouth's inexperience allowed his undersecretary, John Pownall, to play a determinative policy-making role. James High also assigns major influence to an administrative underling.[123] Michael G. Kammen, depicting the declining effect of colonial agents on imperial decisions, sees the process as "symptomatic of the way an entire network of formal and informal lines of transatlantic communication suffered under the strain placed upon them by the factional nature of English politics, the intransigence of the colonists, and the need for financial and administrative reform." [124] This deterioration is not so clear-cut regarding the New York agents. Neither Robert Charles, who served from 1748 to 1770, nor Edmund Burke, his replacement, favored the colonists' exclusive right to tax themselves. If anything, Burke was more circumspect in allowing his position to be known, either to the Americans, whom he little understood, or to his colleagues in Parliament, whose supremacy he upheld.[125] And although there was strong sentiment among Englishmen in favor of the colonial cause, when Burke stood for election in 1774 there was little discussion of the American question.[126]

This may seem strange in view of Burke's reputation, and especially in view of Charles R. Ritcheson's assertion that debate about the colonies produced "the first fully developed issue in British politics since the lingering death of Jacobitism." Not only does Ritcheson argue that "the American problem produced in England an amazing development in imperial thinking," but he also attributes the rebirth of the Tory party to the conservative reaction against American radicalism.[127] It was not until the war began, however, that the transatlantic impact was felt. Recent studies of English politics do not attribute this influence to colonial affairs in the prerevolutionary period.[128] As Esmond Wright has pointed out, America plays a small part indeed in the work of Namier and some of his followers.

Sir Lewis, by confining himself to the political nation, omitted important elements wielding no little influence. Where America was concerned, the omissions are crucially important: dissenters, manufacturers and shopkeepers were highly sympathetic to the colonies. There is little in his pages of the politics of the City of London or of Westminster or of the Yorkshire freeholders; there is even less of that half-world of politics in which Wilkes and Lord George Gordon moved, of the emotions in politics that led Fox and the Duchess of Devonshire to sport the buff and blue of Fairfax County.[129]

This stricture does not apply to all Namierites, however. Ritcheson was influenced by Namier, as was Eric Robson, whose premature death left his account of British policy and the causes of the Revolution somewhat brief and fragmentary.[130] More recently, Bernard Donoughue has made an intensive study of the years immediately preceding the war, examining not only what the North ministry did but also what its alternatives were and what pressures influenced it.[131]

Undoubtedly there will be more work in this vein as the Namierites map out the eighteenth-century political terrain in England for scholars whose main interest is colonial America. Ultimately these studies of the Hanoverians should link with already-existing accounts of the relation between politics and colonial policy in the Stuart period. There are already several substantial books on the transmission of political ideas from England to America during this period, as well as studies which show the degree to which colonials mimicked the political practices of the mother country, especially in the lower houses of the legislatures. Yet for all these influences, which of course transcended politics and could be felt in every area of colonial life, the two societies could not settle their differences except by separation. Was this the inevitable result of cultural divergence, or the consequence of mutual misunderstanding which could have been avoided, or the product of short-sighted policy and careless response? On this question there is not consensus among historians. Perhaps the Anglo-American context is itself too circumscribed to provide the answer and, in the manner of Robert R. Palmer and Hannah Arendt,[132] the scope of study will have to be widened to include Western Civilization.

Notes

CHAPTER 2

1. Richard S. Dunn, "Imperial Pressures on Massachusetts and Jamaica, 1675–1700," p. 63, in this volume. The historical citations that follow are with few exceptions restricted to the essays in this volume. Grateful acknowledgment is given to the authors of the essays for their contributions upon which the present interpretation is based. The responsibility for the interpretation is, of course, entirely my own.
2. Dunn, pp. 60–61.
3. David S. Lovejoy, "Virginia's Charter and Bacon's Rebellion, 1675–1676," pp. 38, 42, 50, in this volume.
4. Dunn, pp. 59–60, 62–63.
5. Dunn, p. 58.
6. Dunn, p. 63.
7. Dunn, pp. 58, 60.
8. Lovejoy, p. 50.
9. Dunn, pp. 61, 64.
10. Dunn, pp. 62–64.
11. Dunn, pp. 61, 71–72.
12. Lovejoy, pp. 48–50.
13. Lovejoy, p. 51.
14. Dunn, p. 65, and *Diary of Samuel Sewall: 1674–1700*, pp. 160–163, in *Collections of the Massachusetts Historical Society*, 5th ser., Vol. V.
15. Dunn, p. 75.
16. See "A Note on Method" at the end of this essay. Easton has defined the political system as "that *behavior or set of interactions through which authoritative allocations (or binding decisions) are made and implemented for a society*." David Easton, "Political Science," p. 285, in David L. Sills, ed., *International Encyclopedia of the Social Sciences* (17 vols.; New York, 1968), Vol. XII.
17. See "A Note on Method." For the meaning of the terms inputs, outputs, demands, support, and feedback see notes 19–22, below.
18. David Alan Williams, "Anglo-Virginia Politics, 1690–1755," pp. 89–91.

In his new book Robert F. Berkhofer, Jr., notes that "the formulation and testing of theory is an integral part of the [behavioral] approach." *A Behavioral Approach to Historical Analysis* (New York and London, 1969), p. 6.

19. *Inputs* are effects that enter the political system in the form of *demands* on the system and *support* for the system. David Easton, *A Systems Analysis of Political Life* (New York, London, and Sydney, 1965), pp. 26–27, 32.

20. *Outputs* of the political system are "the decisions and actions of the authorities." Easton, *A Systems Analysis of Political Life*, p. 28.

21. A *demand* is "an expression of opinion that an authoritative allocation with regard to a particular subject matter should or should not be made by those responsible for doing so." Inputs of *support* are actions or orientations (attitudes, sentiments, or predispositions) which support the political system by promoting goals, ideas, institutions, actions, or persons. Easton, *A Systems Analysis of Political Life*, pp. 38, 157–160.

22. *Feedback* is the process by which the *outputs* (decisions and actions of the authorities) "determine each succeeding round of inputs that finds its way into the political system." Easton, *A Systems Analysis of Political Life*, p. 28.

23. Stanley Nider Katz, "Between Scylla and Charybdis: James DeLancey and Anglo-American Politics in Early Eighteenth Century New York," p. 107, in this volume. See also Katz' *Newcastle's New York: Anglo-American Politics, 1732–1753* (Cambridge, Mass., 1968), a pioneering study and one whose approach, in my opinion, is implicitly behavioral as well as Namieristic.

24. See Jack P. Greene, "Changing Interpretations of Early American Politics," in Ray A. Billington, ed., *The Reinterpretation of Early American History: Essays in Honor of John Edwin Pomfret* (San Marino, Calif., 1966), pp. 151–184. In addition to being an excellent survey of recent literature on the subject, Greene's article presents a pointed interpretation of the American aspect of Anglo-American politics.

25. Katz, p. 97. Thomas C. Barrow, "The Old Colonial System from an English Point of View," pp. 133–34, in this volume.

26. Katz, p. 92.

27. Katz, p. 97.

28. The following discussion of interest groups is based on the article in this volume by Michael G. Kammen, "British and Imperial Interests in the Age of the American Revolution."

29. Alison Gilbert Olson, "The Commissaries of the Bishop of London in Colonial Politics." A competing transatlantic religious interest group, the Dissenters, is traced in Carl Bridenbaugh, *Mitre and Sceptre: Transatlantic Faiths, Ideas, Personalities, and Politics, 1689–1775* (New York, 1962).

30. On the Virginia tobacco interest see Williams, pp. 89–90.

31. Kammen, p. 143.

32. Kammen, p. 143.

33. For example, see Williams, pp. 86–88.

34. For the opposition role of certain Anglican ministers *qua* Commissaries of the Bishop of London see Olson, "Commissaries," p. 113ff.

35. For an interpretation of political colonial parties in which Whigs and

Tories emerge as transatlantic parties see a forthcoming study by Alison Gilbert Olson.

36. Barrow, pp. 133–34. John A. Schutz, "Succession Politics in Massachusetts, 1730–1741," *William and Mary Quarterly*, 3rd ser., XV (1958), 508–520.
37. Katz, p. 97.
38. Katz, p. 99ff.
39. A similarly well connected colonial governor who used his English ties to good advantage was William Gooch. Williams, pp. 88–90.
40. See Figure 2 for an example of the Anglo-American political system in operation.
41. Kammen, p. 149ff.
42. Katz, p. 108.
43. John Shy, "Thomas Pownall, Henry Ellis, and the Spectrum of Possibilities, 1763–1774," p. 163, in this volume.
44. Barrow, pp. 135–37.
45. Shy, p. 183ff.
46. Barrow, pp. 129–31.
47. Katz, p. 108.
48. This discussion of Thomas Pownall follows the interpretation in this volume by John Shy.
49. Pownall advocated American representation in Parliament, a solution unacceptable to Americans. Shy, p. 172.
50. Shy, p. 165.
51. Easton, *A Systems Analysis of Political Life*, pp. 159–160.

C H A P T E R   3

1. David S. Lovejoy, "Equality and Empire: the New York Charter of Libertyes, 1683," *William and Mary Quarterly*, 3rd ser., Vol. XXI (1964), 493–515.
2. William W. Hening, ed., *The Statutes at Large . . . of Virginia* (N. Y., 1823), II, 515–16; Berkeley to Earl of Clarendon, July 20, 1666, Bodleian Library, Clarendon Mss, 84. ff., 230–31 in Virginia 350th Anniversary Celebration Corp. Colonial Records Project, Survey Report, No. X, 53; Newsletter, Oct. 27, 1668, Historical Manuscripts Commission, 25: Twelfth Report, Appendix, Part VII, *The Manuscripts of S. H. LeFleming* (London, 1890), 60.
3. Giles Bland to Sir Joseph Williamson, Apr. 28, 1676, and Bland's "State of Virginia, 1676," *Virginia Magazine of History and Biography*, 20 (1912), 352–53, 356–57; W. N. Sainsbury, ed., *Calendar of State Papers, Colonial, America and West Indies, 1675–76* (London, 1894), #906; John D. Burk, *History of Virginia . . .* II (Petersburg, Va., 1822), Appendix, l–li; Leo F. Stock, ed., *Proceedings and Debates of the British Parliament Respecting North America* (Wash., D. C., 1924), I, 362ff., for debate on tobacco customs. In 1689 the Lords of Trade and Commissioners of Customs reported that Virginia and Maryland tobacco paid £200,000 in customs. Public Record Office, CO324/5/120; John C. Rainbolt, "The Virginia

Vision: a Political History of the Efforts to Diversify the Economy of the Old Dominion, 1650–1706" (unpublished Ph.D. thesis, Univ. of Wisconsin, 1965), particularly ch. IV.

4. HMC 22: 11th Report, App., VII, *Manuscripts of the Duke of Leeds* (London, 1888), p. 10; Stock, ed., *Debates*, I, 362ff. In 1682 merchants in England argued that each white man's work in producing tobacco for a year was worth £7 to the King. *Calendar of State Papers, Colonial, America and West Indies, 1681–85,* #768.

5. Thomas Ludwell to Lord John Berkeley, 1667, quoted in Thomas J. Wertenbaker, *The Planters of Colonial Virginia* (Princeton, N. J., 1922), 90.

6. Hening, ed., *Statutes*, II, 280; L. G. Tyler, writing in 1900, believed that the "suffrage remained practically unchanged" despite the new law. *William and Mary Quarterly*, 1st ser., VIII (1899–1900), 81.

7. HMC, 25: 12th Rep., App., VII, 104.

8. F. H. B. Daniell, ed., *Calendar of State Papers, Domestic, 1675–76* (London, 1907), 85, 98, 134, 154, 342; *Calendar of State Papers, Colonial, 1675–76,* #707.

9. "Causes of Discontent in Virginia, 1676," *Virginia Magazine of History and Biography* 3 (1895–96), 38, #8; *Calendar of State Papers, Colonial, 1675–76,* #707; CO5/1371/Pt. II/153.

10. For an explanation of Virginia taxes, see H. D. Farish, ed., *The Present State of Virginia, and the College* by Henry Hartwell, James Blair, and Edward Chilton (Williamsburg, Va., 1940 ed.), pp. 53–56; Giles Bland suggested a tax on land instead of polls in "The State of Virginia, 1676," *Virginia Magazine of History and Biography,* 20 (1912), 355–56, as did the Isle of Wight County in its grievances following Bacon's Rebellion, CO5/1371/Pt. II/161–62.

11. *Calendar of State Papers, Colonial, 1675–76,* #707, #859; *Calendar of State Papers, Domestic, 1676–77,* 337.

12. *Calendar of State Papers, Colonial, 1669–74,* #63, pp. 22–24, #145–46; H. R. McIlwaine, ed., *Minutes of the Council and General Court of Colonial Virginia, 1622–1632, 1670–1676* (Richmond, 1924), 296.

13. Hening, ed., *Statutes*, II, 519; Burk, *History of Virginia*, II, App., xxxiii–xxxv.

14. *Calendar of State Papers, Colonial, 1669–74,* #572; Berkeley to Treasurer Danby, Feb. 1, 1675, *Virginia Magazine of History and Biography,* 32 (1924), 191–92; Fairfax Harrison, *Virginia Land Grants* (Richmond, 1925), pp. 60, 84, 124, 149–150; Fairfax Harrison, *Landmarks of Old Prince William* (Richmond, 1924), I, 42–43; R. B. Davis, ed., *William Fitzhugh and his Chesapeake World, 1676–1701* (Chapel Hill, 1963), pp. 39–46.

15. H. R. McIlwaine, ed., *Journals of the House of Burgesses of Virginia, 1659/60–1693* (Richmond, 1914), 62; Hening, ed., *Statutes*, II, 311–12; *Calendar of State Papers, Colonial, 1675–76,* #602–604.

16. Berkeley to Lord Arlington, Sept. 21, 1674, Burk, *History of Virginia*, II, App., xxxiii; Berkeley to Danby, Feb. 1, 1675, *Virginia Magazine of History and Biography,* 32 (1924), 191–92.

17. Petition, June 23, 1675, *Calendar of State Papers, Colonial, America and West Indies, 1675–76,* #602, #604.
18. The "Heads" of the charter as approved by the Attorney and Solicitor Generals are in Burk, *History of Virginia,* II, App. xl–xli. For the King's approval, see *ibid.,* lvi–lvii. For agents' explanation of "Heads," see *ibid.,* xlvii–lx. The completed charter draft is in *Virginia Magazine of History and Biography,* 56 (1948), 264–66. See also *Calendar of State Papers, Colonial, 1675–76,* #602–603, #696, #697, I–II, #834.
19. *Ibid.,* #834, #835; William A. Shaw, ed., *Calendar of Treasury Books, 1676–79* (London, 1911), pp. 37–38; W. L. Grant and James Munro, eds., *Acts of the Privy Council, Colonial Series,* I, 1613–1680, p. 661, #1074; Burk, *History of Virginia,* II, App., lviii–lix; C. M. Andrews, *Guide to the Materials for American History to 1783 in the Public Record Office,* I (Washington, D. C., 1912), 271–72.
20. "Journal of the Lords of Trade," June 8, 1676, *Calendar of State Papers, Colonial, 1675–76,* #942; Giles Bland to Sir Joseph Williamson, Apr. 28, 1676, and Bland's "State of Virginia, 1676," both received in June 1676, *Virginia Magazine of History and Biography,* 20 (1912), 352–57; *Acts of the Privy Council, Colonial,* I, 1613–1680, p. 661, #1074; Wilcomb E. Washburn, "The Effect of Bacon's rebellion on Government in England and Virginia," Paper 17 from *Contributions from the Museum of History and Technology,* U. S. National Museum *Bulletin,* 225 (Smithsonian Institution, Washington, D. C., 1962), pp. 142–43.
21. *Calendar of State Papers, Colonial, 1675–76,* #602, #603; Agents' petition to Lord High Chancellor, n.d., Hening, ed., *Statutes,* II, 537; "Remonstrance against the Stoppage of the Charter," n.d., *ibid.,* 534–37.
22. Edward D. Neill, *Virginia Carolorum* (Albany, 1886), pp. 382–83.
23. Moryson to Lord Culpeper, Apr. 14, 1677, *Virginia Magazine of History and Biography,* 21 (1913), 368; Commissioners for Virginia to Mr. Watkins, Apr. 14, 1677, *ibid.,* 367; Fairfax Harrison, *Landmarks of Old Prince William,* I, 194.
24. *Calendar of State Papers, Colonial, 1675–76,* #599; *ibid.,* 1677–80, #308, #360.
25. Burk, *History of Virginia,* II, App. xl–xli; *Virginia Magazine of History and Biography,* 56 (1948), 265; Harrison, *Virginia Land Grants,* p. 35.
26. Additional Manuscripts, 30372, f24b, British Museum; "Enquiries to the Governor of Virginia," Sept. 29, 1670, Hening, ed., *Statutes,* II, 511–17; G. L. Beer, *The Old Colonial System,* I (New York, 1912), 193 and note.
27. Hartwell *et al., The Present State of Virginia,* H. D. Farish, ed., pp. 26, 35; Philip Alexander Bruce, *Institutional History of Virginia in the Seventeenth Century,* II (New York, 1910), 577–78; *Virginia Magazine of History and Biography,* 3 (1895–96), 42–47; Harrison, *Virginia Land Grants,* p. 150 and note 89.
28. Hening, ed., *Statutes,* II, 39, 56, 137; *Virginia Magazine of History and Biography,* 8 (1900–01), 241.
29. For Francis Moryson's arrival and career in Virginia before 1676, see "Colonel Norwood's Voyage to Virginia in 1649," William Maxwell, ed., *Virginia Historical Register,* II (1849), 121–23, 137; HMC 70: *Pepys,* pp.

262–63; *Virginia Magazine of History and Biography*, 8 (1900–01), 108, 167; *ibid.*, 12 (1904–05), 205; *ibid.*, 18 (1910), 413; Hening, ed., *Statutes*, II, 39, 56, 137; Richard L. Morton, *Colonial Virginia*, I (Chapel Hill, 1960), 189, 278–79n; C. M. Andrews, ed., *Narratives of the Insurrections, 1675–1690* (New York, 1915), p. 102; Justin Winsor, *Narrative and Critical History of the United States*, III (Cambridge, Mass., 1884), 148.

For Thomas Ludwell, see *Virginia Magazine of History and Biography*, 1 (1893–94), 174–76; *ibid.*, 3 (1895–96), 133, 156; *ibid.*, 8 (1900–01), 239, 241; *ibid.*, 12 (1904–05), 288–89; *ibid.*, 14 (1906–07), 267, 354; Hening, ed., *Statutes*, II, 39, 56, 137, 313; *Virginia County Records*, VI (March 1909), 83, 119. Thomas and Philip Ludwell were related to the Berkeleys through the formers' maternal great grandfather, *Virginia Magazine of History and Biography*, 1 (1893–94), 174–75. Philip Ludwell, Thomas's brother, married Berkeley's widow soon after the governor's death, *Ibid.*, 25 (1917), 88n.

For General Robert Smith, see *Tyler's Quarterly*, IX (Apr. 1928), 288; *ibid.*, VII (1925–26), 63; *William and Mary Quarterly*, 1st ser., VIII (Jan. 1900), 184; *ibid.*, III (July 1894), 67; *Virginia Magazine of History and Biography*, 9 (1901–02), 46; *ibid.*, 19 (1911), 33–34; *ibid.*, 20 (1912), 360–63.

30. Agents' report to Virginia, n.d., Burk, *History of Virginia*, II, App., xxxvi–xxxvii; "Observations upon the several heads proposed by Mr. Secretary Ludwell and other gentlemen sent from Virginia," *Calendar of State Papers, Colonial, 1675–76*, #403.

31. Burk, *History of Virginia*, II, App., xxxvi–xxxvii.

32. Giles Bland, "The State of Virginia, 1676," *Virginia Magazine of History and Biography*, 20 (1912), 355, 356.

33. Agents' report to Virginia, n.d., Burk, *History of Virginia*, II, App., xxxvii.

34. Agents' explanation of "Heads," *ibid.*, pp. l, lii. The final draft of the charter did not include the two-year limitation upon the King. *Virginia Magazine of History and Biography*, 56 (July 1948), 264–66.

35. Quoted in T. J. Wertenbaker, *Virginia Under the Stuarts, 1607–1688* (Princeton, 1914), p. 136.

36. H. D. Farish, ed., pp. 21–26.

37. *Virginia Magazine of History and Biography*, 1 (1893–94), 175–76; Hening, ed., *Statutes*, II, 280. For duration of the Long Assembly, see T. J. Wertenbaker, *Virginia Under the Stuarts*, pp. 135–36n.

38. Bernard Bailyn, "Politics and Social Structure in Virginia," James Morton Smith, ed., *Seventeenth-Century America: Essays in Colonial History* (Chapel Hill, 1959), pp. 90–115. For other recent discussion of Bacon's Rebellion, see Wilcomb E. Washburn, *The Governor and the Rebel: a History of Bacon's Rebellion in Virginia* (Chapel Hill, 1957) and Wesley Frank Craven, *The Southern Colonies in the Seventeenth Century, 1607–1689* (Baton Rouge, 1949), ch. X.

39. See County Grievances, CO5/1371/Pt. I/151–52b and Pt. II/149–208; also *Virginia Magazine of History and Biography*, 2 (1894–95), 166–73, 380–92 and 3 (1895–96), 35–42, 132–47; Burk, *History of Virginia*, II, 250; Giles Bland, "The State of Virginia, 1676," *Virginia Magazine of History and Biography*, 20 (1912), 255. The Commissioners arrived in Vir-

ginia in January 1677 with instructions from the King to reduce the amount of tobacco paid to legislators. By March 27, after constant urging, the amount agreed upon was 120 pounds of tobacco *per diem, ibid.,* 21 (1913), 240, 362, 365.

40. Agents to ?, March 10, 1676, Burk, *History of Virginia,* II, App., lviii–lix; Agents to Virginia, *Acts of the Privy Council, Colonial,* I, *1613–1680,* p. 661, #1074; "Memorial of the Virginia Agents to one of the Principal Secretaries of State," n.d., Hening, ed., *Statutes,* II, 538–43; "Proposals most humbly offered to his most sacred Ma[tie] by Tho: Ludwell and Rob[t] Smith for the Reducing the Rebells in Virginia to their obedience," *Virginia Magazine of History and Biography,* 1 (1893–94), 433–35; Ludwell to Sec'y Conventry, Apr. 1677, quoted in George Chalmers, *An Introduction to the History of the Revolt of the American Colonies* (Boston, 1845), I, 161–62.

41. CO5/1371/Pt. II/169.

42. *Virginia Magazine of History and Biography,* 3 (1895–96), 135–36, 141–42.

43. Commissioners to Sec'y Coventry, Apr. 5, 1677, *ibid.,* 21 (1913), 366; William Sherwood to Sec'y Williamson, Apr. 13, 1677, *ibid.,* 367.

44. Jan. 22, 1677, William H. Browne, ed., *Archives of Maryland,* V (Baltimore, 1887), 154.

45. *Calendar of State Papers, Colonial, America and West Indies, 1677–1680,* #263.

46. General Assembly to Sir Joseph Williamson, Apr. 2, 1677, H. R. McIlwaine, ed., *Journals of the House of Burgesses, 1659/60–1693,* 98–99; William Blathwayt to the Earl of Carlisle, May 31, 1679, Blathwayt Papers of Colonial Williamsburg, vol. XXII.

47. For the royal charter of 1676, see Burk, *History of Virginia,* II, App., lxi–lxii. The new governor, Thomas Lord Culpeper, may have been responsible for the weak charter. See Hening, ed., *Statutes,* II, 531.

48. For the business of a permanent revenue and Poynings' Law, see *Calendar of State Papers, Colonial, America and West Indies, 1677–80,* #917; British Museum, Abstract of Commissions, etc., Add. Mss, 30372, f24b; Lord Culpeper to William Blathwayt, June 15, 1680, Blathwayt Papers, Colonial Williamsburg, vol. XVII; same to same, July 8, 1680, *ibid.;* Leonard W. Labaree, ed., *Royal Instructions to British Colonial Governors, 1670–1776,* I (New York and London, 1935), 125; Order of the Privy Council, Oct. 30, 1678, *Virginia Magazine of History and Biography,* 24 (1916), 79–80; Rainbolt, *Virginia's Vision,* ch. VII; Leonard W. Labaree, *Royal Government in America* (New York, 1958 edition), pp. 219–22.

CHAPTER 4

1. When I gave this paper at the Rutgers Conference in 1966, I was planning a comparative history of the English mainland and island colonies in America, 1675–1700, a project I have temporarily shelved in order to write a book on the rise of the sugar planters in Jamaica and the other English islands.

2. The secondary literature on late seventeenth-century Massachusetts is infinitely richer than that on Jamaica. For Massachusetts, in addition to titles cited in footnotes below, see Thomas Hutchinson, *History of the Colony and Province of Massachusetts Bay*, ed. L. S. Mayo, 3 vols. (Cambridge, 1936); J. G. Palfrey, *History of New England*, 5 vols. (Boston, 1859–1890); and J. T. Adams, *The Founding of New England* (Boston, 1921). For Jamaica, in addition to titles cited in the footnotes below, see Frank Cundall, *Governors of Jamaica in the Seventeenth Century* (London, 1936); and C. V. Black, *The Story of Jamaica* (London, 1965), Ch. 3–6.

3. Population figures for Massachusetts are drawn from U.S. Bureau of the Census, *Historical Statistics of the United States* (Washington, D.C., 1960), p. 756. The most trustworthy Jamaica estimates for this period are given in *Journal of the Assembly of Jamaica* (14 vols. Jamaica, 1811–1829), I, Appendix, p. 40. Public Record Office (hereafter cited as P.R.O.) C.O. 138/1/80 and C.O. 138/2/113–117. See also F. W. Pitman, *The Development of the British West Indies* (New Haven, 1917), pp. 48, 373. The physical expansion of settlement in Massachusetts can be followed through the creation of new towns. An approximate notion of expansion in Jamaica can be derived from contemporary maps, such as the four maps of Jamaica, all dated in the 1670's, in the Blathwayt Atlas, John Carter Brown Library.

4. For interesting details on the Jamaican economy, circa 1670, see J. Harry Bennett, "Cary Helyar, Merchant and Planter of Seventeenth-Century Jamaica," *William and Mary Quarterly*, 3rd. ser., XXI (1964), 53–76. Comparative West Indian sugar production statistics for the late seventeenth century can be drawn from the following: British Museum [hereafter cited as B.M.] Add. MSS. 8133 C/237; P.R.O. C.O. 318/1/27; C.O. 390/6/31–38, 51–56.

5. For the liquor bottles, see M. C. Link, "Exploring the Drowned City of Port Royal," *National Geographic Magazine*, Vol. 117 (February 1960), pp. 151–183. For the buccaneers, see C. H. Haring, *The Buccaneers in the West Indies in the XVII Century* (London, 1910). The fullest description of Jamaican internal development at this time is in C. A. Lindley's unpublished doctoral dissertation, "Jamaica, 1660–1678" (University of Pennsylvania, 1932).

6. Joseph Jackson to Increase Mather, 6 March 1683/4. Boston Public Library, Mather Papers, V, 53.

7. Curtis Nettels, "England's Trade with New England and New York, 1685–1720," *Publications* of the Colonial Society of Massachusetts, XXVIII, 322–350; Bernard Bailyn, *The New England Merchants in the Seventeenth Century* (Cambridge, 1955), pp. 182–189.

8. My comparative figures on Jamaican and Massachusetts trade with England, circa 1700, are drawn from the following: U.S. Bureau of the Census, *Historical Statistics*, p. 757; P.R.O., C.O. 318/1/27; and B. M. Sloane 2902/151. See also Ralph Davis, *The Rise of the English Shipping Industry* (London, 1962), pp. 298–299. New England totals are always given collectively, hence Massachusetts' exact share is problematical.

9. Figures on Jamaican population and slave importation are drawn from the following: P.R.O., C.O. 138/9/268; C.O. 318/2/11, 73; and T 70/1205/

A43. See also K. G. Davies, *The Royal African Company* (London, 1957), pp. 301–302, 363; F. W. Pitman, *Development of the British West Indies*, pp. 373, 391.

10. The Jamaica slave revolt of 1685 is described in P.R.O., C.O. 138/5/87–102 and C.O. 140/4/84–100. The revolt of 1690 is mentioned in C.O. 138/7/3–4. The slave code of 1664 is in C.O. 139/1/55–58; the slave code of 1683 is printed in *The Laws of Jamaica . . . Confirmed by his Majesty in Council, April 17, 1684* (London, 1684), pp. 140–148; and the slave code of 1696 is in C.O. 139/8/73–82.

11. Shurtleff, *Records of the Governor and Company of the Massachusetts Bay*, IV, pt. 2. The plantation office's New England entry book for 1661–1679 (P.R.O. C.O. 5/903) records no communication between Massachusetts and the crown for an even longer period, 1664–1674.

12. Between July 1675 and May 1677, the Massachusetts General Court levied 32 country rates. A single rate (the normal annual tax levy) was valued at £1553. See Shurtleff, *Records of the Governor and Company of the Massachusetts Bay*, IV, pt. 2.

13. D. E. Leach lists the London imprints on King Philip's War in *Flintlock and Tomahawk* (New York, 1966), pp. 271–273. Leverett's account is in P.R.O., C.O. 5/903/90–97.

14. *Ibid.*, C.O. 138/1/61–82, 134; C.O. 140/1/143–146; William Beeston's Journal in *Interesting Tracts, Relating to the Island of Jamaica* (St. Jago de la Vega, 1800), pp. 281–287. See also A. P. Thornton, *West-India Policy under the Restoration* (Oxford, 1956), Ch. 3.

15. P.R.O., C.O. 139/1/100–101, 117. See also Thornton, *op. cit.*, pp. 167–171 and A. M. Whitson, *The Constitutional Development of Jamaica, 1660–1729* (Manchester, 1929), Ch. 2–3.

16. M. G. Hall, *Edward Randolph and the American Colonies* (Chapel Hill, 1960), pp. 24–25.

17. Coventry to Governor Vaughan of Jamaica, 8 June, 1676. B.M. Add. MSS. 25,120/74.

18. *Interesting Tracts Relating to Jamaica*, pp. 105–117; P.R.O., C.O. 138/3/143–183, 198–241.

19. A. M. Whitson describes the Jamaican constitutional crisis of 1676–1680 in her *Constitutional Development of Jamaica*, Ch. 4. See also Thornton, *West-India Policy*, Ch. 5. Miss Whitson, in my opinion, misunderstands Carlisle's role in this struggle. There is abundant documentation: the *Journals of the Assembly of Jamaica* (14 vols. Jamaica, 1811–1829), I; *Interesting Tracts relating to Jamaica*; P.R.O., C.O. 138/3; and B.M. Add. MSS. 25,120; Sloane 2724; Egerton 2395. The Egerton volume contains an exceedingly interesting journal of the September, 1678 Jamaica Assembly, unused by Miss Whitson.

20. *The Laws of Jamaica . . . Confirmed by his Majesty in Council, April 17, 1684*, pp. 129–139. Whitson, *op. cit.*, ch. 5, recounts the struggle over the revenue act, though she underplays Jamaica's loss of legislative independence. For this phase of the story, the chief sources are: P.R.O., C.O. 138/4, 140/4 and T 64/88; and *A Narrative of Affairs Lately Received from . . . Jamaica* (London, 1683).

21. The rise of Jamaica's sugar planting master class can be traced through the island land patents for the 1660's, 1670's and 1680's, conveniently indexed in the Jamaica Archives, Spanish Town.

22. K. G. Davies gives an authoritative account of Charles II's and James II's active support of the Royal African Company, as well as the company's dealings with the Jamaica planters, in his *The Royal African Company*. The voluminous papers of the Royal African Company in the Public Record Office include copies of letters sent to agent Molesworth (T 70/57) and abstracts of his replies (T 70/12). For the sugar duty of 1685, see G. L. Beer, *The Old Colonial System, 1660–1688* (2 vols. New York, 1912), I, 160–166. Jamaica's reaction to the new tax is in P.R.O., C.O. 138/5/97–105.

23. Information about the projected West India or South American Company can be found in Dalby Thomas, *An Historical Account of the Rise and Growth of the West-India Colonies* (London, 1690); B. M. Sloane 3984/210–211; *Journals of the Assembly of Jamaica*, I, 108–109; P.R.O., C.O. 29/3/471–473 and T 70/57/25–26. The Jamaica address against the project is in *Journals of the Assembly of Jamaica*, I, 123.

24. P.R.O., C.O. 5/903/265–266. M. G. Hall describes the crown prosecution of the Massachusetts charter, 1676–1684, in *Edward Randolph and the American Colonies*, Ch. 2–4. Documentation is more voluminous than for the Jamaica struggle. Among the chief sources are: the printed Massachusetts records; R. N. Toppan and A. T. S. Goodrick, eds., *Edward Randolph* (7 vols., Prince Society Publications, vols. 24–28, 30–31. Boston, 1898–1909); P.R.O. C.O. 5/903, 904 and 905; and two collections of Blathwayt Papers in the Huntington Library and Colonial Williamsburg.

25. P.R.O. C.O. 5/904/213. The Mather Papers, Boston Public Library, many of which are printed in Massachusetts Historical Society *Collections*, 4th ser., VIII, show how fully the Puritans were informed by English Dissenters of the Popish Plot, the Exclusion Crisis, and the Tory Revenge.

26. Philip Haffenden contrasts Charles II's relatively purposeful colonial policy with James II's bombast in "The Crown and the Colonial Charter, 1675–1688," *William and Mary Quarterly*, 3rd ser., XV (1958), 297–311, 452–466. During James II's reign, the plantation office entry books on Massachusetts (P.R.O., C.O. 5/904) and Jamaica (C.O. 138/5–6) show a great slackening of interest and vigor.

27. V. F. Barnes views Andros' regime from a nostalgic imperial perspective in *The Dominion of New England* (New Haven, 1923). M. G. Hall follows Randolph's role in *Edward Randolph*, Ch. 5, and R. S. Dunn describes the transformation of the "moderates" in *Puritans and Yankees*, Ch. 10–11.

28. The negotiations over Albemarle's appointment are in P.R.O., C.O. 138/5/220–335. For background, see Estelle Ward, *Christopher Monck, Duke of Albemarle* (London, 1915), pp. 234–270.

29. The secondary literature on Albemarle's governorship is much skimpier than on Andros' regime. Considerable data can be gleaned from the printed Jamaica Assembly records; from P.R.O., C.O. 138/6 and 140/4; and B. M. Sloane 1599 (Jamaica Council Minutes, 1687–1689).

30. Ward, *Duke of Albemarle*, pp. 304, 327–328; P.R.O., C.O. 138/5/334–335;

C.O. 138/6/119–120; C.O. 140/4/226–228; *Interesting Tracts relating to Jamaica*, pp. 214–215.

31. Dr. Hans Sloane's medical report on the Duke's fatal drinking bout is in B. M. Sloane 3984/283–84.

32. A mass of data illuminating the Massachusetts revolution of 1689 is found in the following three collections: W. H. Whitmore, ed., *The Andros Tracts* (3 vols. Prince Society Publications, vols. 5–7. Boston, 1868–1874); C. M. Andrews, *Narratives of the Insurrections, 1675–1690* (New York, 1915); and M. G. Hall, L. H. Leder and M. G. Kammen, *The Glorious Revolution in America* (Chapel Hill, 1964).

33. P.R.O. C.O. 138/6/144–165, 210–226; C.O. 140/4/261–262, 268, 273–275; *Journals of the Assembly of Jamaica*, I, 134–136.

34. The post-revolutionary confusion in Massachusetts deserves further study. There is a mass of documentation in the unpublished General Court records and in vols. 35–37, Massachusetts Archives.

35. For Mather's unsuccessful negotiations with James II and William III, see K. B. Murdock, *Increase Mather* (Cambridge, 1925), Ch. 13–14. The fascinating details of Mather's lobbying techniques are recorded in his Diary for 1688–1689, American Antiquarian Society. There is further important manuscript material in the Mather Papers, Boston Public Library; in P.R.O. C.O. 5/855 and 5/905; and Carte MSS 81, Bodleian Library.

36. Historical Manuscripts Commission, *Manuscripts of the House of Lords, 1689–1690*, pp. 422–432.

37. Carte MSS 81/756, Bodleian Library. The activities of the Jamaica lobby can be followed in P.R.O., C.O. 137/2 and 138/6. For background, see L. M. Penson, *The Colonial Agents of the British West Indies* (London, 1924).

38. The chief sources for William Beeston's governorship are: the printed Jamaica Assembly records and the following volumes of Jamaica manuscripts in the Public Record Office: 137/1–4 (correspondence with the secretary of state); 138/7–9 (Plantation office entry books); 139/8 (laws) and 140/5–6 (sessional papers).

39. Each of the two chief contestants in the Massachusetts charter negotiation —William Blathwayt and Increase Mather—kept precise records of his role in the struggle. Hence, there is probably more satisfying documentation for this episode than for any other late seventeenth-century Anglo-American constitutional conflict. The prime sources include Mather's Diary for 1691, Massachusetts Historical Society; P.R.O., C.O. 5/856 and 5/905; and Carte MSS 81, Bodleian Library. See also M. G. Hall, ed., "The Autobiography of Increase Mather," American Antiquarian Society *Proceedings*, 71, pt. 2, pp. 322–343.

40. Entry for 9 Sept. 1691, Increase Mather's Diary, Massachusetts Historical Society.

41. For Dudley, see Everett Kimball, *The Public Life of Joseph Dudley*, (New York, 1911).

42. For fuller discussion of post-revolutionary New England's intellectual, political and social structure, see Perry Miller, *The New England Mind*

from Colony to Province (Cambridge, 1953); Bailyn, *The New England Merchants in the Seventeenth Century* and Dunn, *Puritans and Yankees.* For the post-revolutionary West Indies, see Richard Pares, *A West-India Fortune* (London, 1950).

43. For fuller discussion of English mercantilist policy toward the colonies in the late seventeenth century, see C. M. Andrews, *The Colonial Period of American History,* (4 vols.; New Haven, 1934–1938), Vol. 4.

44. The preparations for the 1694 expeditionary force are detailed in P.R.O., C.O. 138/7/197–401. For background, see G. H. Guttridge, *The Colonial Policy of William III in America and the West Indies,* (Cambridge, Eng. 1922).

CHAPTER 5

1. Thomas J. Wertenbaker, *Give Me Liberty* (Philadelphia, 1958); Richard L. Morton, *Colonial Virginia,* 2 vols. (Chapel Hill, 1960); Philip Alexander Bruce, *History of Virginia,* Vol. I, *The Colonial Period, 1607–1763* (Chicago, 1924); Leonidas Dodson, *Alexander Spotswood* (Philadelphia, 1932); Louis B. Wright and Marion Tinling (eds.), *William Byrd of Virginia: The London Diary, 1717–1721* (New York, 1958), 3–46; George M. Brydon, *Virginia's Mother Church,* 2 vols. (Richmond, 1947, Philadelphia, 1950).

2. Michael G. Hall, *Edward Randolph and the American Colonies, 1676–1703* (Chapel Hill, 1960), 138–177; Peter Laslett, "John Locke, The Great Recoinage, and the Origins of the Board of Trade, 1695–1698," *William and Mary Quarterly,* 3rd., XIV (1957), 370–402; Michael Kammen (ed.), "Virginia at the Close of the Seventeenth Century: An Appraisal by James Blair and John Locke," *Virginia Magazine of History and Biography,* LXXIV (1966), 141–169; John M. Hemphill, II, "Virginia and the English Commercial System, 1689–1733" (unpublished Ph.D. dissertation, Princeton University, 1964), ch. 5–8.

3. Stephen S. Webb, "Officer and Governors: The Role of the British Army in Imperial Politics and the Administration of the Amer-Colonies, 1689–1722" (unpublished Ph.D. dissertation, University of Wisconsin, 1965), and, "The Strange Career of Francis Nicholson," *William and Mary Quarterly,* 3rd ser., XXIII (1966), 513–548.

4. William Byrd I to ——— Randolph, 25 July 1690, "Letters of William Byrd I," *Virginia Magazine of History and Biography,* XXVI (1918), 130–131.

5. *Journals of the House of Burgesses,* 1659/60–1693, 316–318; P.R.O., C.O. 5/1305, 35–39, 50–62; P.R.O., C.O. 391/6, 214–223–224, 277–278, 282, 291, 319.

6. Bruce T. McCully, "From the North Riding to Morocco: The Early Years of Governor Francis Nicholson, 1655–1686," *William and Mary Quarterly,* 3rd ser., XIX (1962) 534–556; Webb, "Francis Nicholson," 515–527.

7. Samuel Mohler, "Commissary James Blair" (unpublished Ph.D. dissertation, University of Chicago, 1940), 1–44; Brydon, *Va. Mother Church,* I, 273–326.

8. P.R.O., C.O. 5/1307, 22–23; Gertrude Jacobson, *William Blathwayt* (New Haven, 1932), 305–307.
9. Hall, *Randolph*, 138–177.
10. Robert Walcott, Jr., *English Politics in the Early Eighteenth Century* (Cambridge, Mass., 1956), 82–88; J. H. Plumb, *The Origins of Political Stability: England, 1675–1725* (Boston, 1967), 134–138; Laslett, "John Locke," 390–391.
11. William S. Perry, *Papers Relating to the History of the Church in Virginia* (Hartford, 1870), 3–44.
12. *Executive Journals of the Council*, I, 324–325, 360–364; Gov. Andros to Council of Trade and Plantations, P.R.O., C.O. 391/8, 92–93, P.R.O., C.O. 5/1309, 52.
13. Kammen, "Blair and Locke," 141–170; Laslett, "John Locke," 399–400; Henry Hartwell, James Blair, and Edward Chilton, *The Present State of Virginia and the College*, edited by Hunter Dickinson Farish (Williamsburg, 1940); Lambeth Palace Papers, Library Ref., Class 954, Item 60, Class 1029, Item 22.
14. Jacobson, *Blathwayt*, 297–302; Nicholson to Henry Compton, Bishop of London, 13 February 1697, Fulham Palace, MSS., Maryland, #143; Nicholson to Earl of Bridgewater, 30 March and 22 April 1697, Nicholson Papers, Huntington Library.
15. Lovelace MSS., Bodleian Library, Locke, e9; P.R.O., C.O. 5/1309, #37, 252–259.
16. Stephen Baxter, *William III and the Defense of European Liberty* (New York, 1966), 359–377.
17. David Alan Williams, "Political Alignments in Colonial Virginia, 1698–1750" (unpublished Ph.D. dissertation, Northwestern University, 1959), ch. 1–2; for a differing view, see Webb, "Francis Nicholson," 535–541.
18. Hunter, as with most military and political figures, chose not to place his career in the hands of one man. He was supported in his quest for the Virginia governorship and later the New York office by the Earl of Stair, aide-de-camp to Marlborough, who came from Hunter's county of Ayrshire, by the Earl of Argyll, and by Dr. Arbuthnot, physician to the Queen. Moreover, in 1707 Hunter had made a most advantageous marriage to the wealthy widow of his friend and fellow officer, Lord John Hary, second son of the Marquis of Tweedsdale. James E. Scanlon, "Robert Hunter, Colonial Governor" (unpublished mss., University of Virginia, 1966).
19. Dodson, Spotswood, 251–276; Williams, Political Alignments," ch. 4–5; Byrd, *The London Diary*, 400–401; Exec. Journals of Council, III, 524–525; Webb, "Officers and Governors," 380: the nephews of the Bishop of London were Christopher and John Robinson, Sr., father of the longtime Speaker of the House, John Robinson, Jr.
20. Plumb, *Political Stability*, 159–189.
21. Williams, "Political Alignments," ch. 6. The best insight into the political astuteness of Gooch can be achieved by reading the typescript collection of Gooch's correspondence to England compiled in the Research Library, Colonial Williamsburg, Inc.
22. Gooch to Board of Trade, P.R.O., C.O. 5/1322, 149–152; Board of Trade to Gooch, P.R.O., C.O. 5/1366, 71–74.

23. Hemphill, "Virginia and the English Commercial System," 219–286; J. H. Plumb, *Sir Robert Walpole, The King's Minister* (Boston, 1961), 233–284.

CHAPTER 6

1. Jonathan Belcher to Sir Peter Warren, quoted in George Bancroft, *History of the United States* (Boston, 1872), IV, 142.

   This article is drawn from work done, initially, on a doctoral dissertation: "An Easie Access: Anglo-American Politics in New York, 1732–1753" (unpub. Ph.D. diss., Harvard, 1961). A revised and expanded version was subsequently published as *Newcastle's New York: Anglo-American Politics, 1732–1753* (Harvard U. Press, Cambridge, Mass., 1968). The first half of this article is based upon a portion of Chp. III of *Newcastle's New York*, and the author is grateful to Harvard University Press for permission to reprint parts of pp. 50–58 of the book. The second half of the article is drawn from the dissertation, where a much fuller account of DeLancey's career is presented and documented.

2. Charles McLean Andrews, *The Colonial Period of American History* (New Haven, 1934–1938), IV, 187.

3. Quoted in Andrews, *Colonial Period*, IV, 309.

4. See, for instance, N. C. Hunt, *Two Early Political Associations: The Quakers and the Dissenting Deputies in the Age of Sir Robert Walpole* (Oxford, 1961); Bernard L. Manning, *The Protestant Dissenting Deputies* (ed. Ormerod Greenwood, Cambridge, 1952); Maurice W. Armstrong, "The Dissenting Deputies and the American Colonies," *Church History*, XXIX (1960), 316n6.

5. Carl R. Woodward, *Ploughs and Politicks: Charles Read of New Jersey and His Notes on Agriculture, 1715–1774* (New Brunswick, 1941), p. 97.

6. Lewis Morris to Mrs. Norris, May 14, 1742, *The Papers of Lewis Morris, Governor of the Province of New Jersey from 1738 to 1746*, N.J.H.S., *Collections*, IV, 145. For the history of the New York agency, see Edward P. Lilly, *The Colonial Agents of New York and New Jersey* (Washington, 1936).

7. Robert Hunter to A. Philipse, August 15, 1718, E. B. O'Callaghan and Berthold Fernow, eds., *Documents Relative to the Colonial History of the State of New York* (Albany, 1856–1887) V, 516.

8. Philip Livingston to Robert Livingston, September 23, 1725, Livingston-Redmond Papers, F.D.R. Library. See also William L. Sachse, *The Colonial American in Britain* (Madison, 1956), 93–115, 132–153. For a typical letter of advice to an American in London, see [Lt. John Ormsby Donnellan,) "Advice to a Stranger in London, 1763," *Pennsylvania Magazine of History and Biography*, LXXIII (1949), 85–87.

9. Beverly McAnear, ed., "R. H. Morris: An American in London, 1735–1736," *Pennsylvania Magazine of History and Biography*, LXIV (1940), 164–217, 356–406.

10. [Anon.,] *Of the American Plantations* (1714) in William L. Saunders, ed., *The Colonial Records of North Carolina* (Raleigh, 1886–1890), II, 159.

11. McAnear, "R. H. Morris," pp. 213–214, 403.

12. James DeLancey to Sir John Heathcote, June 17, 1736, 1 A.N.C. XI/B/5 "0", Lincolnshire Archives Committee.

13. Controversy over the character of the DeLancey-Livingston rivalry has taken a new lease on life. See Roger Champagne, "Family Politics versus Constitutional Principles: The New York Assembly Elections of 1768 and 1769," *William and Mary Quarterly*, 3rd ser., XX (1963), 57–79; Lawrence H. Leder, "The New York Elections of 1769: An Assault on Privilege," *Mississippi Valley Historical Review*, XLIX (1962–1963), 675–682; Bernard Friedman, "The New York Assembly Elections of 1768 and 1769: The Disruption of Family Politics," *New York History*, XLVI (1965), 3–24; Patricia U. Bonomi, "Political Patterns in Colonial New York City: The General Assembly Election of 1768," *Political Science Quarterly*, LXXXI (1966), 432–447.

14. Lewis Morris to Marquis of Lothian, March 26, 1735, N-Y.H.S., *Collections*, 1918, pp. 126–127; Collinson to Colden, March 27, 1747, *ibid.*, 1919, p. 369 and various other letters in the N.-Y.H.S. Colden Papers and the British Museum Collinson Papers.

15. Euphemia Norris to Lewis Morris, June 15, 1742, Morris Family Papers, R.U.L.

16. Colden to John Catherwood, November 21, 1749, N-Y.H.S., *Collections*, 1920, p. 159.

17. *D.A.B.*, V, 212–213; Edward Floyd DeLancey, "Memoir of James De-Lancey," *Documentary History of New York* (E. B. O'Callaghan, ed., Albany, 1851), IV, 1037–1059; Stanley N. Katz, "An Easie Access: Anglo-American Politics in New York, 1732–1753," (unpublished Ph.D. dissertation, Harvard, 1961), 209–214. DeLancey acted as lieutenant governor in command of New York from 1753–1755 and from 1757 to 1760.

18. Philip C. Yorke, *The Life and Correspondence of Philip Yorke, earl of Hardwicke, lord high chancellor of England* (Cambridge, 1913), I, 422–423; Norman Sykes, "The Duke of Newcastle as Ecclesiastical Minister," *English Historical Review*, LVII (1942), 62–65; Herring to Hardwicke, June 16, 1743, Add. MSS 35598 f. 19, British Museum; R. Garnett, ed., "Correspondence of Archbishop Herring and Lord Hardwicke during the Rebellion of 1745," *English Historical Review*, XIX (1904), 529. For the correspondence of DeLancey and Herring, see: Herring to Sir G. Heathcote, September 23, 1731, 1 A.N.C. XI/B/4g, Lincolnshire Archives Committee; Rev. Samuel Johnson to Herring, June 29, 1753, *New York Colonial Documents*, VI, 777; DeLancey to Herring, October 15, 1753, William Smith MSS (Archives of the Protestant Episcopal Church), I, no. 4, N-Y.H.S.

19. L. B. Namier, *England in the Age of the American Revolution* (London, 1930), pp. 280–281; L. B. Namier, "Brice Fisher, M.P.: A Mid-Eighteenth Century Merchant and His Connections," *English Historical Review*, XLII (1927), 518–519; L. B. Namier, *The Structure of Politics at the Accession of George III* (2nd ed., London, 1957), pp. 52–54, 56–58; W. Baker to Newcastle, November 21, 1750, Add. MSS 32885 f.478, British Museum;

John Brooke, *The Chatham Administration, 1766–1768* (London, 1956), pp. 105, 128, 283. For a more detailed account of the Bakers' involvement in New York affairs, see Katz, "Easie Access," pp. 228–232.

20. Evelyn D. Heathcote, *An Account of Some of the Families Bearing the Name of Heathcote* (Winchester, 1899), pp. 79–86; Dixon Ryan Fox, *Caleb Heathcote* (New York, 1926), pp. 5–6, 8, 276, 280. For DeLancey's relations with the Heathcotes, see Katz, "Easie Access," pp. 233–236.

21. Heathcote, *Some Families,* pp. 86–87; Mrs. Paget Toynbee, ed., *The Letters of Horace Walpole, Fourth Earl of Orford,* (Oxford 1903–1925) II, 401–402. See the correspondence of Sir John Heathcote in the Ancaster Papers, Lincolnshire Archives Committee.

22. *D.N.B.,* XX, 876–877; Edward Floyd DeLancey, *New York and Admiral Sir Peter Warren at the Capture of Louisbourg, 1745* (n.p., [1896]) pp. 7–9; John Charnock, *Biographia Navalis* (London, 1794–1798), IV, 184–192; [Anon.,] "Biographical Memoir of the Late Sir Peter Warren, K.B., Vice Admiral of the Red Squadron," *The Naval Chronicle,* XII (1804), 257–275 (many inaccuracies); Gerald S. Graham, *Empire of the North Atlantic* (Toronto, 1950), pp. 123, 116–142. For an intensive discussion, see Katz, "Easie Access," pp. 242–257.

23. John Watts to John Watts, Jr., May 5, 1772, Watts Papers, v. 10, N-Y.H.S.

24. David Jones to Robert Charles, April 9, 1748, except, William Smith, Jr. Papers, III, 229, N-Y.P.L. Colden to Clinton, May 9, 1748, Bancroft Transcripts, Colden, I, 77, N-Y.P.L. For Charles' career, see Nicholas Varga, "Robert Charles: New York Agent, 1748–1770," *William and Mary Quarterly,* 3rd ser., XVIII (1961), 211–235.

25. DeLancey to Sir Gilbert Heathcote, September 9, 1729, 1 A.N.C. XI/B/5b, Lincolnshire Archives Committee.

26. Martha Heathcote to [Sir Gilbert Heathcote], May 8, 1732, 1 A.N.C. XI/B/4n; DeLancey to Sir Gilbert Heathcote, May 16, 1732, 1 A.N.C. XI/B/4c; Martha Heathcote to Sir John Heathcote, December 4, 1734 and May 3, 1736, 1 A.N.C. XI/B/4t and 5n, Lincolnshire Archives Committee.

27. Samuel Baker to Sir John Heathcote, November 8, 1735, 1 A.N.C. XI/B/2s, Lincolnshire Archives Committee; William and Samuel Baker to Warren, April 30 and August 1, 1745, Warren MSS, Clements Library.

28. Samuel Baker to Sir John Heathcote, November [2 or 3] and November 8, 1735, 1 A.N.C. XI/B/2s, Lincolnshire Archives Committee.

29. DeLancey to Sir John Heathcote, September 3, 1733, 1 A.N.C. XI/B/4q, Lincolnshire Archives Committee.

30. DeLancey to Sir John Heathcote, June 19, 1734, 1 A.N.C. XI/B/4r Lincolnshire Archives Committee.

31. See note 28. For an account of the hearing of Morris's complaint before the privy council, see Stanley N. Katz, *Newcastle's New York: Anglo-American Politics, 1732–1753* (Cambridge, Mass., 1968), pp. 107–119.

32. DeLancey to Sir John Heathcote, December 9, 1734, 1 A.N.C. XI/B/4s; DeLancey to Sir John Heathcote, July 7, 1735, 1 A.N.C. XI/B/4v, Lincolnshire Archives Committee. DeLancy made a final, unsuccessful effort to secure confirmation of his commission in 1736, through the intercession of Cosby's widow with the Duke of Newcastle. (DeLancey to [Sir John

Heathcote], December 6, 1736, 1 A.N.C. XI/B/4y, Lincolnshire Archives Committee).

33. DeLancey to Sir Gilbert Heathcote, June 21, 1731, 1 A.N.C. XI/B/4e and 4f; DeLancey to Sir John Heathcote, June 21, 1731, A.N.C. XI/B/4d; Thomas Herring to Sir Gilbert Heathcote, September 23, 1731, 1 A.N.C. XI/B/4g; Martha Heathcote to Sir Gilbert Heathcote, December 31, 1731, 1 A.N.C. XI/B/4j; DeLancey to John and Sir Gilbert Heathcote, December 30, 1731, 1 A.N.C. XI/B/4 "1"; Martha Heathcote to Sir John Heathcote, May 3, 1736, 1 A.N.C. XI/B/5n, Lincolnshire Archives Committee.

34. Newcastle to Clinton, October 27, 1747, Clinton MSS, Clements Library; Clinton to Colden, January 31, 1748, Bancroft Transcripts, Colden, I, 59, N-Y.P.L.; Colden to Clinton, February 14, 1748, N-Y.H.S., *Collections*, 1920, p. 13.

35. For a discussion of New York politics, 1743–1753, see Katz, *Newcastle's New York*, pp. 164–242.

36. Clinton to Bedford, April 9, 1750, draft, Clinton MSS, Clements Library.

37. Clinton to Newcastle, February 13, 1748, *New York Colonial Documents*, VI, 416–417.

38. Shirley to Newcastle, January 23, 1753, Add. MSS 32731 f. 100 British Museum; Catherwood to Clinton, March 4, 1751, Clinton MSS, Clements Library; Treasury Minute Book, September 12, 1750, T. 29:31 f. 305, Public Record Office.

39. Catherwood to Clinton, October 10, 1749, Clinton MSS, Clements Library; Clinton to Newcastle, May 30, 1747, *New York Colonial Documents*, VI, 351.

40. William Smith, *The History of the Province of New-York*, N-Y.H.S., *Collections*, 1st ser., [V] II, 145.

41. Clinton to Newcastle, November 9, 1747, *New York Colonial Documents*, VI, 410.

42. Colden to Clinton, November 9, 1749, N-Y.H.S., *Collections*, 1920, p. 150.

43. See Katz *Newcastle's New York*, pp. 187–192, 207–233, for a narrative of these events.

44. Katz, *Newcastle's New York*, p. 212.

45. The Board of Trade report, incorrectly titled "Report of the Privy Council upon the State of New York," is reprinted in *New York Colonial Documents*, VI, 614–703.

46. Smith, *History*, II, 146.

47. Colden to Catherwood, November 21, 1749, N-Y.H.S., *Collections*, 1920, p. 160.

48. McAnear, ed., "R. H. Morris," pp. 176–177.

C H A P T E R   7

1. Dinwiddie wrote the Bishop of London, Aug. 5, 1752, that Stith had "been endeavouring to make a Party of the lower class of People my Enemies, by some low insinuations. . . ." John Blair wrote the Bishop that Stith

"publickly offer'd a large sum of money towards a purse to oppose the Gov^{nr} and he would undertake to break the neck of it. And at his Table he made it a Toast to drink Liberty, Property, and No Pistole (as a Pistole was the fee), also proclaimed the same exasperating words publickly at a Cou(rt) up the Country" (Aug. 15, 1752). Stith himself warned the Bishop in April, "if this Contest between the Governor and the People goes on I'll venture to affirm that his majesty will lose 20 pistoles for one the Gov^{nr} gets" (Lambeth-Fulham Mss., transcripts in the Library of Congress, Vol. XIII). See Gov. Dinwiddie to the Bishop Jan. 29, 1753. William Stevens Perry, ed., *Historical Collections relating to the American Colonial Church*, I, Virginia (Hartford, Conn., 1890), pp. 101–02.

2. See Morgan Dix, ed., *A History of the Parish of Trinity Church in the City of New York*, I (New York, 1898) Ch. XI; Alison G. Olson, "Governor Hunter and the Anglican Church in New York," Ms. article awaiting publication.

3. Richard Peters, *et al.*, to Bishop of London, June 30, 1775, Rev. William Smith to Bishop of London, July 8, 1775 and to the Secretary of the S.P.G., July 10, 1775. William Stevens Perry, D.D., ed., *Historical Collections Relating to the American Colonial Church*, II, Pennsylvania (Hartford, Conn., 1871), pp. 410–12, 473–74, 475–78.

4. Norman Sykes, *Church and State in England in the XVIIIth Century* (Cambridge, England, 1934), pp. 76–91. Outside Virginia the commissaries were not usually members of the provincial councils, whereas English Bishops attended the House of Lords (Sykes, *op. cit.*, p. 47).

5. Blair may possibly have had a predecessor as commissary, one Temple or Semple, but the records are quite obscure. Review by William Wilson Manross of George MacLaren Brydon's *Virginia's Mother Church. Historical Magazine of the Protestant Episcopal Church*, XVI (1947), p. 146. Simeon E. Baldwin, "The American Jurisdiction of the Bishop of London in Colonial Times," *Proceedings of the American Antiquarian Society*, n.s., XIII (1899–1900), p. 192, calls the Rev. William Morell, who came to New England in 1623, the "first episcopal commissary."

   There is no standard life of Blair but see Daniel Esten Motley, "The Life of Commissary James Blair," *The Johns Hopkins University Studies in History and Political Science*, XIX, No. 10 (Baltimore, 1901) and George MacLaren Brydon, *Virginia's Church and the Political Conditions under which it Grew* (Richmond, 1947), Chs. XX and XXI.

6. A general discussion of the appointment of Commissaries is in Arthur Lyon Cross, *The Anglican Episcopate and the American Colonies*, (New York, 1902), Chs. II and III.

7. See, for example, Rev. Caner to Bishop of London, May 6, 1760. Lambeth-Fulham Mss., Vol. VI.

8. Richard Peters wrote the Bishop of London about the clergy of New Jersey, "They have got it into their head that the appointment of Commissaries is like throwing cold water on the design of sending us Bishops and will oppose all Commissarial Powers with all their might." (Nov. 14, 1766). Perry, *Historical Collections Relating to the American Colonial Church, Pennsylvania*, pp. 409–10. See also Rev. William Smith to the Bishop, Nov. 13, 1766, *ibid.*, pp. 413–15.

9. For Maryland see Nelson Waite Rightmyer, *Maryland's Established Church* (Baltimore, 1956) p. 56; for Carolina see Harriet H. Ravenel (Mrs. St. Julien Ravenel) *Charleston, the Place and the People* (New York, 1931), pp. 46–47, John Kendall Nelson, "Anglican Missions in America, 1701–1725, A Study of the Society for the Propagation of the Gospel in Foreign Parts" (unpublished Ph.D. thesis, Northwestern University, Evanston, Ill. 1962, pp. 203–07); and Edward Carpenter, *The Protestant Bishop, Being the Life of Henry Compton, 1632–1713, Bishop of London* (London, 1956), p. 274.

10. Garden to Bishop of London, Feb. 1, 1750. Lambeth Fulham Ms., L.C. transcripts, vol. X. Garden tried George Whitefield before an ecclesiastical court for "not using the Form of Common Prayer in Charlestown Meeting Houses where he has preached" and suspended him, *in absentia*, from exercising his ministerial functions. But Whitefield ignored the suspension locally, and appealed his case to England, where it was never decided. See esp. Frederick P. Bowes, *The Culture of Early Charleston* (Chapel Hill, 1942), p. 24ff.

11. Norman Sykes, *Edmund Gibson, Bishop of London, 1669–1748, A Study in Politics and Religion in the Eighteenth Century* (London, 1926), p. 353. For an example of the difficulties caused by the Commissaries' failure to receive Gibson's commission see Henderson's letters to Gibson, Oct. 27, 1730, Aug. 7, 1731, Oct. 1(1) 1731, Mar. 13, 1731–32, and Secty. Popple to Bishop, May 25, 1732. Lambeth-Fulham Mss., Vol. III.

12. Blair explained to Bishop Gibson that "At first conventions (of the clergy) were once a year. This was found inconvenient especially when the country is in Parties, for, or against a Governor. They are now only upon extraordinary occasions, as the accession of a King or Bishop." Answer to Queries put by the Bishop of London to Persons who were Commissaries to my Predecessor (1724). Perry, *Historical Collections Relating to the American Colonial Church, Virginia*, p. 252.

13. Commissary Dawson to Bishop of London, Mar. 11, 1754, Perry, *Hist. Colls. Colonial Church, Virginia*, pp. 409–11.

14. *Ibid.*, pp. 453–54.

15. Rev. Timothy Cutler to Bishop of London, Apr. 24, 1751. Rev. Brockwell wrote the Bishop (June 8, 1751) that "our then Commissary was not ye strictest Disciplinarian," Lambeth-Fulham Mss., Vol. VI.

16. Rightmyer, *Maryland's Established Church*, pp. 86–112. Hugh Jones and Henry Addison to Bishop (Apr. 27) 1752. Lambeth-Fulham Mss., Vol. III.

17. Commissary Johnston of the Carolinas would not call the clergy of those provinces together after 1710 because ministers who attended meetings were hesitant to concur in any decisions without the consent of absentees for fear that the absentees would complain to the authorities at home. Johnston to Secretary, S.P.G., Jan. 10, 1710/11. Frank J. Klingberg, ed., *Carolina Chronicle: The Papers of Commissary Gideon Johnston, 1707–1716* (Berkeley, 1946), p. 78. Commissary Vesey held no meetings of the New York clergy from 1713 to 1739. Nelson R. Burr, *The Anglican Church in New Jersey*, (Philadelphia, 1954), p. 285.

18. May 23, 1751. Lambeth-Fulham Ms., Vol. VII.

19. Bishop of London to Clergy of Virginia, Apr. 29, 1705. Perry, *Historical*

Collections Relating to the American Colonial Church, Virginia, pp. 145–46.

20. "Any disrespect shown your Government on that or other occasions appears an improper way to support my authority," Apr. 15, 1718. William Stevens Perry, D.D., ed., *Historical Collections relating to the American Colonial Church, Maryland*, IX (Hartford, Conn., 1878), pp. 100–01. See also Summary of a letter (undated) from the Bishop to Henderson (ca. 1717) in Bernard C. Steiner, ed., "Some Unpublished Manuscripts from Fulham Palace Relating to Provincial Maryland," *Maryland Historical Magazine*, XII (1917), pp. 129–30.

21. Sykes, *Edmund Gibson*, pp. 339–40.

22. Quoted in Nelson, "Anglican Missions," p. 58. Clearly as early as 1700 there was a good deal of doubt among royal officials and among the clergy themselves about the propriety of ministers engaging in political partisanship. For example, Col. Quary, a roving royal official in the colonies, complained to the Secretary of the S.P.G., Feb. 12, 1707/08, that the clergy of Pennsylvania were too inclined to engage in political disputes. Perry, *Historical Collections Relating to the American Colonial Church, Pennsylvania*, p. 40. Edward Vaughan, Anglican minister at Elizabeth, New Jersey, spoke of "the freedom I once took in telling Mr. Vesey . . . that it was inconsistent with the Character of a Minister of Peace to foment divisions, to appear in faction and party opposite to Government. (Vaughan to J. Chamberlayne, Nov. 8, 1715, S.P.G., A. Mss., XI, 292, quoted in Nelson, Anglican Missions, pp. 281–83). John Blair wrote the Bishop, August 15, 1752, "A clergyman especially, and much more yo[r] Lo[r]ps Commissary ought to be of a quiet and peaceable spirit," Lambeth-Fulham Ms., L.C. Transcripts, Vol. XIII.

23. Wilkinson to Bishop of London, May 26, 1718. Perry, *Historical Collections Relating to the American Colonial Church, Maryland*, 106–07; Rightmyer, *Maryland's Established Church*, pp. 81–86; Newton D. Mereness, *Maryland as a Proprietary Province* (New York, 1901), pp. 443–46.

24. Jenney to Vestry of Christ Church (1747) Perry, *Historical Collections Relating to the American Colonial Church, Pennsylvania*, pp. 246–49.

25. Mar. 30, 1738. Lambeth-Fulham Mss., Vol. VII.

26. Rev. Nicols to Mr. Stubs, Mar. 20, 1703/4, Perry, *Historical Collections relating to the American Colonial Church, Maryland*, p. 54.

27. John Wolfe Lydekker, "Thomas Bray, 1658–1730, Founder of Missionary Enterprise," *Historical Magazine of the Protestant Episcopal Church* XII (1943) pp. 209–10. Bray's memorial against Seymour is in Perry, *Historical Collections relating to the American Colonial Church, Maryland*, pp. 57–63.

28. Price to Archbishop of Canterbury, May 27, 1739, Perry, *Historical Collections Relating to the American Colonial Church, Massachusetts*, pp. 328–29.

29. Price to Secretary of the S.P.G., May 5, 1744. Perry, *Historical Collections relating to the American Colonial Church, Massachusetts*, pp. 380–82.

30. "Governor Hunter and the Anglican Church in New York," Article in Ms. by Alison G. Olson. Hunter complained in 1712 and 1713 that he was "used like a dog," and had "spent three years of life in such torment and vexation, that nothing in life can make amends for it." (Hunter to Swift, Nov. 1, 1712 and Mar. 14, 1713, F. Elrington Ball, ed., *The Correspondence*

of Jonathan Swift, D.D. II, London, 1910, 10–12, 42.) Quoted in Jordan D. Fiore, "Jonathan Swift and the American Episcopate," *William and Mary Quarterly*, 3rd ser., 11 (1954), p. 432.

31. See for example, Commissary Cummings to Bishop of London, Aug. 1, 1737, Lambeth-Fulham Mss., vol. 7, L.C. transcripts.

32. Spencer Ervin, "The Establishment, Government and Functioning of the Church in Colonial Virginia," *Historical Magazine of the Protestant Episcopal Church*, XXVI (1957), pp. 79–80, 93–95; Samuel Clyde McCulloch, "James Blair's Plan of 1699 to Reform the Clergy of Virginia," *William and Mary Quarterly*, 3rd ser. IX, 1947, p. 72; Charles B. Clark, "The Career of John Seymour, Governor of Maryland," *Maryland Historical Magazine* XLVIII (1953), pp. 134–59. The question is also discussed in Nelson, "Anglican Missions," pp. 587–89.

33. Nicholson to the Clergy of Virginia, Apr. 10, 1700. Perry, *Historical Collections relating to the American Colonial Church, Virginia,* pp. 175–76. Blair accused Nicholson of "convocating the clergy without taking notice of the Bishop's commissary, appointing who shall preach at those convocations, appearing himself in their meetings, and proposing the subject matter of their consultation, holding separate meetings of the Clergy without the Bishop's commissary, putting those separate meetings upon acts of censure and discipline, getting them to sign papers in the name of the Clergy, requiring of some ministers canonical obedience to himself as their bishop. . . ." (Blair's affidavit against Nicholson, May 1, 1704, *Ibid.*, p. 132.) Commissary Henderson complained about Governor Hart's summoning a meeting in a letter to the Bishop of London, July 16, 1720. Perry, *Historical Collections relating to the American Colonial Church, Maryland,* pp. 123–124. See Clergy of Virginia to Bishop of London, Aug. 25, 1703, *William and Mary Quarterly*, 2d ser., XIX (1939), p. 363. Hunter's meetings are referred to in Burr, *Anglican Church in New Jersey*, pp. 284–85.

34. Remonstrance of Price and Church Wardens, July 9, 1732, Lambeth-Fulham Mss., Vol. VI.

35. Summons by Governor and Council, Apr. 21, 1757. Lambeth-Fulham Ms., Vol. XIII. L.C. transcripts; Dawson to Bishop July 9, 1757; Perry, *Historical Collections relating to the American Colonial Church, Virginia,* pp. 453–54.

36. Gooch to Bishop Gibson, June 20, 1734, Lambeth-Fulham Mss., Vol. XII.

37. Governor Hunter, for example, urged the S.P.G. to advise missionaries to be cautious in their attitudes "toward those of different Persuasion as to Ceremonial or Church Discipline." (Hunter to Secretary S.P.G., Feb. 21 to Mar. 21, 1709/10. Letters Rec'd No. 70–73, 80. Quoted in E. B. Greene, "The Anglican Outlook on the American Colonies in the Early Eighteenth Century," *American Historical Review*, XX (1914–15), p. 75.)

38. See, for example, the quarrel between Governor Hunter and Anglican leaders of New Jersey, over the work of the Anglican schoolmaster, Mr. Ellis, at Burlington. Minutes of the S.P.G. January 11, 1716/17, No. 21. S.P.G. Journals III.

39. In 1753, however, Rev. William Smith wrote the Bishop of London asking to be commissary of South Carolina and minister of St. Michaels, the smaller church in Charleston. (May 13, 1753, Lambeth-Fulham Mss., Vol. X.)

40. Mrs. Martha J. Lamb and Mrs. Burton Harrison, *History of the City of New York: Its Origin, Rise, and Progress*, I (New York, 1877), p. 457.

41. In 1765 Peters told the vestry of Christ Church "Do not imagine the least fault in Mr. Penn; he always has, and always will be, well disposed to your churches and to your persons." (Mar. 17, 1765, Rev. Benjamin Dorr, *An Historical Account of Christ Church, Philadelphia, From its Foundation A.D. 1695 to A.D. 1841*, Phila. 1859, pp. 153–54.)

42. Vestry of Trinity Church to Bishop of London, June 7, 1747. Lambeth-Fulham Mss., Vol. V.

43. John Wolfe Lydekker, "Thomas Bray, 1658–1730, Founder of Missionary Enterprise," *Historical Magazine of the Protestant Episcopal Church*, XII (1943), pp. 202–03; Samuel Clyde McCulloch, "Dr. Thomas Bray's Trip to Maryland: A Study in Militant Anglican Humanitarianism," *William and Mary Quarterly*, 3d ser., II (1945), p. 22.

44. For Bray's entertaining see H. P. Thompson, *Thomas Bray* (London, 1954), pp. 50–51. For Henderson see Giles Rainsford to Bishop, April 10, 1721, Lambeth-Fulham Mss. Vol. III.

45. Giles Rainsford wrote the Bishop of Henderson "There is no one clergyman in the whole Province has an estate to support the Dignity of his Lordships Commissary but himself." (Apr. 10, 1721, Lambeth-Fulham Mss., Vol. III,)

46. Alexander Adams to the Bishop of London, Sept. 29, 1752. Lambeth-Fulham Mss., Vol. III.

47. Henderson to Bishop of London, June 18, 1718 (transcript of Lambeth-Fulham ms. says June 17), Perry, *Historical Collections Relating to the American Colonial Church, Maryland*, pp. 109–12. See also Mereness, *Maryland as a Proprietary Province*, p. 445.

48. Mr. Sharpe to Bishop, May 16, 1753, Lambeth-Fulham Ms., XIII.

49. Gooch to the Bishop of London, May 28, 1731 and Aug. 12, 1732. Lambeth-Fulham Mss., Vol. XII.

50. Commissary Wilkinson to Bishop, Aug. 1, 1726; Petition of Maryland Clergy to King (Nov. 24, 1728) Lambeth-Fulham Ms., Vol. III. See also Aubrey C. Land, *The Dulanys of Maryland* (Baltimore, 1955), p. 123.

51. Revs. Wm. Guy, Alex. Garden, Thomas Merrill, and Brian Hunt to Commissary Ball, Oct. 10, 1723. Lambeth-Fulham Ms, Vol. IX. Gov. Nicholson wrote the Bishop Oct. 31, 1724 that he was in sympathy with the clergy's position. Lambeth-Fulham Mss., Vol. IX.

52. Carpenter, *The Protestant Bishop*, pp. 264–65.

53. Sykes, *Edmund Gibson*, pp. 166–75.

54. Glen to Bishop, May 15, 1749, Lambeth-Fulham ms, Vol. X. Rev. McSparran wrote Gibson's successor, March 26, 1751, "Dr. Gibson, the late Bishop of London, tho a very inquisitive and penetrating Prelate, sat several years in y^r See, wth no other knowledge of ye civil State of New England, than y^r it was all under ye jurisdiction of the Govr of ye Massachusetts." Lambeth-Fulham Mss., Vol. VIII.

55. Commissary Cummings to Bishop of London, Aug. 1, 1737, Mar. 30, 1738. Lambeth-Fulham Mss., Vol. VII.

56. Rev. Smith to Secretary, S.P.G., Sept. 1, 1767. Perry, *Historical Collections Relating to the American Colonial Church, Pennsylvania*, pp. 421–22.

57. James Crokatt, a London merchant, was recommended to help the Bishop find an assistant for Commissary Garden of South Carolina (Garden to Bishop, Sept. 16, 1748, Lambeth-Fulham Mss., Vol. X). Nicholas Trott frequently corresponded with the Bishops on provincial affairs in South Carolina (for example, June 17, 1715, Sept. 6, 1728, also Jan. 10, 1729/30, Mar. 28, 1730) Lambeth-Fulham Mss., Vol. IX.

58. For Nicholson's dealings with the Church see Stephen Saunders Webb, "The Strange Career of Francis Nicholson," *William and Mary Quarterly*, 3d ser. XXIII (1966), pp. 520–21, 532–33, 545. Bishop Compton momentarily turned against the governor, 1702–04, but Nicholson later returned to the Bishop's favor. Minutes of the Virginia Council, Aug. 26, 1703, H. L. McIlwaine, ed., *Executive Journals of the Council of Colonial Virginia* II (Richmond, 1927), p. 334. Commissary Bray to R. Quarry, 1702–03. Dr. Bray's Mss. Box 3, 246, Library of Congress Photostats, of Sion College Library.

59. See, for example, Nicholson's sponsorship of a meeting of the clergy in New York, Nov. 1702. Hugh Hastings, ed., *Ecclesiastical Records of the State of New York*, III (Albany, 1902), pp. 1507–08.

60. Steven Fauquier's affidavit against Nicholson, Apr. 25, 1704, Perry, *Historical Collections Colonial Church, Virginia*, pp. 87–93.

61. James Blair's affidavit against Nicholson, Apr. 25, 1704, Perry, *Historical Collections Relating to the American Colonial Church, Virginia*, pp. 93–112. The Address, Apr. 11, 1700, is in *Ibid.*, pp. 116–17, Blair unflatteringly described Nicholson's methods to the Bishop in a letter of May (3), 1704, *ibid.*, pp. 132–33.

62. New England Clergy to George II, Dec. 12, 1727. The meeting was financed by Nicholson. Lambeth-Fulham Mss., Vol. VIII.

63. Commissary Garden to Bishop Gibson, May 26, 1727, Lambeth-Fulham Mss., Vol. IX.

64. *Loc. cit.*

65. Jonathan Gibson to George Gibson, Apr. 27, 1731. Lambeth-Fulham Mss., Vol. XII; Gooch to Bishop Gibson (n.d. but 1732), and June 20, 1734, Jonathan Gibson to Bishop Gibson, May 9, 1741, Lambeth-Fulham Mss., Vol. XII. Gooch also kept on good terms with the Bishop through his brother, the Bishop of Norwich. See for example Gooch to Norwich, Sept. 18, 1727. Gooch Mss., Williamsburg.

66. Drysdale to Bishop of London, May 31, 172(5). Lambeth-Fulham Mss., Vol. XII. Governor Spotswood had also sought Bishop Robinson's support Jan. 27, 1714–15, *The Official Letters of Alexander Spotswood*, Introd. R. A. Brock, II (Richmond, Va., 1885), pp. 88–93.

67. Fauquier to Bishop of London, Nov. 24, 1764. Lambeth-Fulham, Mss., Vol. XIV. Fauquier's wife was a friend of the Bishop's wife.

68. Bishop to Commissary Henderson, April 15, 1718, Perry, *Historical Collections Relating to the American Colonial Church, Maryland*, pp. 100–01.

69. See, for example, Belcher's letters to the Bishop Dec. 12, 1730, Dec. 4, 1730, Nov. 11, 1732, Oct. 5, 1733, Feb. 4, 1733–34, Dec. 9, 1737, Mar. 1, 1738, Lambeth-Fulham Mss., Reel II, Vol. V.

70. J. Winstanley to Bishop of London, July 20, 1728, Lambeth-Fulham Mss., Vol. IX.

71. This was, for example, a problem with the Scot, Commissary Blair. Carpenter, *Protestant Bishop*, pp. 267–68.
72. Nelson, "Anglican Missions," p. 52. See, for example, Matthew Graves to Bishop, July 20, 1750. Lambeth-Fulham Mss., Vol. I, and Commissary Price to the Bishop of London, Oct. 16, 1736, Perry, *Historical Collections Relating to the Colonial Church, Massachusetts*, pp. 315–17. G. MacLaren Brydon has done a study of the origins of the Virginia clergy, "The Clergy of the Established Church and the Revolution," *Virginia Magazine of History and Biography*, XLI, (1935), pp. 11–24.
73. For Welton, see Gov. Keith to Secretary, S.P.G., May 13, 1725. Perry, *Historical Collections Relating to the American Colonial Church, Pennsylvania*, pp. 143–44. For the controversy over Checkley, see Revs. Harris and Mossom to the Bishop of London, Dec. 7, 1725. Perry, *Historical Collections relating to the American Colonial Church, Massachusetts*, pp. 200–02. For Talbot see Minutes of S.P.G., July 1, 1715, No. 8, July 6, 1716, No. 14, Journals of the S.P.G., vol. III; Rev. George Morgan Hills, "John Talbot, the First Bishop in North America," *Pennsylvania Magazine of History and Biography*, III (1879), pp. 32–55, and Edgar Legare Pennington, *Apostle of New Jersey, John Talbot, 1645–1727* (Philadelphia, 1938). See also Henry Wilder Foote, *Annals of King's Chapel from the Puritan Age of New England to the Present Day* I (Boston, 1882), Ch. VII.
74. Dix, ed., *A History of the Parish of Trinity Church*, p. 182.
75. Cummings complained that Peters' agents called upon every member of the Christ Church congregation urging them to support Peters against the Commissary. Cummings to Bishop of London, Aug. 1, 1737, Lambeth-Fulham Mss., Vol. VII.
76. See, for example, Myles to the Bishop, Nov. 3, 1722, Jan. 29, 1724, May 5, 1724, June (23), 1724, June 9 and 25, 1724. Harris to Bishop, June 19, 1724, Dec. 4, 1727, Lambeth-Fulham Mss., Vol. IX. The quarrel between Harris' and Myles' friends continued after Myles' death. Harris' friends wanted him to succeed Myles, Myles' friends generally supported Timothy Cutler. For the division see the lists of signers for and against Harris, Feb. 6, 1728, Lambeth-Fulham Mss., Vol. IX.
77. Alexander Howe to Bishop of London, May 19, 1741; Richard Peters to the Bishop, May 20, 1741, Lambeth-Fulham Mss., Vol. VII.

CHAPTER 8

1. George Bancroft, *History of the United States* (Boston, 1834–1874), IV, 12.
2. George Louis Beer, *British Colonial Policy, 1754–1765* (New York, 1907), 195.
3. *Ibid.*, 31, 314.
4. Oliver M. Dickerson, *The Navigation Acts and the American Revolution* (Philadelphia, 1951), xiv.
5. Wesley Frank Craven, "The Revolutionary Era," *The Reconstruction of American History*, John Higham, editor, (New York, 1962), 49–50.

6. For example, see Dickerson, *Navigation Acts*, 295: there was opposition in America "to the measures enacted after 1763 not because they were trade regulations, *but because they were not laws of that kind.*" See also Bernard Knollenberg, *Origin of the American Revolution, 1759–1766* (New York, 1960), 5: "it seems reasonably clear that until the adoption of the provocative British measures from 1759 to 1765 . . . the stereotyped system of the British government . . . was, on the whole, satisfactory to the colonial 'yokefellows.'"

7. Klaus Knorr, *British Colonial Theories, 1570–1850* (Toronto, 1944), 3: "That set of policies which shaped the relations between Great Britain and her colonial empire . . . is usually referred to as the 'Old Colonial System.' As this system is structurally part of the so-called 'Mercantile System,' the theories underlying it are mercantilist theories."

8. "The American Revolution: A Symposium," *Canadian Historical Review*, vol. XXIII, no. 1 (March, 1942), 1–41.

9. Lieutenant Governor Clarke to Board of Trade, December 15, 1709, in Colonial Office Papers V, 1059, folio 131, Public Record Office.

10. Shirley to Board of Trade, February 26, 1742–43, C. O. V, 883, Ee86, Public Record Office.

11. Clinton to Board of Trade, October 4, 1752, C. O. V, 1064, ff. 144–47, Public Record Office.

12. Treasury to Privy Council, October 4, 1763, House of Lords MSS, 229, British Museum (printed in *Acts of the Privy Council of England: Colonial Series* (London, 1908–1912), IV, 569–572). See also, Thomas C. Barrow, "Background to the Grenville Program, 1757–1763," *William and Mary Quarterly*, 3d ser., Vol. XXII, No. 1 (1965), 93–104.

13. Jonathan Belcher to Board of Trade, March 2, 1736/37, C. O. V, 879, Cc 38, as quoted in Frank W. Pitman, *The Development of the British West Indies, 1700–1763* (New Haven, 1917), 281.

14. Sir Charles Henry Frankland to Duke of Newcastle, Additional MSS. 32693, f. 289, British Museum.

15. Caleb Heathcote to Board of Trade, September 7, 1719, in Dixon Ryan Fox, *Caleb Heathcote* (New York, 1926), 186–89.

16. Robert Livingston's plan of 1701, in *American History Leaflets*, No. 14 (March, 1894), 4.

17. Massachusetts Historical Society, *Collections*, sixth series, VI (Boston, 1893), 3, footnote.

18. Governor Belcher, as quoted in Benjamin Pemberton to Mr. Delafaye, October 8, 1733, C. O. V, 899, ff. 46–47, Public Record Office.

19. William Shirley to Newcastle, July 5, 1741, in *Correspondence of William Shirley . . . 1731–1760*, 2 vols., C. H. Lincoln editor (New York, 1912), I, 37–38.

20. Governor Gooch to Albemarle, September 3, 1739, C. O. V, 1337, ff. 208–209, Public Record Office.

21. As above, footnote 16.

22. Caleb Heathcote to Treasury, January 2, 1715/16, in *Calendar of Treasury Books, 1714–1719*, 185.

23. Thomas C. Barrow, "Archibald Cummings' Plan For A Colonial Revenue," *New England Quarterly* (September, 1963), 383–393.

24. Edward Channing, *A History of the United States* (New York, 1905–1925), III, 48.
25. For example, see William Keith, "A Short Discourse on the Present State of the Colonies in America," C. O. CCCXXIII, 8, ff. 303–314; also, the anonymous "Ways and Means to Raise a Fund to Support Defense," C. O. V, 5, f. 280.
26. Sir Lewis Namier, *Charles Townshend, His Character and Career* (Cambridge, 1959), 16–17.
27. What the Seven Years' War did, in effect, was to offer to the English government two new specific reasons for raising a colonial revenue—imperial defense and England's large war debt—which could be combined with the more general issue of colonial governmental and administrative reform, thus providing a convenient justification and rationalization for the effort to assert English authority in the colonies. See my article, "Background to the Grenville Program," 101–104.
28. John Adams to Hezekiah Niles, February 13, 1818, in the *Works of John Adams*, C. F. Adams ed., 10 vols. (Boston, 1856), X, 286.
29. John Adams to William Tudor, August 16, 1818, in *Works of John Adams*, X, 348.
30. It might be worth suggesting that the very sophistication of the literary debate that took place after 1763—the depth of political theorizing and analysis found in the writing produced immediately before, during, and after the Revolution—arose from that basic fact that the issues involved in the debate between England and her colonies were not peripheral but touched upon the very nature and function of government itself.

CHAPTER 9

1. See G. C. Bolton, "The Founding of the Second British Empire," *Economic History Review*, 2 ser., XIX (1966), 197. An expanded treatment of the themes on this essay appears in my book, *Empire and Interest: The Politics of Mercantilism and the First British Empire, 1660–1800* (New York, 1970), especially Chaps. 5–6.
2. At best we have a textbook by Professor Marshall in which interests provide a recurrent though haphazard theme, a brilliant general essay by Samuel H. Beer, and several new books and articles sensitive to the primary importance of certain interests as determinants of public policy. See Dorothy Marshall, *Eighteenth Century England* (London, 1962); Beer, "The Representation of Interests in British Government: Historical Background," *American Political Science Review*, LI (1957), 613–50; Daniel A. Baugh, *British Naval Administration in the Age of Walpole* (Princeton, 1965), 12 ff. In addition, J. R. Pole has recently described more clearly than ever before the conceptual emergence of interest representation in eighteenth-century Britain. See *Political Representation in England and the Origins of the American Republic* (London, 1966), 443–57, 526–31.
3. *The Structure of Politics at the Accession of George III* (London, 1960, 2nd ed.), 133–34; *Personalities and Powers* (London, 1955), 43; *The*

History of Parliament. The House of Commons, 1754–1790 (London, 1964), I, 109. I do not mean to suggest that Namier was insensitive to the role of interest groups. He devoted considerable attention to the West Indian interest and to a number of lesser ones. But they were not of primary importance to him and he never developed a comprehensive interpretation of their place in 18th-century politics.

4. Namier and Brooke, *The House of Commons, 1754–1790*, I, 46ff.; Robert Walcott, *English Politics in the Early Eighteenth Century* (Oxford, 1956), 110–11, 125; Archibald S. Foord, *His Majesty's Opposition, 1714–1830* (Oxford, 1964), 21–22, 45, 49–50, 60, 69, 89–90, 118, 134, 136, 141, 164, 177, 276, 281, 307–08. But cf. 194–95. For the use of "electoral interests" in the colonial context, see Charles S. Sydnor, *American Revolutionaries in the Making. Political Practices in Washington's Virginia* (New York, 1965), 45, 71.

5. For modern definitions, see Robert MacIver, "Interests" and "Pressure Groups," *Encyclopaedia of the Social Sciences* (New York, 1930–35); Alfred de Grazia, "Nature and Prospects of Political Interest Groups," *The Annals of the American Academy of Political and Social Science*, CCCXIX (1958), 114; Roy C. Macridis, "Interest Groups in Comparative Analysis," *The Journal of Politics*, XXIII (1961), 27 ff.

6. Almond, "A Comparative Study of Interest Groups and the Political Process," *American Political Science Review*, LII (1958), 270–82.

7. Samuel H. Beer, *British Politics in the Collectivist Age* (New York, 1965), 18; J. Steven Watson, *The Reign of George III, 1760–1815* (Oxford, 1960), 55–56.

8. XXXVI (1766), 230.

9. Generalizations throughout this essay are based upon a synthetic examination of the literature concerning some 50 interests.

10. J. H. Plumb, "The Mercantile Interest: the Rise of the British Merchant after 1689," *History Today*, V (1955), 762–67.

11. Eric Williams, *Capitalism and Slavery* (Chapel Hill, 1944), ch. 4, esp. 92–94.

12. J. D. Chambers and G. E. Mingay, *The Agricultural Revolution, 1750–1880* (London, 1966), 121; Baugh, *British Naval Administration*, 15–16.

13. Namier and Brooke, *The House of Commons, 1754–1790*, I, 150.

14. Arthur C. Bining, *British Regulation of the Colonial Iron Industry* (Philadelphia, 1933), 57.

15. Marshall, *Eighteenth Century England*, 167.

16. H. F. Kearney, "The Political Background to English Mercantilism, 1695–1700," *Economic History Review*, 2 ser., XI (1959), 485.

17. Robert Walcott, "The East India Interest in the General Election of 1700–1701," *English Historical Review*, LXXI (1956), 223–39.

18. Williams, *Capitalism and Slavery*, 92–93; Gerrit P. Judd, IV, *Members of Parliament, 1734–1832* (New Haven, 1955), 66; George Louis Beer, *British Colonial Policy, 1754–1765* (New York, 1907), 139.

19. Macridis, "Interest Groups in Comparative Analysis," 33; see also W. J. M. Mackenzie, "Pressure Groups in British Government," *British Journal of Sociology*, VI (1955), 133–48; "Pressure Groups: the 'Conceptual Framework,'" *Political Studies*, III (1955), 247–55.

20. See Michael Kammen, *Empire and Interest: The American Colonies and the Politics of Mercantilism* (Philadelphia, 1970), ch. 4. Gipson has presented his interpretation in volumes 1–3 of his *British Empire Before the American Revolution* (New York, 1959–60, 2nd eds.), and in his Harmsworth inaugural lecture, published as *The British Empire in the Eighteenth Century. Its Strength and Its Weakness* (Oxford, 1952), 23.

21. Franklin to William Shirley, 22 Dec. 1754, *The Papers of Benjamin Franklin*, ed. Leonard W. Larabee, *et al.*, V (New Haven, 1962), 449–51; Franklin to Isaac Norris, 19 March 1759, *ibid.*, VIII, 295–96; Franklin to Hume, 27 Sept. 1760, *ibid.*, IX, 229.

22. The view has been commonly held that "with a few exceptions the period from Sir Robert Walpole to the dismissal of Pitt the Elder saw no drastic alteration in the tranquility and orderliness (or disorderliness) of the system. George III's reign broke the spell." (Franklin B. Wickwire, *British Subministers and Colonial America, 1763–1783* [Princeton, 1966], 10.) Unfortunately it has been assumed that if the system of colonial administration remained tranquil until the 1760's, political and economic society in Britain must also have retained a settled quality. Such was not the case.

23. G. H. Guttridge, *English Whiggism and the American Revolution* (Berkeley, 1942), 58; Dora Mae Clark, *British Opinion and the American Revolution* (New Haven, 1930), 99, 253; see also Namier, *Structure of Politics at the Accession of George III*, 18.

24. Edmund Burke, *A Short Account of a Late Short Administration* (1766) in *The Works of . . . Edmund Burke* (London, 1899), I, 266; Shelburne to Chatham, 4 April 1774, *Correspondence of William Pitt, Earl of Chatham*, eds. William T. Taylor and John H. Pringle (London, 1838–40), IV, 341; Clark, *British Opinion*, 150; Richard B. Morris, *The Peacemakers. The Great Powers and American Independence* (New York, 1965), 418–19, 433, 547n125.

25. Hume to William Strahan, 25 Oct. 1769, *The Letters of David Hume*, ed. J. Y. T. Greig (Oxford, 1932), II, 210.

26. Gipson, *British Empire Before the Revolution*, XI, 449, 474; Bernard Donoughue, *British Politics and the American Revolution. The Path to War, 1773–1775* (London, 1964), 23–24; Benjamin W. Labaree, *The Boston Tea Party* (New York, 1964), 13, 258, 260.

27. *The Jenkinson Papers, 1760–1766*, ed. Ninetta S. Jucker (London, 1949), 106–107, 145–46, 231–32, 274; J. Steven Watson, "Parliamentary Procedure as a Key to the Understanding of Eighteenth-Century Politics," *The Burke Newsletter*, III, (1962), 123–24.

28. See Almond, "A Comparative Study of Interest Groups and the Political Process," esp. 275–76, 280. For the bureaucracy, see Wickwire, *British Subministers, passim.*

29. Ralph Davis, "English Foreign Trade, 1700–1774," *Economic History Review*, 2 ser., XV (1962), 285, 288, 291–92, 295; T. S. Ashton, *An Economic History of England: the 18th Century* (London, 1955), 3, 154, 183.

30. See Mancur Olson, Jr., "Rapid Growth as a Destabilizing Force," *The Journal of Economic History*, XXIII (1963), 529–52.

31. Frances Acomb, *Anglophobia in France, 1763–1789. An Essay in the*

History of Constitutionalism and Nationalism (Durham, 1950), 37–38. See Le Mercier de la Rivière, *L'Ordre Naturel et Essentiel des Sociétés Politiques* (Paris, 1767; 1910 ed.), 27, 155, 267–68.

32. J. G. A. Pocock, "Machiavelli, Harrington, and English Political Ideologies in the Eighteenth Century," *William and Mary Quarterly*, 3 ser., XXII (1965), 582.

33. Mildmay, *The Laws and Policy of England, Relating to Trade* (London, 1765), 101. Italics mine.

34. Charles R. Fay, *Burke and Adam Smith* (Belfast, 1956), 14; Burke, *Thoughts on the Cause of the Present Discontents* (1770), in *The Works of Burke* (London, 1899), I, 473–74. Burke's italics.

35. Gipson, *British Empire Before the Revolution*, XI, 203; Burke, *Speech to the Electors of Bristol . . . 3 November 1774*, in *The Works of Burke*, II, 96–97. Burke's italics.

36. *An Inquiry into the Nature and Causes of the Wealth of Nations*, ed. Edwin Cannan (London, 1950), I, 3, 129, 400, 435–36, 438; II, 18, 85, 114, 142, 146.

37. Josiah Tucker, *The True Interest of Great-Britain Set Forth in Regard to the Colonies. . . .* (1774), in *Josiah Tucker, A Selection from His Economic and Political Writings*, ed. Robert L. Schuyler (New York, 1931), 339; Tucker, *A Letter to Edmund Burke, Esq. . . .* (1775), in *ibid.*, 394; Smith, *Wealth of Nations*, II, 85, 146, 160.

38. "Statement of Trade and Fisheries of Massachusetts," in Connecticut Historical Society *Collections*, XVIII (Hartford, 1920), 271–72; *Letter Book of John Watts . . .* , New-York Historical Society *Collections for 1928*, LXI (New York, 1928), 388; Agnes M. Whitson, "The Outlook of the Continental American Colonies on the British West Indies, 1760–1775," *Political Science Quarterly*, XLV (1930), 69, 73, 76; Weare, "Observations on the British Colonies on the Continent of America," Massachusetts Historical Society *Collections*, 1 ser., I (Boston, 1792), 83–84.

39. Dickinson, *The Late Regulations Respecting the British Colonies on the Continent of America Considered. . . .* (Philadelphia, 1765), in *The Political Writings of John Dickinson* (Wilmington, Del., 1801), I, 58–60; Dulany, *Considerations on the Propriety of Imposing Taxes in the British Colonies* (Annapolis, 1765), in *Pamphlets of the American Revolution, 1750–1776*, ed. Bernard Bailyn (Cambridge, Mass., 1965), I, 624; Franklin to Lord Kames, 1 Jan. 1769, *The Writings of Benjamin Franklin*, ed. A. H. Smyth (New York, 1907), V, 187. In 1776 Carter Braxton of Virginia blamed British tyranny on "a monied interest" which had usurped the power of the Crown (see *Pamphlets of the American Revolution*, I, 182–183).

40. Franklin to David Hall, 14 Feb. 1765, Smyth, *Franklin*, IV, 363.

41. Eric Robinson, "Matthew Boulton and the Art of Parliamentary Lobbying," *The Historical Journal*, VII (1964), 216. See Lillian M. Penson, "The London West India Interest in the Eighteenth Century," *English Historical Review*, XXXVI (1921), 373–92; Eveline C. Martin, *The British West African Settlements, 1750–1821* (London, 1927), 19–26; Bining, *British Regulation of the Colonial Iron Industry*, chs. 2–3; Richard Champion,

Comparative Reflections on the Past and Present Political, Commercial, and Civil State of Great Britain. . . . (London, 1787), 228–29, 264, 320; Kustaa Hautala, *European and American Tar in the English Market During the Eighteenth and Early Nineteenth Centuries,* in *Annales Academiae Scientiarum Fennicae,* CXXX (Helsinki, 1963), 51–52; Francis G. James, "The Irish Lobby in the Early Eighteenth Century," *English Historical Review,* LXXXI (1966), 547, 550, 556. For Burke's caustic comments upon the effect of distance on the North American agents, see his speech On Conciliation, 22 March 1775, in *Edmund Burke on the American Revolution,* ed. Elliott Barkan (New York, 1966), 115–16.

42. Gipson, *British Empire Before the American Revolution,* XI, 243–44, 253. See also Michael G. Kammen, *A Rope of Sand. The Colonial Agents, British Politics and the American Revolution* (Ithaca, 1968), chapters 10 and 12.

43. Compare Arthur H. Buffinton, "The Policy of Albany and English Western Expansion," *Mississippi Valley Historical Review,* VIII (1922), 361–62; Joseph J. Malone, *Pine Trees and Politics. The Naval Stores and Forest Policy in Colonial New England, 1691–1775* (Seattle, 1964), 43; Josiah Tucker, *Letter to Edmund Burke,* 382.

44. Richard Pares, *War and Trade in the West Indies, 1739–1763* (Oxford, 1936), 509; Thomas Pownall to Franklin, and Franklin's reply, *The Complete Works of Benjamin Franklin,* ed. John Bigelow (New York, 1887), IV, 63–64. See also Burke's speech before the House of Commons, 13 Nov. 1770, excerpted in *Burke on the American Revolution,* ed. Barkan, 23.

45. Jackson to Thomas Fitch, 15 Nov. 1765, Conn. Hist. Soc. *Collections,* XVIII, 376; Arthur M. Schlesinger, *The Colonial Merchants and the American Revolution, 1763–1776* (New York, 1957, 2nd ed.), 31; Walter E. Minchinton, "The Stamp Act Crisis: Bristol and Virginia," *Virginia Magazine of History and Biography,* LXXIII (1965), 146–55; R. A. Pelham, "The West Midland Iron Industry and the American Market in the Eighteenth Century," *University of Birmingham Historical Journal,* II (1950), 161–62; Gipson, *British Empire Before the American Revolution,* XII, 122–23.

46. Chilton Williamson, *American Suffrage from Property to Democracy, 1760–1860* (Princeton, 1960), 71–73.

47. Nicholas B. Wainwright, *George Croghan. Wilderness Diplomat* (Chapel Hill, 1959), ch. 10; Peter Marshall, "Lord Hillsborough, Samuel Wharton and the Ohio Grant, 1769–1775," *English Historical Review,* LXXX (1965), 722, 726, 735; Morris, *Peacemakers,* 249.

48. John Mercer to Charlton Palmer, 27 July 1762, in *George Mercer Papers Relating to the Ohio Company of Virginia,* ed. Lois Mulkearn (Pittsburgh, 1954), 46–48; Sewall E. Slick, *William Trent and the West* (Harrisburg, 1947), ch. 11.

49. Lewis B. Namier, *England in the Age of the American Revolution* (London, 1961, 2nd ed.), 262; Carl Bridenbaugh, *Cities in Revolt. Urban Life in America, 1743–1776* (New York, 1955); Charles M. Andrews, "The Boston Merchants and the Non-Importation Movement," Colonial Society of Massachusetts *Publications,* XIX (Boston, 1918), 161–68; Virginia D. Harrington,

The New York Merchants on the Eve of the Revolution (New York, 1935), 173, 204, 244; Arthur L. Jensen, *The Maritime Commerce of Colonial Philadelphia* (Madison, Wisc., 1963); Leila Sellers, *Charleston Business on the Eve of the Revolution* (Chapel Hill, 1934); cf. Lucy S. Sutherland, *The City of London and the Opposition to Government, 1768–1774* (London, 1959); Donald Read, *The English Provinces. c. 1760–1960* (London, 1964), ch. 1; W. H. Chaloner, "Manchester in the Latter Half of the Eighteenth Century," *Bulletin of the John Rylands Library*, XLII (1959), 40–60.

50. *Causes and Consequences of the American Revolution*, ed. Esmond Wright (Chicago, 1966), 212; Namier and Brooke, *The House of Commons, 1754–1790*, I, 161. In 1769 Barré again chastised the House: "So full a House upon this occasion [the Wilkes affair] is an impeachment of parliament. Upon the American affairs you had not above half the number." *Sir Henry Cavendish's Debates of the House of Commons During the Thirteenth Parliament of Great Britain*, ed. John Wright (London, 1841–43), II, 126.

51. See the interesting discussion in Julian P. Boyd's introduction to *The Susquehanna Company Papers. Memorial Publications of the Wyoming Historical and Genealogical Society* (Wilkes-Barre, 1930–33), II, xi.

52. See Ralph Davis, "The Rise of Protection in England, 1669–1786," *Economic History Review*, 2 ser., XIX (1966), 314.

53. Gipson, *British Empire Before the Revolution*, XI, 92–93; Edith M. Johnston, "The Career and Correspondence of Thomas Allan, c. 1725–1798," *Irish Historical Studies*, X (1957), 313 ff. The pamphlet by William Knox, *The Interests of the Merchants and Manufacturers of Great Britain . . .* , was inspired by North's ministry in 1774 in order to shape mercantile opinion. See Jack M. Sosin, *Agents and Merchants. British Colonial Policy and the Origins of the American Revolution, 1763–1775* (Lincoln, Nebr., 1965), 219–20.

54. R. B. Rose, "Eighteenth-Century Price Riots and Public Policy in England," *International Review of Social History*, VI (1961), 283–90; Eric Hobsbawm, "The Machine-breakers," *Past and Present*, I (1952), 57–70; Jonathan D. Chambers, "The Worshipful Company of Framework Knitters (1657–1778)," *Economica*, IX (1929), 324–29; William R. Riddell, "Pre-Revolutionary Pennsylvania and the Slave Trade," *Pennsylvania Magazine of History and Biography*, LII (1928), 18–19; Arthur Lee to Joseph Reed, 18 Feb. 1773, Reed MSS, New-York Historical Society.

55. B. D. Bargar, "Matthew Boulton and the Birmingham Petition of 1775," *William and Mary Quarterly*, 3 ser., XIII (1956), 30; Clark, *British Opinion and the American Revolution*, 89.

56. Burke to Richard Champion, [10] Jan. 1775, *The Correspondence of Edmund Burke*, III, ed. George H. Guttridge (Chicago, 1961), 95–96. My italics.

57. The Rev. James Madison to St. George Tucker, 20 Sept. 1775, in Charles Crowe, "The Reverend James Madison in Williamsburg and London, 1768–1771," *West Virginia History*, XXV (1964), 275; Clark, *British Opinion and the American Revolution*, 99–100.

58. J. Steven Watson has shown that between 1760 and 1775 there was so

much business to be handled that Parliament was unable to function properly. "Parliamentary Procedure as a Key to the Understanding of Eighteenth-Century Politics," *Burke Newsletter*, III (1962), 107–28.

59. For the important distinction between power and influence in Anglo-American politics, see Pole, *Political Representation*, 422–23.

60. Quoted in Carl L. Becker, *The Declaration of Independence* (New York, 1958), 84. My italics.

C H A P T E R   1 0

1. Their host was Joseph Cradock, who wrote of the evening in his *Literary and Miscellaneous Memoirs*, (4 vols.; London, 1826), II, 178–80.

2. *Ibid.*, I, 253, 277–78; also J. G. Sulzers, *Tagebüch . . . 1775 und 1776* (Leipzig, 1780), 122. Ellis' book is *A Voyage to Hudson's Bay . . . in the Years 1746 and 1747* (London, 1748). For his other offspring, see his will in Somerset House, London, willbook "Pitt," f. 777.

3. There are two biographies, one by an English descendant, Charles A. W. Pownall (London, 1908), which is predictably biased and unscholarly, though interesting and informative; the other by John A. Schutz (Glendale, California, 1951), which is scholarly but disappointing. A better account of his parliamentary career is in Sir Lewis Namier and John Brooke, *The House of Commons, 1754–1790* (London, 1964), III, 316–318. To "make a figure" is of course Chesterfield's admonition to his son, since made famous by Namier as a key to British political behavior in the mid-18th century.

4. [Philip Thicknesse], *The Modern Characters from Shakespeare* (London, 1778), 68: quotation from *As You Like It* (Act II, Scene VII) on "G - - - - r P - -n - - l." By contrast, Thicknesse had only compliments for his friend Ellis; see John Nichols, *Literary Anecdotes* (London, 1812–1815), IX, 533.

5. Cradock, *Memoirs*, II, 179.

6. The specific office tendered to him by Hillsborough is my conjecture, but there is no doubt about the offer itself; Henry Ellis to William Knox, 30 December 1767, Knox papers, 1/25, William L. Clements Library, Ann Arbor, Michigan. The summary of this letter in *Historical Manuscripts Commission, Various Collections*, VI (Dublin: 1909), 95, is misleading. The other points concerning Ellis' career are discussed below.

7. William W. Abbot, *The Royal Governors of Georgia* (Chapel Hill, 1959), 57–83, contains an excellent account of his governorship.

8. *A Voyage to Hudson's Bay*, xvii–xviii, 93–94, and 212 ff.

9. On his thinking as governor, see especially his memorial to the Board of Trade, 5 October 1756, which was sent on to the Treasury because it requested funds for presents to the Indians; in Treasury papers 1/367, Public Record Office, London. His work for Egremont is documented in the Egremont papers (Public Record Office, London, 30/37), vol. 14, ff. 65–66, and vol. 22, ff. 37–41, 67–92, and 105–110. Some of these items are signed by Ellis; others are in his hand; the remainder in one way or another reflect the influence of his position and thinking. William Knox,

John Pownall (the brother of Thomas), Maurice Morgann, and certainly Halifax himself were others who contributed actively to the formulation of an American policy in this critical period, although it is difficult to be precise in the allocation of credit within a welter of anonymous memoranda. Knox, who served under Ellis in Georgia and whose ideas matched those of his patron, was most likely the author of a series of "Hints" on American policy, done either for Ellis or directly for Egremont. The formulation of policy for the West is discussed most fully in Jack M. Sosin, *Whitehall and the Wilderness* (Lincoln, Nebraska, 1961), pp. 37–65, while military policy is treated in my *Toward Lexington* (Princeton, 1965), 52–58. Neither book quite finds and fits together all the pieces of this very interesting puzzle. In particular, a comparison of handwriting now leads me to believe that it was Ellis himself who drew up the "Plan of Forts and Garrisons" (or "Plan of Forts and Establishments" as it is in the early draft in the Egremont papers, PRO 30/47/22, ff. 84–87) which Egremont sent to the Board of Trade for its guidance. The belief that Ellis drafted the Proclamation of 1763 is expressed in Francis Maseres to Fowler Walker, Quebec, 19 November 1767, *The Maseres Letters*, ed. W. Stewart Wallace (Toronto, 1919), 62–63. Evidence of Ellis' ideas and influence is also found in *The Papers of Sir William Johnson*, ed. Alexander C. Flick, et al., (14 vols.; New York, 1921–65), III, 294, and X, 209; in Governor Lyttleton of Jamaica to William Knox, Spanish Town, 30 December 1762, Knox papers, I/11, Clements Library; and especially in Knox's memoir of the Earl of Shelburne in *Historical Manuscripts Commission, Various Collections*, VI, 282–283.

10. 8 December 1773, Knox papers, II/5, Clements Library. In other letters, he frequently admitted to laziness.

11. In a letter to Knox, 17 October 1772, Knox Papers, I/57, Clements Library, he speaks of a friendly visit to "Beckett," Barrington's country house.

12. Ellis to Knox, Marseilles, 23 March 1774, *Historical Manuscripts Commission Various Collections*, VI, 111.

13. Caroline Robbins, *The Eighteenth Century Commonwealthman* (Cambridge, Mass., 1959), 312.

14. Schutz, *Pownall*, 11; and *The Papers of Benjamin Franklin*, eds. Leonard W. Labaree and Whitfield J. Bell, V (New Haven and London, 1962), 339–340n., where the date of the first edition of *Administration of the Colonies* is mistakenly given as 1765 instead of 1764. See also Labaree, *Royal Government in America* (New Haven, 1930), 43, for an earlier expression of the same opinion.

15. To William Tudor, Quincy, 4 February 1817, *The Works of John Adams*, ed. Charles F. Adams (Boston, 1856), X, 243.

16. There is a bibliography of his writings in Schutz, *Pownall.*

17. *Administration*, 1764 ed., 1. Compare the sympathetic if sarcastic response which these words evoked in James Otis, *Rights of the British Colonies Asserted and Proved* (Boston, 1764), 40–41.

18. I have transposed the order of these quotations, but their sense is unaltered.

19. In the extensive analysis of the book by Schutz there is no hint that Pownall proposed, or at the very least condoned, taxation of the colonies (p. 189). Other lapses in Schutz's treatment of *Administration of the*

Colonies make his analysis positively misleading. For example: p. 192, to the effect that neither Indian affairs nor the military establishment were discussed in the first or later editions; p. 207, which implies that the first two editions did not discuss taxation at all; p. 209, where it is suggested that the "considerable person" mentioned by Pownall in the fourth edition was the Earl of Chatham, when the fifth edition (p. 29n.) states that it was the Duke of York; p. 188, where Schutz says that Pownall accepted the idea of "balanced government" as the guarantor of liberty, when in fact his mind was notably free of that particular cliché of 18th century political thought. On this last point, Harrington's influence helps to understand Pownall's position; see J. G. A. Pocock, "Machiavelli, Harrington, and English Political Ideologies in the Eighteenth Century," *William and Mary Quarterly*, 3d series, XXII (October 1965), 549–583. To my knowledge Edmund S. and Helen M. Morgan are the only historians to state clearly what Pownall actually said about taxation: *The Stamp Act Crisis* (Chapel Hill: 1953), 74. A recent treatment is G. H. Guttridge, "Thomas Pownall's *The Administration of the Colonies*: the Six Editions," *William and Mary Quarterly*, 3d series, XXVI (January 1969), 31–46.

20. Pownall to Pitt, 24 January 1765, Chatham papers, Public Record Office, London, 30/8/53, ff. 170–171, in which Pownall expressed uncertainty about revealing his identity as the author of *Administration*, whose first edition was anonymous. Later he claimed that the second and third editions (1765, 1766) were not "dedicated" to Grenville, but only "addressed" to him; yet the running head in the second edition reads "DEDICATION."

21. Pownall to Halifax (?), 23 July 1754, ed. Beverley McAnear, *Mississippi Valley Historical Review*, XXXIX (March 1953), 745.

22. See note 9 for my own belief that Ellis himself drew up the "Plan of Forts and Garrisons" of early 1763, the final version of which proposed a regional division of the supreme military command.

23. The idea of Parliamentary representation for the colonies is of course not original; it was proposed by, among others, Governors William Shirley and Francis Bernard of Massachusetts, James Otis, Benjamin Franklin, and William Knox. Richard Koebner, *Empire* (Cambridge, 1961), 175–177, implies that Pownall first presented these ideas in the third edition (1768). More serious is Koebner's distortion of Pownall's point of view; for Pownall, the shift in the center of power was a danger to be averted while there was still time, not an inevitable development, as Koebner would have it.

24. Dowdeswell to Rockingham, 16 January 1766, Rockingham papers, R1–558, Wentworth-Woodhouse Muniments, Sheffield City Library.

25. Pownall to Samuel Cooper, 9 May 1769, in Frederick Griffin, *Junius Discovered* (Boston, 1854), 229.

26. *William and Mary Quarterly*, 3d series, XXII (October 1965), 549–583.

27. See James Harrington, "A System of Politics" in *The Oceana . . . and His Other Works* (London, 1737), ed. John Toland, 496. See also Koebner, *Empire*, 59–67, and especially the notes, on Harrington's categories and their etymology.

28. The best account of his political career at this point is in Sir Lewis Namier and John Brooke, *House of Commons, 1754–1790*, III, 316–318.

29. I refer here to the work of R. A. Humphreys, Charles R. Ritcheson, John

Brooke, Jack M. Sosin, and John Norris, though the conclusion is my own.

30. These page references are to the annotated copy of the 1768 edition in the British Museum, accession number C.60.i.9.

31. Koebner uses these marginal comments to reach even harsher conclusions about Burke; *Empire*, 184–192.

32. For example, there are such suggestions in two recent, important, and erudite works written from totally opposed points of view: Bernhard Knollenberg, *Origin of the American Revolution, 1759–1766* (New York, 1960), 13–24; and Lawrence H. Gipson, *The British Empire Before the American Revolution*, XI (New York, 1965), 70–82.

33. For example, see Koebner, *Empire*, 125.

34. Edmund S. Morgan, "The American Revolution: Revisions in Need of Revising," *William and Mary Quarterly*, 3d series, XIV (January 1957), 3–15. Even Professor Morgan indulges in "if-history"; see p. 12.

35. On this, see Koebner, *Empire*, 85ff.

36. Sir Lewis Namier and John Brooke, *Charles Townshend* (London, 1964), 27–28, 37–45, 76–77, 138–142, and especially 179.

37. Here I must register strong disagreement with Koebner, *Empire*, especially pp. 117–118, where the incoherence of imperial thought is stressed, and p. 125, where it is said that there was no systematic conception of empire in 1763. The opposite was more nearly true, and Koebner's own analysis of Pownall, Franklin, and Francis Bernard will, if read carefully, support that opinion. This is a remarkable book, from which I have learned a great deal, but Koebner was perhaps excessively literal in his treatment of these ideas, and moreover seems to have been led by his aim of depriving the idea of "empire" of any emotional content to seek diversity rather than coherence in the thought of this epoch.

C H A P T E R   1 1

1. John Higham, "The Cult of 'American Consensus': Homogenizing Our History," *Commentary*, XXVII (1959), 93–100. Daniel Boorstin's aptly-titled *The Amercians: The Colonial Experience* (New York, 1958) bore the brunt of Higham's attack. In 1960 Boorstin wrote: "We all suffer powerful temptations to homogenize experience, to empty each age of its vintage flavor in order to provide even larger receptacles into which we can pour an insipid liquid of our own making." *America and the Image of Europe: Reflections on American Thought* (New York, 1960). David Noble draws an interesting parallel between the intellectual development of Boorstin and a radical historian of the past, Charles A. Beard, in *Historians Against History* (Minneapolis, 1965). On Beard, Turner and Parrington, see Richard Hofstadter, *The Progressive Historians* (New York, 1968).

2. See Irwin Unger, "The 'New Left' and American History: Some Recent Trends in United States Historiography," *American Historical Review*, LXXII (1966–1967), 1237–1263.

3. *The Liberal Tradition in America* (New York, 1955). Hartz, however, has been criticized for not giving due weight to the vestiges of feudalism in

early America. See Arthur Mann's review of his book, *William and Mary Quarterly*, Third Series, XII (1955), 653–655. All following references to this journal concern the Third Series.

4. Louis Hartz, et al., *The Founding of New Societies: Studies in the History of the United States, Latin America, South Africa, Canada and Australia* (New York, 1964). As the title suggests, Hartz favors the use of comparative history. A similar attempt is made by Silvio Zavala, *The Colonial Period in the History of the New World*, Abridgement in English by Max Savelle (Mexico City, 1962).

5. Richard Schlatter, "The Puritan Strain," in John Higham, ed., *The Reconstruction of American History* (New York, 1962), 25–45; Howard Mumford Jones, *O Strange New World* (New York, 1964). Staughton Lynd, one of the leading New Left historians, has objected to Jones' method on the grounds that "the cultural history of a given period is . . . more influenced by the non-cultural activities of the same period than by the cultural history of the preceding period." He classifies Jones' book among the "many latter day quests for a homogeneous, timeless American consensus." *Commentary*, XXXIX (1965), 86–88.

6. R. M. Gummere, *The American Colonial Mind and the Classical Tradition: Essays in Comparative Culture* (Cambridge, Mass., 1963); R. L. Middlekauff, "A Persistent Tradition: The Classical Curriculum in Eighteenth-Century New England," *William and Mary Quarterly*, XVIII (1961), 54–67; Id., *Ancients and Axioms* (New Haven, 1963). The persistence of the classics, and the refusal to use new methods of teaching them (as urged by Locke), is obviously not a testimony to American adaption and pragmatism.

7. Published in Chapel Hill, 1968.

8. Published in Cambridge, Mass., 1959. Recent studies of seventeenth-century English thought include J. G. A. Pocock, *The Ancient Constitution and the Feudal Law: A Study of English Historical Thought in the Seventeenth Century* (Cambridge, Eng., 1959); W. H. Greenleaf, *Order, Empiricism and Politics: Two Traditions of English Political Thought, 1500–1700* (New York, 1964); G. E. Aylmer, "Place Bills and the Separation of Powers: Some Seventeenth-Century Origins of the 'Non-Political' Civil Service," *Transactions of the Royal Historical Society*, Fifth Series, XV (1965), 45–69. Two works that consider the implications for America are M. J. C. Vile, *Constitutionalism and the Separation of Powers* (New York, 1967) and W. B. Gwyn, *The Meaning of the Separation of Powers* (New Orleans, 1966).

Scholars who have followed Miss Robbins' lead or, at least, substantiate her findings include Mary Maples Dunn, whose *William Penn, Politics and Conscience* (Princeton, 1967), illustrates the influence of classical republican thought on a prominent trans-Atlantic figure. Bruce I. Granger, in *Political Satire in the American Revolution, 1763–1783* (Ithaca, 1960), demonstrates the persistence of the Whig mentality in the satirical themes used by the Patriots. George F. Sensabaugh shows the continuing impact of one of Miss Robbins' classical Republicans; he concludes that John Milton was the most important link between seventeenth-cenutry libertarian ideas and the American Revolution. See *Milton in Early America* (Princeton, 1964). Though Richard Buel is primarily interested in relating political theory to the actual location of power in "Democracy and the American Revolution: A Frame of Reference," *William and Mary Quarterly*, XXI (1964), 165–190, he does note that by "1760 local political magnates devoid of trans-Atlantic connections had acquired an elaborate conceptual arsenal from the dissenting tradition in English thought. . . ." Pauline Maier, in explaining American attachment to John Wilkes in spite of Franklin's advice, points out that the Wilkesite party was "composed of 'commonwealthmen' in Caroline Robbins' sense." *Ibid.*, XXII (1965), 549–583. Staughton Lynd, who judges the Founding Fathers to have been overly conservative, finds *The Intellectual Origins of American Radicalism* (New York, 1968) in the wilder varieties of English dissent during the Interregnum, that is, in the generation before Locke *et al.*

9. Published at Chapel Hill, 1965.

10. B. Bailyn, "Political Experience and Enlightenment Ideas in Eighteenth-Century America," *American Historical Review* LXVII (1961–1962), 339–351; E. S. Morgan, "The American Revolution Considered as an Intellectual Movement," in A. M. Schlesinger, Jr., and Morton White, eds., *Paths of American Thought* (Boston, 1963), 11–33. Both men argue that Americans took ideas seriously, that ideas were transmitted from England to America and that in America these ideas were used to justify what already existed. Bailyn's emphasis is political and economic, whereas Morgan's is religious. In *Liberty and Authority: Early American Political Ideology, 1689–1763* (Chicago, 1968), Lawrence Leder also argues for the importance of theory to Americans, but in placing freedom of the press at the foundation of ideological development, he de-emphasizes the importance of borrowing from England.

11. In "The Declaration of Independence and Eighteenth-Century Logic," *William and Mary Quarterly*, XVIII (1961), 463–483, Wilbur S. Howell attempts to show "that an unmistakable parallelism exists between the argumentative structure of the Declaration and the theory of argumentative structure set forth in the most significant of the logics and rhetorics of Jefferson's time." Paul S. Boyer contends, in "Borrowed Rhetoric: The Massachusetts Excise Controversy of 1754," *Ibid.*, XXI (1964), 328–351, that the most interesting feature of that controversy was "the way it was decisively conditioned by a similar upheaval which had occurred in Great Britain two decades earlier." In their provocative article, "England's Cultural Provinces, Scotland and America," *Ibid.*, XI (1954), 200–213, John Clive and Bernard Bailyn point out that the origins of the Scottish Renaissance and the eighteenth-century flowering of America were not only similarly middle-class, but alike insofar as a sense of inferiority to England was a source of creativity. (Caroline Robbins has also noted the peculiar reaction of the provinces—in her case, Ireland and Scotland—to Commonwealth ideas.) Felix Gilbert, in *To the Farewell Address: Ideas of Early American Foreign Policy* (Princeton, 1961), sees an analogy between England's retreat from the continental alliance system and the North American colonies' separation from England. (Gilbert's study and Gerald Stourzh's *Benjamin Franklin and American Foreign Policy* [Chicago, 1964], both of which emphasize the importance which Americans attached to

ideas, provide a sobering counterpoint to Boorstin's *The Americans;* see especially Boorstin's concluding chapter on isolationism as the logical product of home defense.) For a narrative approach to the same subject, see Max Savelle, *The Origins of Anglo-American Diplomacy: The International History of Angloamerica, 1492–1763* (New York, 1967); a much abbreviated form, under the title "The International Approach to Early Angloamerican History, 1492–1763," appears in R. A. Billington, ed., *The Reinterpretation of Early American History* (San Marino, 1966).

Erwin C. Surrency has discussed the English origins and colonial deviation from this model in "The Courts in the American Colonies," *American Journal of Legal History,* XI (1967), 253–276, 347–376.

12. Richard S. Dunn, "Seventeenth-Century English Historians of America," in James M. Smith, ed., *Seventeenth Century America* (Chapel Hill, 1959), 195–225.

13. Published in New York, 1968.

14. The breadth of the franchise is the focus of Robert E. Brown's *Middle-class Democracy and the Revolution in Massachusetts, 1691–1780* (Ithaca, 1955) and Robert E. and B. Katherine Brown, *Virginia, 1705–1786: Democracy or Aristocracy?* (East Lansing, 1964). Brown states his thesis baldly in "Reinterpretation of the Revolution and Constitution," *Social Education,* XXI (1957), 102–105, 114. Jack P. Greene evaluates the Browns' work in "Changing Interpretations of Early American Politics," Billington, *Reinterpretation,* 156–159.

The Browns' view of a widely-held franchise has been substantiated by other scholars: Charles S. Grant, *Democracy in the Connecticut Frontier Town of Kent* (New York, 1961); Lucille Griffith, *The Virginia House of Burgesses, 1750–1774* (Northport, Ala., 1963); Chilton Williamson, *American Suffrage, from Property to Democracy, 1760–1860;* Richard P. McCormick, *The History of Voting in New Jersey* (New Brunswick, 1953). For an opposing view, see John Cary's "Statistical Method and the Brown Thesis on Colonial Democracy," and Brown's rebuttal, *William and Mary Quarterly,* XX (1963), 251–276. However, most historians have rejected the idea that middle-class democracy was philosophically or temperamentally aceptable to colonial Americans. See especially Roy N. Lokken, "The Concept of Democracy in Colonial Political Thought," *Ibid.,* XVI (1959), 568–580, and J. R. Pole, "Historians and the Problem of Early American Democracy," *American Historical Review,* LXVII (1961–1962), 626–646.

15. Published in New York, 1966.

16. Perhaps too great an awareness of this pitfall contains its own dangers. Note, for example, the absence of an explicit comment as to whether Americans had achieved a distinctive way of life in Louis B. Wright's, *The Cultural Life of the American Colonies, 1607–1763* (New York, 1957).

17. It is significant but not surprising that a sociologist has attempted such an approach. See Sigmund Diamond, "From Organization to Society, Virginia in the Seventeenth Century," *American Journal of Sociology,* LXIII (1958) 457–475.

18. Published in New York, 1964. Another recently-published textbook of note is David Hawke's *The Colonial Experience* (Indianapolis, 1966).

19. Greene's book was published at Chapel Hill in 1963, the same year in which F. G. Spurdle's *Early West Indian Government: Showing the Progress of Government in Barbadoes, Jamaica and the Leeward Island, 1660–1783* (Palmerston, N.Z.) was issued. Although Spurdle does not deal with the question of motivation, his description of the lower houses' acquisition of power parallels Greene's account. George Metcalfe, in *Royal Government and Political Conflict in Jamaica, 1729–1783* (London, 1965), argues that the lower house saw itself as the equal of Parliament. See also Maureen McGuire, "Struggle over the Purse: Governor Morris v. the New Jersey Assembly," *Proceedings of the New Jersey Historical Society*, LXXXII (1964), 200–207.

For explanations of the decline of the council relative to the assembly, see H. Hale Bellot "Council and Cabinet in the Mainland Colonies," *Transactions of the Royal Historical Society* V (1955), 161–176, and M. Eugene Sirmans, "The South Carolina Royal Council, 1720–1763," *William and Mary Quarterly*, XVIII (1961), 373–392. The plight of the executive is depicted in Beverley McAnear, *The Income of the Colonial Governors of British North America* (New York, 1967), which actually concerns only a few governors in mid-eighteenth-century New York, and Carole Shammas, "Cadwallader Colden and the Role of the King's Prerogative," *New-York Historical Society Quarterly*, LIII (1969), 103–126. A man of unusual political skill is depicted in Richard P. Sherman's *Richard Johnson, Proprietary and Royal Governor of South Carolina* (Columbia, 1966). Although he successfully juggled colonial and imperial interests, Johnson was finally undermined by local predators.

20. M. Eugene Sirman's *Colonial South Carolina: A Political History, 1663–1763* (Chapel Hill, 1966) substantiates Greene's findings about the importance of constitutional principle.

21. *The New England Merchants in the Seventeenth Century* (Cambridge, Mass., 1955).

22. Published at Princeton, 1962.

23. See also Bailyn's "Politics and Social Structure in Virginia," in Smith, *Seventeenth-Century America*, 90–115; R. S. Dunn, "The Barbados Census of 1680: Profile of the Richest Colony in English America," *William and Mary Quarterly*, XXVI (1969), 3–30.

24. A. P. Thornton's excellent *West India Policy Under the Restoration* (New York, 1956) is testimony to the fact that institutional history is still being written, though Thornton admits that "to seek in isolation a 'colonial policy' amid the confusions of politics is somewhat to distort the outlook of seventeenth-century statesmen . . ." Significantly, Lawrence A. Harper has called this work a supplement to G. L. Beer's *The Old Colonial System* (see *American Historical Review*, LXII [1956], 120–121).

25. Published in New York, 1967.

26. Lawrence H. Leder, "The Glorious Revolution and the Pattern of Imperial Relationships," *New York History*, XLVI (1965), 203–211; Michael G. Kammen, "The Causes of the Maryland Revolution of 1689," *Maryland Historical Magazine*, LV (1960), 293–333; O. Burton Adams, "The Virginia Reaction to the Glorious Revolution, 1688–1692," *West Virginia History*, XXIX (1967), 6–12; Richard S. Dunn, "The Rejection of the Glorious

Revolution in the English West Indies," Paper delivered at Mississippi Valley Historical Association Convention, Omaha, Nebraska, May 3, 1962; M. G. Hall, L. H. Leder, and M. G. Kammen, eds., *The Glorious Revolution in America: Documents on the Colonial Crisis of 1689* [Massachusetts, New York, Maryland] (Chapel Hill, 1964).

27. *Edward Randolph and the American Colonies, 1676–1703* (Chapel Hill, 1960).

28. "William Blathwayt, Imperial Fixer: From Popish Plot to Glorious Revolution," *William and Mary Quarterly*, XXV (1968), 3–21; "The Strange Career of Francis Nicholson," *Ibid.*, XXIII (1966), 513–548.

29. "Governor Fletcher's Recall," *Ibid.*, XX (1963), 527–542; "The Problem of Anglo-American Politics in Bellomont's New York," *Ibid.*, XXVI (1969), 191–217.

30. "The Crown and the Colonial Charters, 1675–1688," *Ibid.*, XV (1958), 297–311, 452–466. Michael G. Hall, on the other hand, sees no relationship between the attacks on municipal charters in England and colonial charters abroad. All were isolated incidents; there was no overall policy. Richard S. Dunn, in "The Downfall of the Bermuda Company: A Restoration Farce," *Ibid.*, XX (1963), 378–512, takes exception to Haffenden regarding Bermuda, noting "that Stuart 'despotism' had its careless and casual side, and that there was plenty of room for local disorder within the so-called English imperial system." Stuart procedure lay somewhere between policy and pragmatism.

31. "William Penn, Parliament, and Proprietary Government," *Ibid.*, XVIII (1961), 176–195.

32. Joseph E. Illick, *William Penn the Politician* (Ithaca, 1965). Several of Penn's allies have recently been the subjects of first-rate biographies. J. P. Kenyon's portrait of *Robert Spencer, Earl of Sunderland, 1641–1702* (New York, 1957), shows the philosopher's strong influence on the Board of Trade, as does Peter Laslett in "John Locke, the Great Recoinage, and the Origins of the Board of Trade: 1695–1698," *William and Mary Quarterly*, XIV (1957), 370–402.

33. Published in New York, 1968.

34. Exceptions to this statement are Richard S. Dunn's "The Trustees of Georgia and the House of Commons, 1732–1752," *Ibid.*, XI (1954), 551–564; Alison G. Olson, "The British Government and Colonial Union, 1754," *Ibid.*, XVII (1960), 22–34; Philip Haffenden, "Colonial Appointments and Patronage under the Duke of Newcastle, 1723–1739," *English Historical Review*, LXXVIII (1963), 417–435; Reed Browning, "The Duke of Newcastle and the Imperial Election Plan, 1749–1754," *Journal of British Studies*, VII (1967–1968), 28–47.

35. Robert Walcott, "The Later Stuarts (1660–1714): Significant Work of the Last Twenty Years (1939–1959)," *American Historical Review*, LXVII (1961–1962), 352–370. Walcott's own work, however, constitutes an attack on earlier interpretations; see *English Politics in the Early Eighteenth Century* (Cambridge, Mass., 1956). J. H. Plumb's *The Growth of Political Stability in England, 1675–1725* (London, 1967) is a counter-attack on Walcott as is Geoffrey Holmes', *British Policies in the Age of Anne* (London, 1967). Dennis Rubini's *Court and Country, 1688–1702* (London,

1967) lies somewhere between Walcott's view of the extreme fractionaliza-
tion of politics and Plumb's emphasis on Whig-Tory party rivalry. John
M. Beattie has argued that the Crown played an important policy-making
role in *The English Court in the Reign of George I* (Cambridge, Eng.,
1967).

36. "British Politics preceding the American Revolution," *Huntington Library
Quarterly*, XX (1956–1957), 301–320. See also Richard Pares, *Limited
Monarchy in Great Britain in the Eighteenth Century* (London, 1957), and
Sir Lewis Namier, *Crossroads of Power: Essays on Eighteenth-Century
England* (New York, 1962), especially the closing essay, "Monarchy and
the Party System."

37. Published in Cambridge, Mass., 1968.

38. An initial approach to Namier may be made through David I. Gaines'
"Namier on Eighteenth-Century England," *Historian*, XXV (1962–1963),
213–225. In addition to explaining his work and his followers, Gaines shows
how the novice can sample Namier. In *George III and the Historians*
(New York, 1959), Herbert Butterfield has raised objections to the
Namierite approach. He is answered by C. L. Mowat "George III: The
Historians' Whetstone," *William and Mary Quarterly*, XVI (1959), 121–
128, and Jacob M. Price, "Party, Purpose and Pattern: Sir Lewis Namier
and his Critics," *Journal of British Studies*, I (1961–1962), 71–93. See also
the controversy between Harvey C. Mansfield and Robert Walcott in *Ibid.*,
II (1962–1963), 28–55; III (1963–1964), 85–119.

A discussion of Namier's life in relationship to his work can be found
in essays by Arnold Toynbee ("Lewis Namier, Historian," *Encounter*, XVI
[1961], 39–43), J. H. Plumb ("The Grand Inquisitor," *Spectator* [Oct. 11,
1957], 484), Henry M. Winkler ("Sir Lewis Namier," *Journal of Modern
History*, XXXV [1963], 1–19), J. L. Talmon ("The Ordeal of Sir Lewis
Namier: The Man, the Historian, the Jew," *Commentary*, XXXII [1962],
237–246), Sir Isaiah Berlin ("L. B. Namier," *Encounter*, XXII [Nov. 1966],
32–42), and Ved Mehta (*Fly and the Fly-Bottle* [Boston, 1962]).

39. "England knows not democracy as a doctrine, but has always practiced it
as a fine art." *England in the Age of the American Revolution* (2nd ed.;
New York, 1961), 6. An important recent critique is Jack P. Greene, "The
Plunge of the Lemmings: A Consideration of Recent Writings on British
Politics and the American Revolution," *South Atlantic Quarterly*, LXVII
(1968), 141–175.

40. Published in New York, 1962.

41. On Parliament and the Parliamentarians see A. S. Foord, *His Majesty's
Opposition, 1714–1830* (New York, 1964); Sir Lewis Namier and John
Brooke, *The History of Parliament: The House of Commons, 1754–1790*
(3 vols.; New York, 1964); J. H. Plumb, *Sir Robert Walpole* (2 vols.;
Boston, 1956–1961)—the second volume has not been as well received as
the first, and there is a third forthcoming; John B. Owen, *The Rise of the
Pelhams* (Evanston, 1964); Lewis W. Wiggin, *The Faction of Cousins: A
Political Account of the Grenvilles, 1733–1763* (New Haven, 1958)—gen-
erally regarded as an applied misunderstanding of Namier.

Recent work in administrative history includes Sir Herbert Richmond,
The Navy as an Instrument of Policy, 1558–1727 (New York, 1953);

Daniel A. Baugh, *British Naval Administration in the Age of Walpole* (Princeton, 1965); Stephen B. Baxter, *The Development of the Treasury, 1660–1702* (Cambridge, Mass., 1957).

42. Published in Princeton, 1966.

43. Published in New Haven, 1960.

44. Published in Cambridge, Mass., 1967. Barrow's book includes an analysis of the Acts of Trade and Navigation. See also Herbert A. Johnson and David Syrett, "Some Nice Sharp Quillets of the Customs Law: The *New York* Affair, 1763–1767," *William and Mary Quarterly*, XXV (1968), 432–451.

45. On the accomplishments of the imperial historians, see Robert L. Middle-kauff, "The American Continental Colonies in the Empire," in R. W. Winks, ed., *Historiography of the British Empire-Commonwealth* (Durham, N.C., 1966). See also Philip D. Curtin, "The British Empire and Commonwealth in Recent Historiography," *American Historical Review*, LXV (1959–1960), 72–91. Carl Ubbelohde's *The American Colonies and the British Empire, 1607–1763* (New York, 1968) is a useful short survey.

46. Gipson's fourteen volumes were published in Caldwell, Idaho and New York between 1936 and 1969; the first three have been revised and repub-lished in New York. The fourteenth is a bibliographical guide. See also Gipson's "The Imperial Approach to Early American History" in Billington, *Reinterpretation*.

The quotation is from A. R. M. Lower, "Lawrence H. Gipson and the First British Empire: an Evaluation," *Journal of British Studies*, III (1963–1964), 57–78. See also R. B. Morris' eulogy, "The Spacious Empire of Lawrence Henry Gipson," *William and Mary Quarterly*, XXIV (1967), 169–178.

47. Charles Wilson, " 'Mercantilism': Some Vicissitudes of an Idea," *Economic History Review*, Second Series, X (1957–1958), 181–188; W. D. Grampp, "The Liberal Elements in English Mercantilism," *Quarterly Journal of Economics*, LXVI (1952), 465–501.

Relationships between theory and practice are put forward in J. E. Far-nall, "The Navigation Act of 1651, the First Dutch War, and the London Merchant Community," *Economic History Review*, XVI (1963–1964), 439–454, and George L. Cherry, "The Development of the English Free-Trade Movement in Parliament, 1689–1702," *Journal of Modern History*, XXV (1953), 103–119. In "Mercantilist Policies and the Pattern of World Trade, 1500–1750," *Journal of Economic History*, XXVII (1967), 39–55, Rudolph C. Blitz argues that "the structure of contemporary world trade, combined with certain monetary conditions, justified on purely favorable economic grounds the Mercantilist preoccupation with a favorable balance of trade and the lack of faith in an automatic adjustment."

48. Published in Cleveland, 1961.

49. Herbert Heaton, in a witty but somewhat alarming essay ("Clio's New Overalls," *Canadian Journal of Economics and Political Science*, XX [1954], 467–577), predicts: "The American cult of quantities is no mere turning tide. It is a tidal wave, on which Clio's little craft seems likely to be sunk by a swarm of vessels manned by statisticians, econometricians, and macro-economists. . . ." Evidence that this trend has affected the writing of colo-

nial American history is Bernard and Lotte Bailyn's, *Massachusetts Shipping, 1697–1714: A Statistical Study* (Cambridge, Mass., 1959), and Robert Paul Thomas' "A Quantitative Approach to the Study of the Effects of British Imperial Policy upon Colonial Welfare: Some Preliminary Findings," *Journal of Economic History*, XXV (1965), 615–638. Thomas attempts "to measure, relative to a hypothetical alternative, the extent of the burdens and benefits stemming from imperial regulation of the foreign commerce of the thirteen colonies." He concludes that the benefits outweighed the burdens. Jacob M. Price has misgivings about Thomas' model and suggests refinements in calculations, as well as firmer definitions of terms. *Ibid.*, 655–659. Also critical of Thomas is Roger L. Ransom; see "British Policy and Colonial Growth: Some Implications of the Burden from the Navigation Acts," *Ibid.*, XXVIII (1968), 427–435, and Thomas' response, *Ibid.*, 436–440.

Other studies in this vein include James F. Sheperd, "A Balance of Payments for the Thirteen Colonies, 1768–72," *Ibid.*, XXV (1965), 691–695; John J. McCusker, "Colonial Tonnage Measurement: Five Philadelphia Merchant Ships as a Sample," *Ibid.*, XXVII (1967), 72–91, and commentary by Gary M. Walton, *Ibid.*, 293–397; Gary M. Walton, "Sources of Productivity Change in American Colonial Shipping, 1675–1775," *Economic History Review*, XX (1967), 67–78; *Ibid.*, "A Measure of Productivity Change in American Colonial Shipping," *Ibid.*, XXI, (1968), 268–282. A survey of earlier work appears in Lawrence A. Harper's "Recent Contributions to American Economic History: American History to 1789," *Journal of Economic History*, XIX (1959), 1–24. Harper is currently compiling a massive bibliography at the University of California, Berkeley.

50. Published in New York, 1965.
51. *The Rise of the English Shipping Industry in the Seventeenth and Eighteenth Centuries* (New York, 1962); "Merchant Shipping in the Economy of the Late Seventeenth Century," *Economic History Review*, IX (1956–1957), 59–73; "English Foreign Trade, 1660–1700," *Ibid.*, VII (1954–1955), 150–166; "English Foreign Trade, 1700–1774," *Ibid.*, XV (1962–1963), 285–303. Davis briefly summarizes his work in *A Commercial Revolution; English Overseas Trade in the Seventeenth and Eighteenth Centuries* (London, 1967).
52. "The Commercial Empire of the Atlantic, 1607–1783," *Economic History Review*, XV (1962–1963), 205–218, including a select bibliography. Rather less useful is John H. Andrews', "Anglo-American Trade in the Early Eighteenth Century," *Geographical Review*, XLV (1955), 99–110.
53. *The Tobacco Adventure to Russia: Enterprise, Politics, and Diplomacy in the Quest for a Northern Market for English Colonial Tobacco, 1676–1722* (Philadelphia, 1961). See also K. G. Davies, *The Royal African Company* (London, 1957).
54. Robert Walcott, "The East India Interest in the General Election of 1700–1701," *Economic History Review*, LXXI (1956), 223–239; Lucy Stuart Sutherland, *The East India Company in Eighteenth-Century Politics* (Oxford, 1952). Miss Sutherland begins her book with an acknowledgement to Namier. (Since she hardly mentions America, her book might well be supplemented with Benjamin W. Labaree's *The Boston Tea Party* [New

York, 1964]). In "The London Entrepôt Merchants and the Georgia Colony," *William and Mary Quarterly*, XXV (1968), 230–244, Geraldine Meroney also shows the political influence of the merchants.

55. J. H. Plumb, "The Mercantile Interest: The Rise of the British Merchant after 1689," *History Today*, V (1955), 762–767.

56. Byron Fairchild, *Messrs. William Pepperell: Merchants at Piscataqua* (Ithaca, 1953); Glenn Weaver, *Jonathan Trumbull: Connecticut's Merchant Magistrate* (Hartford, 1956); James B. Hedges, *The Browns of Providence Plantations: Colonial Years* (Cambridge, Mass., 1952); Mack Thompson, *Moses Brown, Reluctant Reformer* (Chapel Hill, 1962); L. H. Leder and V. P. Carosso, "Robert Livingston (1654–1728); Businessman of Colonial New York," *Business History Review*, XXX (1945), 18–45; L. H. Leder, *Robert Livingston, 1654–1728, and the Politics of Colonial New York* (Chapel Hill, 1961); C. M. Waller, *Samuel Vetch: Colonial Enterprises* (Chapel Hill, 1960); Philip L. White, *The Beekmans of New York in Politics and Commerce, 1647–1877* (New York, 1956); *Id.*, ed., *The Beekman Mercantile Papers, 1746–1799* (3 vols.; New York, 1956); Aubrey C. Land, *The Dulanys of Maryland* (Baltimore, 1955); Alice Barnwell Keith, ed., *The John Gray Blount Papers* [vol. 1, 1764–1789], (Raleigh, 1952).

57. Benjamin W. Labaree, *Patriots and Partisans: The Merchants of Newburyport, 1764–1815* (Cambridge, Mass., 1962).

58. "The Blount Papers: Notes on the Merchant 'Class' in the Revolutionary Period," *William and Mary Quarterly*, XI (1954), 98–104.

59. Bailyn does note that the major coastal cities had closer cultural relations with England than with the backwoods villages in the seventeenth century, but as officialdom, composed of nationals in the provinces, became a definition of class, the orientation of the merchants became more American. "Communications and Trade: the Atlantic in the Seventeenth Century," *Journal of Economic History*, XIII (1953), 378–387. See also "Kinship and Trade in Seventeenth-Century New England," *Explorations in Entrepreneurial History*, VI (1953–1954), 197–206. His discussion of American merchant families in relationship to the Namier approach is in "The Beekmans of New York: Trade, Politics, and Families," *William and Mary Quarterly*, XIV (1957), 598–608.

60. A. L. Jensen, "Inspection of Exports in Colonial Pennsylvania," *Pennsylvania Magazine of History and Biography*, LXXVIII (1954), 275–297; Newton B. Jones, "Weights, Measures and Mercantilism. The Inspection of Exports in Virginia, 1742–1820," in Darrett B. Rutman, ed., *The Old Dominion* (Charlottesville, 1964), 122–134; C. Robert Haywood, "The Influence of Mercantilism on Social Attitudes in the South, 1700–1763," *Journal of the History of Ideas*, XX (1959), 577–586; *Ibid.*, "Mercantilism and Colonial Slave Labor, 1700–1763," *Journal of Southern History*, XXIII (1957), 454–464; Id., "The Mind of the North Carolina Advocates of Mercantilism," *North Carolina Historical Review*, XXXIII (1956), 139–165; Id., "Mercantilism and South Carolina Agriculture, 1700–1763," *South Carolina Historical Magazine*, LX (1959), 15–27.

Victor L. Johnson, in "Fair Traders and Smugglers in Philadelphia, 1754–1763," *Pennsylvania Magazine of History and Biography*, LXXXIII

(1959), 125–149, shows how imperial policies aimed to end illicit trade with France had the ironical effect of hurting the fair traders, making evasion of the law more respectable and generally alienating all merchants. C. R. Haywood, in "The Mind of the North Carolina Opponents of the Stamp Act," *North Carolina Historical Review*, XXIX (1952), 317–343, claims that the people of that province remained faithful to the "Old Colonial System" until 1765.

61. James High, "The Origins of Maryland's Middle Class in the Colonial Aristocratic Pattern," *Maryland Historical Magazine*, LVII (1962), 334–345, points to the middle class's dislike of mercantilism. Keach Johnson's articles on the genesis of Maryland's iron industry, the iron trade and the search for English subsidies (*Ibid.*, LI [1951], 27–43; *Journal of Southern History*, XIX [1953], 157–176; *William and Mary Quarterly*, XVI [1959], 37–60) do not contain a commentary on this issue.

In *Pine Trees and Politics: The Naval Stores and Forest Policy in Colonial New England, 1691–1775* (Seattle, 1965), Joseph J. Malone describes a policy which contributed to the deterioration of relations between England and her colonies. Jere R. Daniell, in "Politics in New Hampshire under Governor Benning Wentworth, 1741–1767," *William and Mary Quarterly*, XXIII (1966), 76–105, shows that Wentworth's twenty-five years in office, the longest of any colonial governor, were the result not only of influential friends in England but also of his policy of protecting local lumbermen against imperial regulation. Patronage and a constant willingness "to espouse causes to win support" also largely account for the success of *William Shirley, King's Governor of Massachusetts* (Chapel Hill, 1961), according to John A. Schutz.

62. E. James Ferguson, "Currency Finance: An Interpretation of Colonial Monetary Practices," *William and Mary Quarterly*, X (1953), 153–180; Richard M. Jellison, "Antecedents of the South Carolina Currency Acts of 1736 and 1746," *Ibid.*, XVI (1959), 556–567; R. M. Weir, "North Carolina's Reaction to the Currency Act of 1764," *North Carolina Historical Review*, XL (1963), 183–199; D. L. Kemmerer, "A History of Paper Money in Colonial New Jersey, 1668–1775," *Proceedings of the New Jersey Historical Society*, LXXIV (1956), 107–144. Ferguson notes that most historians are still looking at the financial and monetary problems of the colonies from the perspective of nineteenth-century advocates of hard money (in this regard, see Malcolm Freiberg, "Thomas Hutchinson and the Province Currency," *New England Quarterly*, XXX [1957], 190–208). According to Ferguson, paper money did not serve the aims of a particular class but the community.

63. For a contrary view, see Theodore Thayer, "The Land-Bank System in the American Colonies," *Journal of Economic History*, XIII (1953), 145–159.

64. Jack P. Greene and Richard M. Jellison, "The Currency Act of 1764 in Imperial-Colonial Relations, 1764–1776," *William and Mary Quarterly*, XVIII (1961), 485–518. Surveys of imperial policy during the pre-Revolutionary crisis include I. R. Christie, *Crisis of Empire: Great Britain and the American Colonies, 1754–1783.* (London, 1966) and Neil R. Stout, "Goals and Enforcement of British Colonial Policy, 1763–1775," *American Neptune*, XXVII (1967), 211–220.

65. The foregoing discussion of trade has ignored the literature on the West Indies in the eighteenth century. Most important is the work of Richard Pares; see especially *Yankees and Creoles: The Trade Between North America and the West Indies Before the American Revolution* (Cambridge, Mass., 1956); *Merchants and Planters* (New York, 1960); "The London Sugar Market, 1740–1769," *Economic History Review*, IX (1956), 254–270; and R. B. Sheridan "The Molasses Act and the Market Strategy of the British Sugar Planters," *Journal of Economic History*, XVII (1957), 62–83; "The Commercial and Financial Organization of the British Slave Trade, 1750–1807," *Economic History Review*, XI (1958), 249–263; "The Rise of a Colonial Gentry: A Case Study of Antigua, 1730–1775," *Ibid.*, XIII (1961), 342–357; "The Wealth of Jamaica in the Eighteenth Century," *Ibid.*, XVIII (1965), answered by R. P. Thomas, "The Sugar Colonies of the Old Empire: Profit or Loss for Great Britain?" *Ibid.*, XXI (1968), 30–45; with a rejoinder by Sheridan, *Ibid.*, 46–61. A noneconomic approach to Anglo-American relations regarding the West Indies can be found in J. Harry Bennett, *Bishops and Bondsmen: Slavery and Apprenticeship on the Codrington Plantations of Barbadoes, 1710–1838* (Berkeley and Los Angeles, 1958).

66. Genevieve Miller, "Smallpox Innoculation in England and America: A Reappraisal," *William and Mary Quarterly*, XIII (1956), 476–492; R. H. Shryock, *Medicine and Society in America, 1660–1860* (New York, 1960); Whitfield J. Bell, *John Morgan, Continental Doctor* (Philadelphia, 1965).

   James Logan's scientific interests, in accord with his other scholarly endeavors, were self-consciously European. See F. B. Tolles, *James Logan and the Culture of Provincial America* (Boston, 1957).

67. I. Bernard Cohen, *Franklin and Newton: An Inquiry into Speculative Newtonian Experimental Science and Franklin's Work in Electricity as an Example Thereof* (Philadelphia, 1956).

68. E. G. Swem, *Brothers of the Spade. Correspondence of Peter Collinson of London, and of John Custis, of Williamsburg, Virginia, 1734–1746.* (Barre, Mass., 1957); Brooke Hindle, *The Pursuit of Science in Revolutionary America, 1735–1789* (Chapel Hill, 1956); Id., *David Rittenhouse* (Princeton, 1964).

69. W. S. Sachse, *The Colonial American in Britain* (Madison, 1956). See also L. B. Wright and Marion Tinling, eds., *William Byrd of Virginia: The London Diary (1717–1721) and Other Writings* (New York, 1958); Leonard W. Cowie, *Henry Newman: An American in London, 1708–43* (London, 1956); Leonard W. Labaree, "Benjamin Franklin's British Friendships," *Proceedings of the American Philosophical Society*, CVIII (1964), 423–428; David S. Lovejoy, "Henry Marchant and the Mistress of the World," *William and Mary Quarterly* (1955), 375–398.

70. Quoted in E. R. R. Green, "Scotch-Irish Emigration, An Imperial Problem," *Western Pennsylvania Historical Magazine*, XXV (1952), 193–209. See also Mildred Campbell, "Social Origins of Some Early Americans" in Smith, *Seventeenth-Century America*, 63–89; Id., "English Emigration on the Eve of the American Revolution," *American Historical Review*, LXI (1955–1956), 1–20; George R. Mellor, "Emigration from the British Isles to the New World, 1765–1775," *History*, XXXIX (1955), 68–83; Ian C. C.

Graham, *Colonists From Scotland: Emigration to North America, 1707–1783* (Ithaca, 1956); Duane Meyer, *The Highland Scots of North Carolina, 1732–1766* (Chapel Hill, 1957); Joseph G. Leyburn, *The Scotch-Irish: A Social History* (Chapel Hill, 1962); R. J. Dickson, *Ulster Emigration to Colonial America, 1718–1775* (New York, 1966); E. G. Hartmann, *Americans from Wales* (Boston, 1967).

71. There are, of course, new editions of original accounts, such as Andrew Burnaby's *Travels Through Middle Settlements in North America in the Years 1759 and 1760* (Ithaca, 1960).

72. Published in New York, 1962. William H. Nelson, in *The American Tory* (Oxford, 1961), views the establishment of an American Episcopate as one of the major projects of his protagonists between 1750 and 1770 and notes that "their weakness lay in the fact that they held social or political opinions which could prevail in America only with British assistance."

73. "From the Covenant to the Revival," in J. W. Smith and A. L. Jamison, eds., *The Shaping of American Religion* (Princeton, 1961).

74. *Religion and the American Mind, From the Great Awakening to the Revolution* (Cambridge, Mass., 1966).

Heimert's point of view appears to be substantiated by David Lovejoy's "Samuel Hopkins: Religion, Slavery, and the Revolution," *NEQ*, LX (1967), 227–243, and W. G. McLoughlin's *Isaac Backus and the American Pietistic Tradition* (Boston, 1967).

75. Morgan's review of Heimert appears in *William and Mary Quarterly*, XXIV (1967), 454–459. His earlier view is to be found in "The American Revolution as an Intellectual Movement," in Schlesinger and White, *Paths of American Thought*. The more recent one is "The Puritan Ethic and the American Revolution," *William and Mary Quarterly*, XXIV (1967), 3–43.

76. "The Anglican Church in Restoration Colonial Policy," Smith, *Seventeenth-Century America*, 166–191.

77. "English Bishops and Imperial Jurisdiction, 1660–1725," *Historical Magazine of the Protestant Episcopal Church*, XXXII (1963), 175–188. The first "imperial bishop" was Henry Compton, the protagonist of Edward Carpenter's *The Protestant Bishop* (London, 1956). Carpenter discusses Compton's interest and involvement in American affairs.

78. Spencer Ervin, "The Establishment, Government and Functioning of the Church in Colonial Virginia," *Historical Magazine of the Protestant Episcopal Church*, XXVI (1957), 65–110; Norman Sykes, *From Sheldon to Secker: Aspects of English Church History, 1660–1768* (New York, 1959). See also Sykes' *William Wake: Archbishop of Canterbury, 1657–1737* (Cambridge, Eng., 1957), the biography of a man who was a constant proponent of an American episcopate.

79. Spencer Ervin, "The Anglican Church in North Carolina," *Historical Magazine of the Protestant Episcopal Church*, XXV (1956), 102–161; Glenn Weaver, "Anglican-Congregationalist Tensions in Pre-Revolutionary Connecticut," *Ibid.*, XXVI (1957), 269–285.

Of course, Ervin is dealing with the South, neglected by Bridenbaugh. See also Ervin's, "The Established Church of Colonial Maryland," *Ibid.*, XXIV (1955), 232–292.

80. Kellaway's book was published in London, 1961. Armstrong's article is

"The Dissenting Deputies and the American Colonies," *Church History*, XXIX, (1960), 298–320. The English and American Quakers also were in close contact, but apparently they were not concerned with the episcopacy question. See F. B. Tolles, *Quakers and the Atlantic Culture* (New York, 1960).

81. *Called unto Liberty: A Life of Jonathan Mayhew, 1720–1766* (Cambridge, Mass., 1964). By way of contrast at Yale, Anglicanism was the agency of liberal thought. See L. L. Tucker, "The Church of England and Religious Liberty at Pre-Revolutionary Yale," *William and Mary Quarterly*, XVII (1960), 314–328.

82. George W. Pilcher, "Virginia's Newspapers and the Dispute over the Proposed Colonial Episcopate, 1771–1772," *Historian*, XXIII (1960), 98–113.

83. *The Colonial Wars, 1689–1762* (Chicago, 1964).

84. "Imperialism in Massachusetts during the Governorship of William Shirley, 1741–1756," *Huntington Library Quarterly*, XXIII (1959–1960), 217–236. The tendency among historians to attach virtue to frontier tactics should be qualified by John K. Mahon's argument that only the regular soldiery— "first the redcoats and then their American counterparts"—could be depended upon to rout the Indians. See "Anglo-American Methods of Indian Warfare, 1676–1794," *Mississippi Valley Historical Review*, XLV (1958–1959), 254–275.

85. *Toward Lexington: The Role of the British Army in the Coming of the American Revolution* (Princeton, 1965); "Quartering His Majesty's Forces in New Jersey," *Proceedings of the New Jersey Historical Society*, LXXVIII (1960), 82–94. See also Jack P. Greene, "The South Carolina Quartering Dispute, 1757–1758," *SCHM*, LX (1959), 193–204. Both Jesse Lemisch, in "Jack Tar in the Streets: Merchant Seamen in the Politics of Revolutionary America," *William and Mary Quarterly*, XXV (1968), 371–407, and Neil R. Stout, "Manning the Royal Navy in North America, 1763–1775," *American Neptune*, XXIII (1963), 174–185, show the impressment of Americans to have been a source of conflict between England and the colonies. Stout points out, however, that the presence of the army was a more important irritant.

86. In addition to his religious approach to the Revolution, Carl Bridenbaugh has come forward with an urban perspective in *Cities in Revolt: Urban Life in America, 1743–1776* (New York, 1955). The two interpretations may be complementary, insofar as Bridenbaugh sees the role of the cities as one of preparing the American people socially and intellectually to embrace nationalism. But his emphasis on the impact of the Enlightenment suggests a spirit of tolerance which runs counter to the attitudes responsible for the fear of an American episcopate.

Bridenbaugh's urban analysis should be supplemented with John Alden's regional account, *The South in the Revolution, 1763–1789* (Baton Rouge, 1957).

87. Originally in *William and Mary Quarterly*, XIV (1957), 3–15, it is now part of the Bobbs-Merrill Reprint Series in History. A year earlier, Morgan had put forward his own version of the period in *The Birth of the Republic: 1763–1789* (Chicago, 1956).

88. "David Ramsay and the Causes of the American Revolution," *American Historical Review*, XVII (1960), 51–77.

    Christopher Collier, in "Recent Interpretations of the Causes of the American Revolution," *Social Studies*, LII (1961), 43–49, rejects the opinions of both Morgan and Smith. Noting John Adams' fear that a good history of the Revolution would never be written because the participants were dying and the best sources for later generations were among the Tory papers being carried off to Canada or England, Collier concludes: "For over a century Adams' judgment was thoroughly borne out." Thomas C. Barrow, viewing the historiographical controversies, has suggested an analogy between the Revolution and contemporary colonial wars of liberation in "The American Revolution as a Colonial War for Independence," *William and Mary Quarterly*, XXV (1968), 452–464. See also Merrill Jensen, "Historians and the Nature of the American Revolution," Billington, *Reinterpretation*.

89. Published at Chapel Hill. Given the impact of this book on writing about the Revolution, it is probably not too much to say that its publication marked the founding of a school of thought concerning the Revolution. Exception is taken to the Morgans' view on the determinative effect of the Stamp Act in Benjamin F. Newcomb's "Effects of the Stamp Act on Colonial Pennsylvania Politics," *William and Mary Quarterly*, XXIII (1966), 257–272.

90. "The Revolutionary Era," in Higham, *Reconstruction of American History*, 46–63. See also Peter Marshall, "Radicals, Conservatives and the American Revolution," *Past and Present*, XXIII (1962), 44–56.

91. Thus, Greene aptly titled his essay "The Flight from Determinism," *South Atlantic Quarterly*, LXI (1962), 235–259. Greene's *The Reappraisal of the American Revolution in Recent Historical Literature* (Washington, 1967) draws upon this article but contains a more extensive bibliography.

92. "Rhetoric and Reality in the American Revolution," *William and Mary Quarterly*, XXIII (1966), 3–32. There is more than a passing similarity between Wood's approach and Richard Hofstadter's in *The Paranoid Style in American Politics* (New York, 1965).

93. For a different interpretation of the purpose of the Progressive historians, see William H. Nelson, "The Revolutionary Character of the American Revolution," *American Historical Review*, LXX (1964–1965), 998–1014. Admitting that Americans did not have an old regime to dismantle, thus making the Revolution seem conservative, Nelson argues that significant changes did, in fact, take place.

94. Published in Cambridge, Mass., 1965. A revised and expanded version of this essay, which puts less emphasis on radical thought, has appeared as *The Ideological Origins of the American Revolution* (Cambridge, Mass., 1967). See also Thomas R. Adams, *American Independence: The Growth of an Idea. A Bibliographic Study of the American Political Pamphlets Between 1764 and 1776 Dealing with the Dispute Between Great Britain and Her Colonies* (Providence, 1965).

95. This is also the view of Cecelia M. Kenyon, who carefully defines her terms as she makes her analysis. See "Republicanism and Radicalism in the

American Revolution: An Old-Fashioned Interpretation," *William and Mary Quarterly*, XIX (1962), 153–182.

96. L. H. Butterfield, et al., eds., *The Adams Papers: Earliest Diary of John Adams* (Cambridge, Mass., 1966); *Diary and Autobiography of John Adams* (4 vols.; Cambridge, Mass., 1963) Lester J. Cappon, ed., *The Adams-Jefferson Letters: The Complete Correspondence between Thomas Jefferson and Abigail and John Adams* (2 vols.; Chapel Hill, 1959); Leonard W. Labaree, et al., eds., *The Papers of Benjamin Franklin* [1706–1766] (13 vols.; New Haven, 1959–1964); Harold C. Syrett, et al., eds., *The Papers of Alexander Hamilton* [1768–1791] (9 vols., New York, 1961–1965); Julian Boyd, et al., *The Papers of Thomas Jefferson* [1760–1791] (18 vols., Princeton, 1950–1969); William T. Hutchinson, et al., eds., *The Papers of James Madison* [1751–1783] (6 vols.; Chicago, 1962–1969).

97. Recent biographies of the Founding Fathers include Page Smith's *John Adams* (2 vols.; Garden City, N.Y., 1962); William S. Hanna's *Benjamin Franklin and Pennsylvania Politics* (Stanford, 1964); Broadus Mitchell's *Alexander Hamilton* (2 vols.; New York, 1957–1962); Louis M. Hacker's *Alexander Hamilton in the American Tradition* (New York, 1957); John C. Miller's *Alexander Hamilton: Portrait in Paradox* (New York, 1959); Dumas Malone's *Jefferson and His Time* (3 vols.; Boston, 1948–1962); Irving Brant's *James Madison* (6 vols.; Indianapolis, 1941–1962). The greatest range of treatment is that accorded George Washington. One may choose between Douglas Southall Freeman's seven volume portrait, *George Washington, a Biography* (New York, 1948–1957), and Marcus Cunliffe's slim but provocative depiction, *George Washington: Man and Monument* (Boston, 1958). There is also Curtis P. Nettels' eulogistic *George Washington and American Independence* (Boston, 1951); Bernard Knollenberg's "warts and all" rendition, *George Washington: The Virginia Period, 1732–1775* (Durham, N.C., 1954); and James T. Flexner's attempt at a middle-of-the-road appraisal, *George Washington: The Forge of Experience, 1732–1775* (Boston, 1965) and *George Washington in the American Revolution, 1775–1783* (Boston, 1968). Materials necessary to reconstruct the life of Patrick Henry are virtually non-existent; but see the attempt made by Robert D. Meade, *Patrick Henry: Patriot in the Making* (2 vols.; Philadelphia, 1957–1969). All of these studies, some of which are excellent, fall into one or another of the traditional biographical approaches.

The same may be said of the portraits of less well-known Patriots. John Cary, in *Joseph Warren: Physician, Politician, Patriot* (Urbana, 1961), has ranked his protagonist with Sam Adams as a pre-revolutionary leader in Massachusetts, while John T. Zimmerman, in "Charles Thompson, the Sam Adams of Philadelphia," *Mississippi Valley Historical Review*, XLV (1958), 464–480, has performed a similar service. Three other Pennsylvanians of varying political stripe have been carefully studied; see C. Page Smith, *James Wilson: Founding Father, 1742–1798* (Chapel Hill, 1956); John F. Roche, *Joseph Reed: A Moderate in the American Revolution* (New York, 1957); David L. Jacobson, *John Dickinson and the Revolution in Pennsylvania, 1764–1776* (Berkeley and Los Angeles, 1965). Two quite different New Yorkers are the subjects of Howard Thomas' *Marinus Willett:*

Soldier-Patriot, 1740–1830 (Prospect, N.Y., 1954) and George Danger-field's *Chancellor Robert R. Livingston of New York, 1746–1813* (New York, 1960). See also Katherine Anthony's *First Lady of the Revolution: The Life of Mercy Otis Warren* (Garden City, N.Y., 1958) and W. M. Dabney and Marion Dargan's *William Henry Drayton and the American Revolution* (Albuquerque, 1962).

98. Craven, "The Revolutionary Era," 63. A recent and very useful historiographical guide is Esmond Wright's *Causes and Consequences of the American Revolution* (Chicago, 1966).

99. The refinement of tools for handling economic questions, which reserves their consideration for specialists, may account for the decline of this approach. The geography of the Chesapeake region, relations between planters and English merchants, the impact of Scottish intrusion, the nature of credit, the monetary situation and the volume of debt are factors presently being utilized to explain pre-revolutionary Virginia. See A. P. Middleton, *Tobacco Coast: A Maritime History of Chesapeake Bay in the Colonial Era* (Newport News, 1953); Jacob M. Price, "The Economic Growth of the Chesapeake and the European Market, 1697–1775," *Journal of Economic History*, XXIV (1964), 496–516 (includes discussion of Price's paper by Mancur Olson); *Id.*, "The Rise of Glasgow in the Chesapeake Tobacco Trade," *William and Mary Quarterly*, XI (1954), 179–199; James H. Soltow, "Scottish Traders in Virginia, 1750–1775," *Economic History Review*, XII (1959), 83–98; S. M. Rosenblatt, "The Significance of Credit in the Tobacco Consignment Trade: A Study of John Norton & Sons, 1768–1775," *Economic History Review*, XIX (1962), 383–399; Jacob M. Price, "Who Was John Norton? A Note on the Historical Character of Some Eighteenth-Century London Virginia Firms," *Ibid.*, 400–407; Robert Polk Thompson, "The Tobacco Export of the Upper James River Naval District, 1773–1775," *Ibid.*, XVIII (1961), 393–407; John M. Hemphill II, "Documents Relating to the Colonial Tobacco Trade," *Maryland Historical Magazine*, LII (1957), 153–156; Aubrey C. Land, "Economic Base and Social Structure: The Northern Chesapeake in the Eighteenth Century," *Journal of Economic History*, XXV (1965), 639–659 (includes discussion of Land's paper by J. M. Price); Emory G. Evans, "The Rise and Decline of the Virginia Aristocracy in the Eighteenth Century: The Nelsons," in Rutman, *The Old Dominion*, 62–78; L. H. Gipson, "Virginia Planter Debts before the American Revolution," *Virginia Magazine of History and Biography*, LXIX (1961), 259–277; Emory G. Evans, "Planter Indebtedness and the Coming of the Revolution in Virginia," *William and Mary Quarterly*, XIX (1962), 511–533. Clarence L. Ver Steeg's "The American Revolution Considered as an Economic Movement," *Huntington Library Quarterly*, XX (1957), 361–372, is a consideration of the change brought by the Revolution.

100. Staughton Lynd is probably the strongest proponent of this point of view; see *Anti-Federalism in Duchess County, New York: A Study of Democracy and Class Conflict in the Revolutionary Era* (Chicago, 1962). Elisha P. Douglass, arguing similarly in *Rebels and Democrats: The Struggle for Equal Political Rights and Majority Rule During the American Revolution* (Chapel Hill, 1955), also concentrates his attention on the post-1775

period. This interpretation is rejected, though not very convincingly, by Richard B. Morris in "Class Struggle and the American Revolution," *WMQ*, XIX (1962), 3–29. See also Morris' *The American Revolution Reconsidered* (New York, 1967).

101. Published in Princeton, 1965.

102. *Rhode Island Politics and the American Revolution, 1760–1776* (Providence, 1958). Lovejoy's view is substantiated in Mack Thompson's "The Ward-Hopkins Controversy and the American Revolution in Rhode Island: An Interpretation," *William and Mary Quarterly*, XVI (1959), 363–375.

103. Becker's argument that home rule was no more important than who should rule at home is less subject to revision than his contention that the latter conflict was between upper and lower economic groups. New York politics, as seen by most scholars today, was characterized by the clash of aristocratic groups. See Bernard S. Mason, "The Heritage of Carl Becker: The Historiography of the Revolution in New York," *New-York Historical Society Quarterly*, LIII (1969), 127–147; Id., *The Road to Independence: The Revolutionary Movement in New York, 1773–1777* (Lexington, Ky., 1966); Don R. Gerlach, *Philip Schuyler and the American Revolution, 1773–1777* (Lincoln, Neb., 1964); Milton M. Klein, "Prelude to Revolution in New York," *William and Mary Quarterly*, XVII (1960), 439–462 (here, as in his "Rise of the New York Bar," *Ibid.*, XV [1958], 334–358, Klein emphasizes the importance of constitutional principles and the role of lawyers); Id., "Democracy and Politics in Colonial New York," *New York History*, LVII (1959), 221–246; Roger Champagne, "Family Politics versus Constitutional Principles: The New York Assembly Elections of 1768 and 1769," *William and Mary Quarterly*, XX (1963), 57–79 (principles and politics are accorded equal importance); *Id.*, "New York and the Intolerable Act, 1774," *New-York Historical Society Quarterly*, XLV (1961), 195–207; *Id.*, "New York's Radicals and the Coming of Independence," *Journal of American History*, LI (1964–1965), 21–40; L. H. Leder, "The New York Election of 1769: An Assault on Privilege," *Ibid.*, XLIX (1962–1963), 675–682. The lone dissent from this point of view is Bernard Friedman's "The New York Assembly Elections of 1768 and 1769: The Disruption of Family Politics," *New York History*, XLVI (1965), 3–24, which assigns an importance to the Sons of Liberty that even Becker shrank from.

104. "The Coming of the Revolution in Virginia: Britain's Challenge to Virginia's Ruling Class, 1763–1776," *William and Mary Quarterly* (1962), 323–343. See also John G. Mathews, "Two Men on a Tax: Richard Henry Lee, Archibald Richie, and the Stamp Act," in Rutman, *The Old Dominion*, 96–108.

105. Jack P. Greene, in "Bridge to Revolution: The Wilkes Fund Controversy in South Carolina, 1769–1775," *Journal of Southern History*, XXIX (1963), 19–52, argues that "royal government in South Carolina broke down four years earlier than it did in any of the other colonies" because of the controversy surrounding the Assembly's gift of £1500 to John Wilkes in 1769. But Richard Walsh, in *Charleston's Sons of Liberty: A*

Study of the Artisans, 1763–1789 (Columbia, 1959), sees the genesis of conflict in the radical persuasion of the 2,000 or more artisans who joined the Sons of Liberty and the John Wilkes Club in the mid-1760's.

106. William W. Abbott, *The Royal Governors of Georgia, 1754–1775* (Chapel Hill, 1959); Kenneth Coleman, *The American Revolution in Georgia, 1763–1789* (Athens, Ga., 1958); Herbert E. Klingelhofer, "The Cautious Revolution: Maryland and the Movement toward Independence, 1774–1776," *Maryland Historical Magazine*, LX (1965), 261–313.

107. Merrill Jensen, "Democracy and the American Revolution," *Huntington Library Quarterly*, XX (1956–1957), 321–342; Jackson Turner Main, "Government by the People: The American Revolution and the Democratization of the Legislatures," *William and Mary Quarterly* (1966), 391–407; *Id.*, "Social Origins of a Political Elite: The Upper House in the Revolutionary Era," *Huntington Library Quarterly*, XXVII (1963–1964), 147–158. Jensen's *The Founding of a Nation: A History of the American Revolution, 1763–1776* (New York, 1968) is detailed rather than interpretive.

108. A recent attempt at synthesis of this material has, perhaps significantly, been undertaken by a layman. See Dan Lacy, *The Meaning of the American Revolution* (New York, 1964).

109. In addition to the closing volumes of *The British Empire before the American Revolution*, see *The Coming of the Revolution, 1763–1775* (New York, 1954).

110. *Whitehall and the Wilderness: The Middle West in British Colonial Policy, 1760–1775* (Lincoln, Neb., 1961); *Agents and Merchants: British Colonial Policy and the Origins of the American Revolution, 1763–1775* (Lincoln, Neb., 1964); "The Massachusetts Acts of 1774: Coersive or Preventative?," *Huntington Library Quarterly*, XXVI (1962–1963), 235–252.

111. *Origin of the American Revolution: 1759–1776* (New York, 1960).

112. Dickerson's *The Navigation Acts and the American Revolution* (Philadelphia, 1951) and "The Attempt to Extend British Customs Controls over Intercolonial Commerce by Land," *South Atlantic Quarterly*, L (1951), 361–368, may be contrasted to *The Maritime Commerce of Colonial Philadelphia* (Madison, 1963), in which Arthur L. Jensen argues that the merchants in Pennsylvania entered the revolutionary movement with the utmost reluctance. Dickerson's "British Control of American Newspapers on the Eve of the Revolution," *New England Quarterly*, XXIV (1951), 453–468, conflicts with Arthur M. Schlesinger's observation, in *Prelude to Independence: The Newspaper War on Britain, 1764–1776* (New York, 1958), that only newspapers with an American point of view could survive. Dickerson's detective work in "The Commissioners of Customs and the 'Boston Massacre,'" *New England Quarterly*, XXVII (1954) is based on circumstantial evidence.

113. "Background to the Grenville Program, 1757–1763," *William and Mary Quarterly*, XXII (1956), 93–104.

114. A. S. Johnson, "The Passage of the Sugar Act," *Ibid.*, XVI (1959), 507–514; C. R. Ritcheson, "The Preparation of the Stamp Act," *Ibid.*, X (1953), 543–559. For a contemporaneous dissent from Grenville's plan,

see Jack P. Greene's "'A Dress of Horror': Henry McCulloh's Objections to the Stamp Act," *Huntington Library Quarterly*, XXVI (1962–1963), 253–262.

115. In addition to *The Stamp Act Crisis*, Edmund S. Morgan has gathered together sixty-five documents in *Prologue to Revolution: Sources and Documents on the Stamp Act Crisis, 1764–1766* (Chapel Hill, 1959). See also W. E. Minchinton, "The Stamp Act Crisis: Bristol and Virginia," *Virginia Magazine of History and Biography*, LXXIII (1965), 145–155. For New York see Neil R. Stout, "Captain Kennedy and the Stamp Act," *New York History*, XLV (1964), 44–58, and Michael D'Innocenzo and John J. Turner, "The Role of New York Newspapers in the Stamp Act Crisis, 1764–66," *New-York Historical Society Quarterly*, LI (1967), 215–232, 345–365.

116. L. H. Gipson, "The Great Debate in the Committee of the Whole of Commons on the Stamp Act, 1776, as Reported by Nathaniel Ryder," *Pennsylvania Magazine of History and Biography*, LXXXVI (1962), 10–41; A. S. Johnson, "British Politics and the Repeal of the Stamp Act," *South Atlantic Quarterly*, LXII (1963), 169–188.

117. Jack M. Sosin, "A Postscript to the Stamp Act: George Grenville's Revenue Measures: A Drain on Colonial Specie?," *American Historical Review*, LXIII (1957–1958), 918–923.

118. For Ferguson's and related articles, see footnote 62.

119. "Genesis of the Currency Act of 1764. Virginia Paper Money and the Protection of British Investments," *William and Mary Quarterly*, XXII (1965), 33–74; "The Currency Repeal Movement: A Study of Imperial Politics and Revolutionary Crisis, 1764–1767," *Ibid.*, XXV (1968), 177–211. A less satisfactory explanation, but one which traces the problem down to 1773, when the Act of 1764 was amended, is Jack M. Sosin's "Imperial Regulation of Colonial Paper Money, 1764–1773," *Pennsylvania Magazine of History and Biography*, LXXXVIII (1964), 174–198.

120. "The Currency Act of 1764 in Imperial-Colonial Relations, 1764–1776," *William and Mary Quarterly*, XVIII (1961), 485–518. Jellison and Greene see the currency controversy as a psychological reminder of colonial subordination, whereas Sosin (footnote 119) depicts the amended Act of 1773 as a constitutional admission of Parliamentary authority. Both points of view may be simultaneously correct, which serves to demonstrate the manner in which divergent sympathies obscure an understanding of Anglo-American relations during the pre-revolutionary crisis.

121. "The British Credit Crisis of 1772 and the American Colonies," *Journal of Economic History*, XX (1960), 161–186.

122. The former point of view is put forward in David Lovejoy's "Rights Imply Equality: The Case Against Admiralty Jurisdiction in America, 1764–1776," *William and Mary Quarterly*, XVI (1959), 459–484, while the latter can be found in Carl Ubbelohde's *The Vice-Admiralty Courts and the American Revolution* (Chapel Hill, 1960). Joseph E. King, in "Judicial Flotsam in Massachusetts-Bay, 1760–1765," *New England Quarterly*, XXVII (1954), 366–381, traces the development of antagonism toward the vice-admiralty courts in that colony.

123. B. D. Barger, *Lord Dartmouth and the American Revolution* (Columbia,

S.C., 1965); F. B. Wickwire, "John Pownall and British Colonial Policy," *William and Mary Quarterly*, XX (1963), 543–554; James High, "Henry McCulloh: Progenitor of the Stamp Act," *North Carolina Historical Review*, XXIX (1952), 24–38.

124. "The Colonial Agents, English Politics, and the American Revolution," *William and Mary Quarterly*, XXII (1965), 244–263. Kammen's *A Rope of Sand: The Colonial Agents, British Politics, and the American Revolution* (Ithaca, 1968) deals with the years 1756 through 1775, divided them into two periods at 1766 when, he claims, the agents reached the height of their influence. There is a fuller and more careful treatment of British domestic politics here than in Sosin's *Agents and Merchants*.

125. Nicholas Varga, "Robert Charles, New York Agent, 1748–1770," *William and Mary Quarterly*, XVIII (1961), 210–235; Ross J. S. Hoffman, *Edmund Burke, New York Agent, with his Letters to the New York Assembly . . . 1761–1776* (Philadelphia, 1956). See also Carl B. Cone, *Burke and the Nature of Politics* (Lexington, Ky., 1957) and John Brooke, "Burke in the 1760's," *South Atlantic Quarterly*, LVIII (1959), 548–556, a review of the first volume of T. W. Copeland, ed., *The Correspondence of Edmund Burke* [v. I, 1744–1768; v. II, 1768–1774; v. III, 1774–1778] (Chicago, 1958–1961).

126. Robert Rea, in *The English Press in Politics, 1760–1774* (Lincoln, Neb., 1963), demonstrates the great influence of the London newspapers' sympathy for America. Also pertinent are M. Dorothy George's *English Political Caricature: A Study of Opinion and Propaganda* (2 vols.; Oxford, 1959); Albert M. Lyles, "The Hostile Reaction to the [anti-] American Views of Johnson and Wesley," *Journal of the Rutgers University Library*, XXIV (1960–1961), 1–12; Jennings B. Sanders, "The Crisis of London and American Revolutionary Propaganda, 1775–1776," *Social Studies*, LVIII (1967), 7–12. P. T. Underdown, "Henry Cruger and Edmund Burke: Colleagues and Rivals at the Bristol Election of 1774," *William and Mary Quarterly*, XV (1958), 14–34.

127. *British Politics and the American Revolution* (Norman, Okla., 1954).

128. Richard Pares, *King George III and the Politicians* (New York, 1953); J. Steven Watson, *The Reign of George III, 1760–1815* (New York, 1960); Sir Lewis Namier and John Brooke, *Charles Townshend* (New York, 1964); P. D. G. Thomas, "Charles Townshend and American Taxation in 1767," *English Historical Review*, LXXXIII (1968), 33–51; John Brooke, *The Chatham Administration, 1766–1768* (New York, 1956). O. A. Sharrard's laudatory biography, *Lord Chatham* (3 vols.; London, 1952–1958) is not in the Namierite category, nor is Alan Valentine's *Life and Times of Lord North* (2 vols.; Norman, Okla., 1967).

129. *Fabric of Freedom, 1763–1800* (New York, 1961).

130. *The American Revolution in its Political and Military Aspects, 1763–1783* (New York, 1955).

131. *British Politics and the American Revolution: The Path to War, 1773–75* (New York, 1964).

132. R. R. Palmer, *The Age of the Democratic Revolution. A Political History of Europe and America, 1760–1800* [vol. I, The Challenge] (Princeton, 1959); Hannah Arendt, *On Revolution* (New York, 1963). Carl Briden-

baugh also used this perspective, noting the pervasive effect of the Enlightenment and comparing urban development in America to Europe, in *Cities in Revolt*. See also David B. Davis's excellent study, *The Problem of Slavery in Western Culture* (Ithaca, 1966), and Richard Koebner's *Empire* (1961).

Index

This book was set in Caledonia Linotype and printed by letterpress on P & S Wove manufactured by P. H. Glatfelter Co., Spring Grove, Pa. Composed, printed and bound by H. Wolff Book Manufacturing Company Inc., New York, N. Y.